# UNDERSTANDING VAGUENESS

# UNDERSTANDING VAGUENESS

AMITA CHATTERJEE

PRAGATI PUBLICATIONS
DELHI

PRAGATI PUBLICATIONS
9926 Library Road,
Azad Market, Delhi 110006

First Published 1994



ISBN: 81-7307-020-2

Published by Pramod Kapoor for Pragati Publications,
9926 Library Road, Azad Market, Delhi 110006

Typeset by Vikas Print Communication Services, New Delhi 110026
and Printed at Efficient Offset Printers, Delhi 110035

*In memory of my father*

AMITES C. BANERJI

# Contents

# Acknowledgements

My debts are many—I doubt that I shall be able to acknowledge them all. Yet let me try. I am indebted:

To the University Grants Commission for financially supporting my project on 'Understanding Vagueness' and the Department of Philosophy, Jadavpur University, for reducing my normal teaching load;

To Dr Mihir K. Chakraborty of the Department of Pure Mathematics, Calcutta University, who has initiated me into the problems centering around vagueness, explained the existing mathematical solutions and collaborated with me in devising mathematical representation techniques of vague sentences as well as of approximate reasoning;

To Professor Pranab Kumar Sen, Department of Philosophy, Jadavpur University, who has always listened to my half-baked ideas patiently, pointed out the errors in my argument with his characteristic incisive analyses, prevented me from being led up the garden path, and given me access to his invaluable personal collection of important works on the topic;

To all the members of the Friday Seminar Group who have smoothed my steps with alternative suggestions without being too critical;

To the members of the Calcutta Logic Circle who have infused me with enthusiasm by their unambiguous presence in workshops where I vaguely presented my all the more vague thoughts on the logic of vague sentences;

To the teachers and research scholars of the Centre for Knowledge Based Systems, Department of Electrical Engineering, Jadavpur University, for inviting me to deliver lectures on Fuzzy Logic, allowing me to use their library, and letting me know how the AI researchers tackle the problem of vagueness;

To all my colleagues at the Department of Philosophy, Jadavpur University, who have always boosted my morale by showing sufficient interest in the progress of my work, especially Dr M.N. Mitra and Dr T.K. Sarkar who were ever ready to discuss any difficult problem and provided me with information on the latest publications on the topic which they have come across;

To Srimati Mahua Banerjee who has worked with me on Sorites Paradox for her Ph.D. dissertation and has very efficiently completed a considerable part of the literature survey;

To Sri Buddhadeva Bhattacharya who out of affection for me has very kindly taken the trouble of contacting Tulika Print Communication and has done the cover design, copy editing and styling of the pages in spite of his illness and busy schedule;

To Tulika Print Communication Services for preparing the manuscript painstakingly on DTP;

To Smt. Alakananda Brahma who has helped me in preparing the bibliography;

To Shefali (Dr S. Moitra) for her friendship, her views, her careful reading of the whole manuscript, for all her love and concern for me;

To my husband who could have doubted whether the term 'his wife' applies to me or not for the past one year but did not, despite my total neglect of all social commitments;

To everybody else who has directly and indirectly helped me in some way, big or small, out of their goodness.

# Preface

The topic of vagueness lies at the interface of mathematical and philosophical logic, philosophy of language and artificial intelligence. Natural language with its loosely structured grammar, vague predicates and ambiguous sentences has often posed difficulties to all who have wanted to use it as a vehicle of precise thoughts. Consequently we find that at one stage natural language received derogatory treatment from logicians and philosophers of science. Frege, Russell, Quine and other stalwarts of classical logic considered natural language essentially defective and those defects irremediable. So they tried to replace it by some ideal language. But since then much water has flown down the river and we have learnt to have more respect for natural language. We have realized that 'Philosophy cannot for ever confine itself to theories, of the logical structure of make-believe languages' (Putnam, 1983), simply because no ideal language is adequate for communication, not even for philosophical discourse. So instead of resorting to ideal language we now try to discover the logical form of natural language sentences and to translate them into proper canonical notation.

Three years back I was writing a research paper on the regimentation of natural language for a volume on *Foundations of Logic and Language* to be prepared by the members of the Logic Group of our department. In the course of my research I tried to identify the problematic expressions of a natural language that defy easy translation into canonical notation and found that vague expressions form one such stubborn kind. Subsequently I found that a vast literature has already developed around the problem of vagueness, many alternative logics have been formulated, many mathematical solutions have been worked out, many computer programmes have been sketched; yet a lot of confusion persists at the theoretical level.

At first I had no ambitious project before me. I just wanted to clarify the issues for my own sake. The more I entered into the heart of the problem, the more I surveyed the existing literature, the more fascinated I became. I noticed that there is a surprising lack of coordination amongst researchers of different branches. Mathematicians are proving theorem after theorem, computer scientists are feeding machines with innumerable new programmes, but they are all blissfully unaware of the related philosophical problems. The philosophers, on the other hand, are busy finding ways out of the sorites type paradox but are simply not interested in the techniques adopted by computer scientists for processing natural language or developing artificial intelligence or decision theory. I felt that only a concerted effort by all concerned with vagueness can satisfactorily solve the related problems. Hence my endeavour in writing the following pages with a view to bringing the researchers in different fields closer to one another.

For quite some time now it has been an established fact that the scene of logic as a whole—even that of philosophical logic—is dominated by mathematicians and computer scientists. The philosophers, bogged down by the bogey of technicalities, either occupy some fringe area or watch from the other side of the fence. They are becoming more and more estranged from the mainstream of logical pursuit. This estrangement is almost complete in India. Everybody will agree with me that this is not a happy situation. I had, therefore, two objectives in front of me when I decided to take up a book-length study on Vagueness. First, to state clearly and in the simplest possible terms the almost esoteric logical writings on vagueness for those brilliant academics who can contribute a lot to the problem area if they do not feel hindered by technicalities. Second, to bring the foundational philosophical problems arising out of vagueness to the notice of those scientists who are eternally devising schemes to avoid applicational difficulties. My objectives being what they are, I could not avoid being eclectic. But the perspective is my own and I have offered relevant modifications to the existing logical techniques and solutions of the sorites paradox.

Any discourse on the nature and problems of vagueness is bound to present some initial difficulty. The reason thereof has been explained by Dummett very clearly:

> The topic of vagueness is a very difficult one . . . it is, . . . evident that we have an intuitive sympathy with Frege's view that a vague expression is one which is, to that extent, defective in sense: any account of vagueness which failed at least to explain this intuitive feeling would be inadequate. At the same time we have also a contrary intuition, that vagueness is an indispensable feature of our language, that we could not operate with language as we do unless many of its expressions displayed this feature: and it is equally a requirement on any satisfactory account of vagueness that it should at least explain our having this intuition also (Dummett, 1973b).

I am, however, more in sympathy with Wittgenstein's view that vagueness is no defect of language. The first chapter of this work is devoted to explaining this thesis. Another important point that we have established in this chapter is that not all expressions of a natural language are vague but many are.

The second chapter is a critique of the position that vagueness necessarily leads to incoherence in language. So this chapter may be viewed as a culmination of the first. Here I have refuted two important assertions about vagueness: *(a)* Vague observational expressions are sure to lead to inconsistency; and *(b)* we should give up the notion of phenomenal properties. The main thrust of the rebuttal is as follows. 'Observational expressions' are to be interpreted more liberally; the paradoxical argument is a non-starter at a purely phenomenal level, so phenomenal predicates need not be given up. We can explain away the apparent inconsistency originating from the tolerant nature of observational predicates and can even formulate some semantic rules for them.

In the third chapter I have raised the most controversial issue, whether vagueness is a feature of representation or a feature of reality. The vagueness-in-reality thesis is generally countered with the argument of the impossibility of indeterminate identity. But I have shown that the above-said argument is not sufficient to disprove vague objects.

Next I have discussed in detail the different logical approaches towards vague sentences. Though I do not disagree with Williamson in upholding that the last thing to give up is a principle of classical logic yet I have been compelled by the nature of vague sentences to admit a modified version of fuzzy logic as the adequate model for representing vague sentences of which the classical logic is a special case. The most crucial thesis that I have expounded here is that identity induced by a vague concept is approximate.

Talk about vague predicates has always led to talk about the sorites paradox. So I felt that a survey of the whole field of the sorites paradox would be in order. I have discussed and rejected different solutions to the sorites paradox before declaring the solutions by approximate reasoning or by approximate identity to be the right solutions.

The logic of vague sentences that I have developed on the basis of fuzzy logic is adequate for modelling both essential vagueness and epistemic vagueness. Computer scientists, however, have offered a logic of layered sets to represent sentences involving epistemically vague predicates. So a resumé of the theory of layered sets has been included here.

In a natural language we have expressions affected by the possibility of vagueness. Arguments involving such open-textured observational expressions can be best handled with a type of non-monotonic reasoning, viz. circumscriptive reasoning.

In the last decade a new logic has come up with immense possibilities. This branch is known as the logic of rough sets. Rough sets can avoid the problems that arise in fuzzy set theory in connection with assignment of membership degree. The logic of rough sets, I think, will be an equally good alternative logic, if not a better one, for vague sentences. This logic is yet to be fully worked out and I came to know about it very recently. I hope to reformulate the topic of vagueness in terms of rough sets in the near future. Till such time, I shall continue to hope that this humble work of mine will be of some help to the readers, at least in the restricted field of the logic of vagueness, and that my efforts will be construed as something 'more than designing wall paper'.

*Department of Philosophy* AMITA CHATTERJEE
*Jadavpur University, Calcutta*
*December 1993*

# CHAPTER 1

# Varieties of Vagueness

## 1.1 INTRODUCTION

> 'Inexact' is really a reproach, and 'exact' is praise. And that is to say what is inexact attains its goal less perfectly than what is more exact.[1]

Thus observes Wittgenstein in one of the very familiar passages of *Philosophical Investigations*. Here, Wittgenstein has recorded our general attitude towards exactitude and inexactitude, towards precision and imprecision. Indeed, in our ordinary vocabulary the former has become associated with approbation and the latter with disapprobation. We should not therefore think that the penchant for precision is a peculiarity of the pedants. It is not only a mathematician or a scientist or a logician who considers precision a panacea; people in general have extolled it as a virtue and thus very naturally disparaged anything that is imprecise or inexact. There is however no single idea of imprecision. We shall see as we proceed that imprecision may be of different varieties. I propose to deal with a particular type of imprecision, viz. vagueness, in this book.

Though the lure of precision is almost irresistible, yet we find vagueness as a phenomenon permeating our thought and our language. Here, however, we shall confine ourselves to the study of lack of precision in language.

That vague expressions in our language give rise to difficult problems and so deserve a special attention was first realized by the Megarian philosophers. Thereafter, queries in this area were shelved for a very long time, say, almost two thousand years. But at the turn of this century, there has been a renewed interest in this area and the problems centring around vagueness have been approached from various different standpoints—philosophical, logico-mathematical, linguistic, 'semantic' and computational. These approaches differ among themselves not only in perspectives, but also in goals. The objectives set before these are really varied like: explanation of the general nature of vague sentences, solving the paradoxes arising out of vagueness, providing algebraic representation of vague sentences, determining truth conditions for them, to account for successful human communication in spite of vagueness, finding out the best possible way of making such sentences intelligible to machines and so on. I must admit that all these approaches have achieved some limited success with respect to their specified goals. But what is still needed, I feel, is a global approach to vagueness and the problems related to it. It will, therefore, be my endeavour in this work to develop a unified approach with a view to considering as many aspects of vagueness as possible.

We start our discussion with a proposition which nobody wants to dispute: that there are some vague expressions in a natural language, e.g. 'tall', 'bald', 'heap', 'red', etc. Such an admission immediately evokes a number of questions like what is vagueness, are only some expressions vague or are all expressions vague, is vagueness necessarily a defect of language, does it serve any useful purpose, is vagueness eradicable, what is the root of vagueness, is vagueness a feature of reality, etc. All these questions are interrelated and the latter ones cannot be answered without settling first what we mean by vagueness. I am, therefore, going to take up this point presently. To determine the nature of vagueness I shall draw heavily on two seminal papers of Peirce[2] and Russell.[3]

## 1.2 DEFINITION

C.S. Peirce offered a definition of a vague proposition in 1902, which could capture the essence of vagueness. He wrote:

> A proposition is vague when there are possible states of things concerning which it is *intrinsically* uncertain whether, had they been contemplated by the speaker, he would have regarded them as excluded or allowed by the proposition. By intrinsically uncertain we mean not uncertain in consequence of any ignorance of the interpreter, but because the speaker's habits of language were indeterminate.[4]

An analysis of the above definition will bring out all the salient features of a Vague expression. Peirce has defined vagueness in the context of a proposition. A proposition is vague if at least one of its components is vague. We shall see later that almost every component of a proposition may be vague. So vagueness of a proposition depends on the vagueness of the terms constituting it. And a term is vague *a la* Peirce if there are cases in which there is no definite answer as to whether or not the term applies. Take, for instance, the term 'old'. A man over sixty years is definitely old, a man below forty is definitely not; but we cannot decide whether the term applies or not when somebody's age ranges between fifty-five and sixty.

The characteristic feature of vagueness that we have so far grasped is that vague expressions lack sharp boundaries. Perhaps this is why the most common examples of vague terms are colour words. Colours in a spectrum are arranged continually and various shades of one colour always merge into the shades of another. So colour predicates do not have clear-cut boundaries. It is often found that being called upon to identify a shade lying between red and orange, people fail to characterize it as either red or orange. For, it may be the case that when compared with a typical shade of red, the given shade appears to be orange but it may also appear red when compared with a typical shade of orange. (There are some problems, I admit, regarding identification of 'typical' shade which I shall take up later.) Thus any assertion with reference to a given shade like 'This shade is red' turns out to be neither true nor false. Such a consequence seems unacceptable at first glance for the following reasons. It hurts our common sense and goes against classical logic. Since the shade in question lies in a region of the colour spectrum bounded by red and orange, our common sense tells us, the shade must be either a shade of red or a shade of orange. But our perception does not unhesitatingly back any of the alternatives. Nor can we say that the given shade is both red and orange for we usually take red and orange to be exclusive colours. Hence we have to admit that the given shade is neither red nor orange.

Such being the state of affairs, the proposition 'This shade is red' cannot be true for the shade *may be* orange, nor can it be false for the shade *may be* red hence the proposition is neither true nor false. But the classical two-valued logic has taught us that a proposition is either true or false, there is no other possibility.

A discerning mind may point out that not all instances of a vague proposition are that troublesome. Some instances of it are definitely true, some are definitely false; only some referring to shades occupying the 'penumbral'[5] region of the spectrum cannot possess any definite truth value. So, if we decide by consensus to have no truck with such cases, the problems can be avoided. But unfortunately the penumbra or the fringe is not sharply defined. A fringe is 'itself bounded by a fringe of higher order, and that in turn by another and so on *ad infinitum.*'[6] So Russell rightly concludes, 'all the vagueness which apply to the primary use of words apply also when we try to fix a limit to their indubitable applicability.'[7]

Let us consider the above-said region of the colour-spectrum once again where shades of red finally merge into shades of orange passing through shades of orangish red and reddish orange. One may think that the portion of the colour spectrum starting from orangish red and ending with reddish orange constitute the fringe or penumbra. But all the shades in the colour chart corresponding to the spectrum segment mentioned above are so arranged that no two successive stages are distinguishable and therefore it is not possible for us to determine exactly with which shade the fringe starts or ends. So there will always be a fringe of fringe of fringe. . . . and we are back to square one again.

Still someone may persistently object and maintain that in spite of there being fringes, our communication goes through. So existence of borderline cases should not bother us. I admit that the objection is valid to some extent. The borderline cases may not always present us with practical difficulties but definitely raise some doubt about our theoretical scheme of classification.

Peirce has also said in his definition that a vague expression is intrinsically uncertain. That means, uncertainty over application of a vague term is not due to our insufficient knowledge-base or 'intellectual laziness.'[8] We may amass a host of relevant data on the neuro-physiological condition and other aspects of the life of a 59-year-old man, still we shall not be able to decide whether he is old or not. For our language, or more broadly our conceptual scheme is such that we shall never be able to specify how old is old. Moreover, the issue here is not whether we can or cannot draw a line between 'old' and 'not-old' but the point is that the line should not at all be drawn. Hence terms like 'old' and 'bald' are essentially vague and not merely epistemically vague.

But why shouldn't we draw such a line? Because that would go against a distinctive feature of vague terms, viz. their *tolerance*. By *tolerance* is meant that vague terms are immune to small changes, only a big change raises doubt about the application of the term. The notion can be clarified better with the help of examples. 'Tall' is a vague term associated with the concept of tallness. Let us suppose that the concept allows that a man whose height is 5' 11" is tall. If another man differs in height from the former by no more than 0.1 inch, he will also be definitely tall. That is, a marginal change with respect to height will not make the term 'tall' inapplicable. Similar will be the case with 'heap'. If one grain is removed from a heap, then also the term 'heap' applies to that particular collection. But how much tolerance may a vague term possess? Logically there cannot be a limit to it. If with every successive reduction in height the same vague term continues to apply, every successive stage should be tolerated by the concept. But then a midget will be tall just as a giant is and a null collection of sand will form a heap. This is the infamous *sorites paradox* and its source can rightly be traced to the tolerability of vague expressions.

A hasty reaction to the above puzzle usually results in an attempt to prevent the fall along the sliding slope by drawing an arbitrary line, by dividing a continuum into some arbitrary segments. But this approach would rob the vague expressions of their explanatory power.[9] Not only that, this would also sin against ordinary usage. Suppose that we have decided arbitrarily that a heap should comprise at least 1000 grains. Then every time we are to pour *a heap* of sand we have to count the grains first to decide whether we have exactly a heap at our disposal or not. This is surely ludicrous.

Even then, for our practical convenience we do draw such dividing lines, e.g. we set a minimum limit to the voting age at 18 years. But that does not guarantee that a child or an adolescent, to be precise, becomes an adult all of a sudden with the sunrise on her nineteenth birthday and right at that moment her behaviour starts conforming to the adult pattern. So the problem remains. If vague expressions are not allowed tolerance, they become useless. On the other hand, if tolerance is extended too far, the *sorites paradox* is the inevitable consequence.

Unlike Peirce, Russell considers both vagueness and precision to be characteristics of representation and defines vagueness in contrast with accuracy.[10] One structure, according to Russell, is accurate representation of another if there is a one-one correlation between the terms, as well as between the relations of the two structures. An accurate map will be an example of such representation. A representation, on the other hand, is vague when the relation of the representing system to the represented system is not one-one but one-many. For example, a map which is so inaccurately drawn that it may appear to be a map either of South America or of Africa.

This definition, however, is over-extensive since it fails to distinguish vagueness from generality.[11] A term is general when it refers to a number of objects. Hence a mapping from a general term to its referents will be one many. But a term, e.g. 'triangle', may be general without being vague. So vagueness should be distinguished from generality.

### 1.3 VAGUENESS AND IMPRECISION

The shortcoming of Russell's definition makes us conscious of the fact that though imprecision is an essential aspect of vagueness, whatever is imprecise cannot be said to be vague. So, at this point, I would like to draw attention to some other forms of imprecision with which vagueness should not be confused.

Vagueness has often been confounded with relativity. Though vagueness and relativity sometimes go together, the latter can be eliminated without removing the former. Take, for instance, the property of being above average in height.[12] This property is relative, for the average height varies from race to race. The average height for a Pathan is greater than the average height for a Bengali, and the average height for a Bengali is greater than the average height for a Pygmy. But the expression, 'is above average in height' is not vague, provided there is a device for calculating the average height of people living in a community. The expression 'tall' is, on the other hand, vague as well as relative. What is tall for a member of the Royal Gorkha Brigade is not tall for a member of the Royal Scottish Guard. We can easily remove this relativity by changing the expression 'tall' to 'tall for a Gorkha'. But vagueness inherent in the term 'tall' remains in 'tall for a Gorkha' too for the latter term is as tolerant as the former.

Vagueness is also to be differentiated from ambiguity. An ambiguous expression has more than one meaning, e.g. 'bank'. Now we fail to give any definite answer to a question containing an ambiguous word just as it is the case with a question containing a vague word, say, 'bald'. But the similarity ends here. If we hesitate to answer when somebody asks whether a particular person has gone to the bank or not, it is because we do not know in which sense the word 'bank' has been used in that particular context. In fact, the above question is not one single question at all. There are two questions lumped into one. So once the ambiguity is removed and the question is specified, there should not be any difficulty in answering the question. But when we hesitate to answer the question: 'Is he bald?' our hesitation is of a different kind; our indecision is irremovable if the person in question exemplifies a borderline case of the concept bald. As a result, though only one question is involved here, neither 'yes' nor 'no' will be the correct answer.

Vagueness is also different from the metaphorical or figurative use of language.[13] Consider the sentences:

> 'He has blue blood in his vein.'
> 'He was born with a silver spoon in his mouth.'

Ordinarily speaking, blood cannot possibly be blue, nor can anybody be born with a silver spoon. But here 'blue' and 'silver spoon in his mouth.' have been used in an extended sense which is parasitic on the ordinary sense of a word. A competent user of language with a little stretch of imagination is able to find out the connection between the established sense and the extended sense of a word and the metaphor becomes intelligible. If some one raises the objection that even then the extended sense does not exactly match the established sense and some imprecision still lingers, our answer will be: (*a*) metaphor was never meant to be that precise and (*b*) this type of imprecision does not make metaphors vague in our sense.

It is on very rare occasions that special features of vagueness have been carefully noted. Most people, even writers with a technical approach to the subject, have used the word 'vague' rather indiscriminately. One example of such indiscrimination is evident in Termini's opening sentence. 'Vagueness, Approximation, Error, Imprecision, Accuracy, etc. all share the same "family resemblance".'[14] I strongly disagree with this remark of Termini. Error, imprecision, etc. are considered defects of language and rightly too, but vagueness is not a defect. Accuracy, error and imprecision also have an evaluative ring around them. If vagueness is placed somewhere in between error and accuracy, we are bound to consider it in terms of value/disvalue. Approximation is the methodological counterpart of a theory which upholds that the nature of objects is precise and we are continuously trying to approximate it, or that the end of our endeavour is beyond our reach, in spite of that we are trying to bridge the gap all the time and there is a uniform way of approaching the objects of our enquiry. These are speculations which require an elaborate support system and we should not prejudge these issues. Besides, vagueness does not necessarily involve the notion of approximation. I am, therefore, against bringing vagueness and approximation under the same head without adding many restrictive clauses to the latter.

But in the field of artificial intelligence especially in knowledge-based systems we find once again vagueness, approximation and imprecision being systematically conflated. Here vagueness has been considered under the generic name ignorance along with ambiguity, imprecision and inaccuracy and the methods to be adopted for handling them have also been classified under one type, viz. approximate reasoning. According to the scholars of AI, vagueness applies to observed facts or data and arises due to noise, resolution, lack of focus/contrast, imprecise definition and masking. It is obvious from the list of sources of vagueness that they do not make any distinction between essential and inessential vagueness. Moreover, the sort of vagueness with which they are concerned is mainly epistemological; so it is at least theoretically possible to remove imprecision by extending our knowledge base, by precisifying definitions and by eliminating all other extraneous impediments. We shall discuss later how to deal with epistemological vagueness within a given knowledge base when we are not in a position to rectify the inadequacies of the system.

## 1.4 IS VAGUENESS SUBJECTIVE?

The query might appear superfluous since in the very definition of vagueness uncertainty has been declared intrinsic and essential vagueness has been distinguished from epistemic vagueness on this ground. Still a suspicion might lurk in the back of one's mind that vagueness is subjective. For vagueness, we have already seen, is a matter of degree. Not all propositions involving the same vague expression are equally vague. The degree of vagueness usually depends on the range of borderline cases, and the fixing of range in its turn depends on the purpose and attitude of the user. When, for example, colours are gradually arranged in a chart ranging from various shades of red through shades of orange to yellow, or chairs are so arranged in an exhibition that the first one is a Chippendale piece and the last one is a stump of tree, an ordinary observer is quite certain about the identity of the extreme instances, but is undecided only about the objects distant from both the ends. But two persons, or even the same person on different occasions, may not agree with the range of the doubtful cases. (There may be disagreement among people regarding the extreme instances as well. A person who means by chair only Louis XIV Chaise may think that Chippendale chairs are not chairs at all; whereas to a breathless vagabond a tree-stump may be chair enough. But both these persons are uncommon persons, hence my emphasis is on an ordinary person.) Then how can one maintain that vagueness is not subjective? The answer has been suggested by Black.[15] Black assumes that while the vagueness of a word involves variations in its application by the users of language in which it occurs, such variations must themselves be systematic and obey statistical laws. To prove that such an assumption is not ungrounded Black made some experiments[16] with vague symbols the results of which clearly exhibited some statistical regularity and, therefore, he concludes that vagueness is objective.

I do not have any quarrel with Black's contention. Still I have to say that there is a lacuna in Black's answer. Black has not explained why such variations in application be systematic. The explanation, I think, is somewhat like this. Members of the same linguistic community share the same socio-biological traits and almost similar cultural background. That is why, there is uniformity in fixing the range of a vague term. I do not of course mean that the cut-off point between a sure case and a doubtful case will always be the same; I only want to emphasize that the ranges of a fringe fixed by different persons belonging to the same linguistic community more or less coincide. This fact, however, does not disprove the context-dependent character of a vague expression.

## 1.5 ARE ALL EXPRESSIONS VAGUE?

An answer to this question presupposes a specific domain of discourse. It is obvious that when we raise such a question, we raise it in the context of a particular language, more specifically, a particular natural language. Any natural language contains two types of expressions—non-technical and technical. Technical expressions are introduced in a language together with their stipulative definitions; the meaning of non-technical expressions, on the contrary, are determined by some established convention. So the latter are more prone to vagueness. The scope of our enquiry, therefore, can be further narrowed down. We want to find out whether or not all non-technical expressions of a natural language are vague.[17]

Someone may legitimately ask: are we thereby upholding that technical expressions of scientific discourses are totally free from all sorts of imprecision? If yes, then what did Russell mean when he said that all symbols, technical or non-technical, used by human beings are bound to be vague and precision can be found only in the extra-terrestrial realm? Let us take up the first question first. Our answer is: yes, technical expressions introduced by stipulative definitions are free from vagueness in our sense, though not from all sorts of imprecision. The reason for taking such a stand is as follows. If a triangle is defined as a figure bounded by three straight lines, having three sides and three angles the sum of which equals 180°, then a figure is either a triangle or a non-triangle, it cannot be more or less a triangle. If a red object is defined as indistinguishable in hue from a uniformly reflecting surface illuminated with monochromatic light of wavelength between 580.27 and 702.35 nm, then an object is either red or not red, there is no ground for indecision.

Russell, however, wanted to put on record a different point. Russell saw vagueness as a property of human representation.[18] As human faculty of representation, he maintains, has some inherent limitation, there always remains a gap between the system represented and the representing system. So accuracy is an ideal limit.

Let me elucidate this point. Russell being a realist instinctively believes that there are objects in the world and objects are as they are. These objects may be represented to us through our senses or representation may be conceptual. Objects of our everyday experience are represented through sense data. There the limits of our physiological constitution constitute the limits of our sense representations. Russell rightly observes, 'Knowledge that we can obtain through our sensations is not as fine-grained as the stimuli to those sensations.'[19] Even an object of mathematical representation, as long as it is a human representation, cannot be accurate.

Even if objects of our perception are reduced to waves in motion, as was done by the theoretical scientists till 1920 and qualitative expressions in our language are replaced by some quantitative expressions, the problem will not be solved. For, accuracy of any measuring instrument used for determining the quantitative parameters can always be doubted. There imprecision may enter through two loopholes. The matching has to be done by a human being with limited physiological capacity and even 'an ideal instrument' cannot really be ideal, since the materials constituting it are governed by the laws of physics and are subject to physical limitations and changes. So some amount of imprecision always remains in spite of all precautions taken. At this point, I would like to draw attention to the fact that Russell did not always make a careful distinction between vagueness and other kinds of imprecision.

Let us now go back to the original problem: are all expressions of a particular natural language vague or not. One may not be ready to go the whole way with Russell to declare that even logical and mathematical symbols are vague, still it has to be granted that Russell has offered a sufficiently convincing explanation why observational terms of our language are vague. His thesis has been corroborated by physiologists and psychologists.

Russellian way, however, is not the only way to show the pervasive character of vagueness. It may be shown to follow from the very definition (Peirce's) of vague expression. An expression is vague if it has borderline instances. By this definition not only 'tall', 'young', 'bald', 'heap', 'child', 'blue', etc. are vague, but expressions like 'book', 'bird', 'pearl', 'chair', 'table', 'cat', etc. also become vague. Let us suppose that we mean by 'book' a collection of pages of printed material expressing ideas having a thematic unity, then how do we distinguish it from a sizable monograph or for that matter a slender monograph from a long learned paper? Thus it can be shown that all non-technical expressions of a natural language possess a penumbra occupied by doubtful cases.

But this is a thesis we cannot accept willingly. How are we to understand what a vague expression is if there is no precise expression? Haig Khatchadourian[20] attempts to rescue non-vague expressions of a natural language by giving a different definition of vagueness. I shall put in summary form the main contention of Khatchadourian. 'Vague' and 'precise' are polar words. One can be understood only in terms of the other. If all ordinary words were vague, then the distinction between 'vague' and 'non-vague' becomes meaningless. One cannot maintain that vagueness of ordinary words could be understood only by comparing and contrasting them with exact words of logic and mathematics. In fact, we learnt to distinguish between vague and non-vague expressions in the context of natural language long before mathematics and logic were systematized. According to Khatchadourian, existence of a fringe should not have been taken as a distinguishing mark as well as the defining condition of a vague expression. The distinguishing criteria as envisaged by Khatchadourian are as follows. For any non-vague expression, ordinary or technical, there exists a set of relatively fixed and well-defined linguistic rules that conventionally govern its usage. There exist some uncontested paradigms for non-vague expressions. A non-vague expression possesses some 'defining features' as its connotation, as well as a denotation. It also expresses a concept that conveys some definite content. Of course, that concept may be open-textured.[21] A vague expression, on the other hand, is not governed by any well-defined rule, its usage can always be contested in principle. Here Khatchadourian sounds a caution. We need not think that all contestable expressions are vague, though the converse undoubtedly holds. The connotation of a vague expression does not possess any defining feature, though sometimes its instances may have some 'family resemblance', but sometimes even family resemblance cannot be traced. A vague expression does not possess any definite content either; only when contrasted with a gibberish it appears to have a definite content.

From the above account two points become obvious and Khatchadourian himself admitted one of them. That is, he is not using vague in our sense. Another point that merits observation is that in his enthusiasm to salvage non-vague expressions of our language from Russell's blow, he has gone to the other extreme. If we follow his account, no ordinary expression can ever be vague. For, whatever has uniform usage in language, maintains Khatchadourian, cannot be vague. But there are vague expressions in our language which we use constantly and even succeed in communicating with them. So, contrary to his claims, he fails to distinguish between vague and non-vague expressions of ordinary language. In his theory an expression can be vague only in one of its eccentric, non-typical usages. The examples of vague expressions which he has mentioned in his essay are technical adaptations of ordinary words by philosophers, e.g. 'copy' by Plato, 'emanation' by Plotinus, 'objectification' by Fichte, 'dread' by Heidegger and so on. But paradoxically for this interpretation, non-vague expressions will also lead to the Sorites Paradox.

In spite of Khatchadourian's insistence on the point that this understanding of 'vague' is the 'ordinary' understanding and ours is only an extension of it, I persist in believing that there is nothing 'extraordinary' about our way of understanding vagueness and we shall be able to draw a distinction between 'essentially vague' expressions and 'inessentially vague' expressions[22] remaining within our ambit.

It is true that human intellect is endowed with a power such that it can arrange almost all instances coming under a particular concept in a graded scale. But not all concepts are naturally so graded. Some concepts have a built-in order in which instances falling under it are arranged and the ordered scale extends up to the diametrically opposite concept. We cannot even properly grasp such a concept without taking into consideration the inherent order associated with it. Concepts related to 'young', 'child', 'bald', 'short', 'green' and all the polar words like hot-cold, fat-thin, etc., are such concepts. 'Young', 'middle aged' and 'old', and 'childhood', 'adolescence' and 'adulthood' are stages in the life span of an individual human being, the former emphasizing its physiological aspect and the latter its psychological aspect. But there is no sharp line of demarcation among any of these stages, one smoothly passes on to the other. Such graded series possess two important characteristics. First, there is a distinct order or direction in the series such that if g–7, for instance, is a borderline case of green and g–6 precedes g–7 then g–6 is a better case of green than g–7. Second, each stage of the series is 'non-discriminably different' from the immediately preceding stage as well as from the immediately succeeding one. Besides, all such concepts by virtue of their inherent nature possess the property of tolerance and can absorb small differences among its instances. Moreover, we cannot by fiat introduce any sharp demarcating line in the series associated with the concept without robbing it of its explanatory value. Such concepts and their linguistic expressions are essentially vague.

In relation to an inessentially vague concept too, instances can be ordered in a graded scale if we arbitrarily choose a paradigm instance of that concept and arrange every other instance in an ordered scale considering their similarity/dissimilarity with the paradigm. But for understanding these concepts it is not necessary to consider the associated graded scale. And if for pragmatic reasons we introduce a sharp dividing line and place a so-called 'borderline case' definitely at one side of the divide, the functional role of the original concept does not change. Consider for instance the expression 'Bird' and let birdiness be the concept associated with it.[23] Now, depending on our notion of a bird, we may select *robin* as the paradigm instance of birdiness and arrange other instances on a graded scale, like, robin, parrot, kite, chicken, duck, pelican, penguin, ostrich, bat. It is evident that for understanding the notion of a bird, understanding this order is not necessary. Besides in these cases we have some licence in selecting the members of the penumbra. Supposing by our definition, a bird has wings, it flies, it has a beak, it lays eggs, etc. But our definition has not said anything about the creatures whose wings can be used as flippers and who swim under water. So we shall be undecided about whether a penguin is a bird or not, we may list it as a borderline case of a bird. But if we grant by decision the status of bird to penguin, it will not harm the original concept of birdiness. So 'bird' is not an essentially vague word. Similar analysis applies to 'book', 'table', 'chair', 'pearl', 'cat' and all other inessentially vague words. In our ordinary everyday communication these inessentially vague expressions are treated as non-vague.

V.C Chappell[24] would have surely objected to this newfangled distinction between essentially and inessentially vague expressions on the ground that we have actually accomplished nothing by this move. First we have wronged against ordinary language by obliterating the distinction between 'vague' and 'clear' since both vague and clear words have 'undecidable cases' with regard to the question of their application. But as 'vague' cannot be properly understood without contrasting it with 'clear' we have revised the language and have introduced a new pair of words to express the same distinctions previously expressed by the words 'clear' and 'vague'.

This objection has some point. I concede that our move is not strictly in accordance with ordinary usage. We would have been very happy if we could retain the ordinary distinction between vague and clear words. But that was not to be. For there is no logical justification for making such a distinction. Yet we had to explain the established usage in this context. Hence we uphold the most plausible alternative.

### 1.6 DIFFERENT TYPES OF VAGUE EXPRESSIONS

It is yet to be seen what types of linguistic expressions are liable to be affected by vagueness. We shall take up this task right now.

Vagueness can affect both singular and general terms of a language. To quote Quine:

> A singular term naming a physical object can be vague in point of boundaries of that object in space time, while a general term can be vague in point of marginal hangers-on of its extension.[25]

Thus Mount Everest is vague if it is not settled how far from the summit of Mount Everest one can be and still claim to be on Mount Everest. The general term 'Mountain', on the other hand, is vague for we do not know where a mountain ends and where it begins. Consequently we cannot decide whether any raised terrain above a certain height is to be considered a mountain or not; sometimes we cannot even tell whether there is one mountain or two mountains.

Singular terms may be affected by yet another type of vagueness. If a singular term is of the form 'the ø', in other words, if the singular term in question is a definite description and ø is vague, then 'the ø' is vague. That is to say, the vagueness of 'the ø' is derivative.

Countable nouns like 'heap', 'flock', 'herd', etc. are all vague because the number of elements belonging to collections referred to by countable nouns are never specified.

That many adjectives are vague is evident from the examples already used. 'Tall', 'bald', and other non-numeral adjectives are taken as paradigmatic vague expressions by everybody dealing with vagueness.

Adverbs like 'slow', 'fast' also possess the characteristic features of vagueness listed above. But comparative expressions like 'taller than', 'slower than' are not vague even though 'tall', 'slow', etc. are. Quantifiers like 'most', 'few', 'many', 'rather', 'almost' are vague. Black names them pseudo-quantifiers as opposed to the so-called 'respectable' quantifiers, viz. 'all', 'any'.[26] This derogatory christening smacks of Fregean sentiments. Recently such quantifiers have gained respectability due to the efforts of the non-standard and fuzzy logicians.

Now vagueness pertaining to different types of linguistic expressions may be of different sorts. I have already made it clear that vague expressions in our language are rule guided. Sometimes there is only one criterion of application of a vague expression, here vagueness is unidimensional. Instances of such expressions can be plotted on one single line. At one extreme of the line the vague expression is applicable, at the other extreme it is inapplicable but in between lies the zone where we cannot tell whether the expression is applicable or not, e.g. 'red'. But there are some terms which are associated with multiple criteria of usage. But these criteria are neither singly necessary nor jointly sufficient for application of a vague term to its reference. Naturally instances of one such expression is to be plotted against a number of intersecting lines. The best illustration of such a term having multiple criteria has been provided by Wittgenstein in *Philosophical Investigations*.[27] Anybody familiar with the literature must have guessed that I am referring to his classic example of 'game' for which he has listed a set C of typical characteristics $C_1, \ldots, C_n$. Now, some event to be a game must possess a number of characteristics from this set. Though the criteria are widely different and the event referred to by 'game' are divergent yet all of them can have the name 'game' as there is a 'family resemblance' present among these events. But how many of them, or in what combination, these characteristics will constitute an adequate criteria for application of 'game' cannot be determined *a priori.* Actually the grouping varies from context to context. This sort of vagueness can be traced in inessentially vague expressions too.

Expressions affected by simple vagueness give rise to the sorites paradox quite naturally. But the paradox is not obvious with expressions having multiple criteria of application. For in the latter case we have to decide upon the paradigm first and that is a tricky affair. Only then by comparing other cases with the paradigm can we arrange all of them in a linear order.

To make this point intelligible let us go back to the example of 'game'. Let us spell out some elements of the set of characteristic features C.[28] Let $C_1$ be—there are rules that govern the activity, $C_2$: there is the possibility of winning, $C_3$: it is pleasant diversion, and $C_4$: the players must exercise some specific skill. Now, if we take the cluster $C_1$, $C_3$ and $C_4$, then 'patience' is a game, if, on the other hand, we make $C_2$ a necessary condition, then 'patience' is definitely not a game. If only $C_3$ is considered adequate then 'ring-a-ring-a-roses' becomes a game, otherwise not. But which one of these games is to be taken as paradigmatic? That will depend on which of the clusters we consider to be aptly representing the concept of game. If we think that the notion of winning is an inalienable feature of a game, then 'patience' and 'ring-a-ring-a-roses' will be placed lower down the scale but tennis, football, etc. will come at the top. This ordering will change if we understand 'game' in a different manner. So to tackle complex vague expressions we have to decide which are the quorum features[29] from a set of typical features the possession of which will determine a positive or a negative instance of the expression. But there will be every possibility of having difference of opinion among the users of the expression unless we can settle issues like why a particular cluster is representative of the paradigm, why some of the features should carry more weight than others, etc. Again, there may be expressions in our language, such as, 'neurotic' for which we cannot even exhaustively enumerate the relevant conditions forming the set C. Therefore, we shall always be unsure about the typical use of such an expression. In spite of these hurdles, once we fix the paradigm and arrange all instances falling under a particular concept in a series, the paradox can be formulated.

## 1.7 IS VAGUENESS ERADICABLE?

One important question that we cannot but raise at this point is whether vagueness is eradicable. This question once again has two facets (i) whether it is possible to eradicate vagueness and (ii) whether it is advisable to eradicate vagueness. Alston[30] and Waismann[31] have offered incisive arguments to show that total eradication of vagueness from our thought and natural language is impossible. Without going into the details of the topic I shall just mention two important arguments in favour of the thesis of the impossibility of removal of vagueness from our language. The first one is the argument from impossibility of attaining precision through quantization. Not all qualitative expressions of a language are amenable to quantization. Besides as we have already seen in 1.5, human power of measurement is limited. The second argument is the one from the open texture of all 'observational' expressions. We have dealt with this point in the previous section but we will reformulate it by introducing Waismann's phrase 'open-texture'.

In the very last section we have admitted the possibility of there being some expressions in our language such that we cannot precisely grasp their criterion of application simply because we can never exhaust enumerating their relevant characteristic features. Waismann points out that such expressions may have infinite possibilities. We may temporarily choose a set of quorum features for a term and on the basis of that try to demarcate between the region of application and non-application of that term; but there may arise a situation where we shall be in a fix as to the question whether or not to apply the term. Waismann starts with the example of an ordinary cat which is four-legged, furry and miaows. But what about the Chesire Cat of Lewis Carroll who grins or the pet of Russell which can grow hungry even without existence? Should we call them cat or not? To eliminate vagueness one may decide not to include features of 'grinning' or 'getting hungry without existing' into the set of characteristic features of cat and thus making the Cheshire Cat or the Russellian Cat non-cats. But one may have to face hundreds of such situations because of the 'open-texture' or ever-expanding possibilities of an 'observational' term. So Waismann rightly concludes that it is not possible to eliminate this kind of vagueness completely since no concept can be defined 'in such a way that every nook and cranny is blocked against entry of "doubt".'[32]

Another attempt at eliminating vagueness was made by the ideal language philosophers who tried to remove vagueness of natural language by translating natural language expressions into an ideal language. But even introduction of an ideal language will not solve all our problems. For one thing we have to admit that an ideal language has much less expressive power and can never supplant natural language. Besides, an ideal language to be useful has got to be interpreted and that interpretation once again cannot be given in another ideal language. So one will have to rely on some natural language for interpretation and in the process the ideal language will be contaminated.

But why should anyone try to eliminate vague expressions in the first place? At this juncture I feel that I shall present the briefest possible outline of the famous Frege-Wittgenstein[33] controversy over vagueness just to show how very differently philosophers have reacted to this particular issue. Frege always thought that vagueness is a defect of natural language and unless vagueness is removed, no coherent semantics of natural language can be arrived at. Of course, by semantics Frege means the classical two-valued semantics and Frege is right in maintaining that such a framework cannot accommodate vague expressions. It is doubtful that natural language can ever be free of vagueness so Frege concluded that it cannot be the proper vehicle of precise thought. That is why Frege developed his concept script which, according to him, alone can represent our precise thoughts properly. Wittgenstein in *Philosophical Investigations* countered Fregean thesis and upheld that vagueness is an indispensable feature of natural language and we need not try to remove it for whatever is 'inexact' is not necessarily 'unusable'.[34] On the contrary, we have to accept the fact that many natural language expressions are vague. We can communicate by using them, not only in spite of their vagueness but also because of their vagueness. To quote from Wittgenstein:

> One might say that the concept 'game' is a concept with blurred edges.—'But is a blurred concept a concept at all?' Is an indistinct photograph a picture of a person at all? Is it always even an advantage to replace an indistinct picture by a sharp one? Isn't the indistinct one often exactly what we mean?[35]

A few pages later he writes:

> We want to say there can't be any vagueness in logic. The idea now absorbs us, that the ideal 'must' be found in reality.[36]

This is actually a dig at the Fregean thesis that we can never have any vague concept or an incomplete object in reality. Wittgenstein does not subscribe to this position simply because it goes against one of our very powerful intuitions that we could not operate with language as we do unless many expressions of natural language displayed vagueness. This is the sum and substance of the Wittgensteinian polemics.

Let us now go back to the second question: whether it is advisable to eradicate vagueness. Time and again, some scholars have drawn our attention to the need for vague expressions in natural language. According to them, vagueness is not an out and out undesirable feature of our language. There are situations where vagueness of language is rather a boon, e.g. in political discourses and diplomatic encounter.[37] Quine in *Word and Object* pointed out long ago what other 'good purposes are often served by not tampering with vagueness'. According to him, vagueness is not incompatible with precision. Vague expressions can convey certain items, especially about cultural objects, more effectively than precise expressions.

As he writes:

> A painter with a limited palette can achieve more precise representation by thinning and combining his colors than a mosaic worker can achieve with his limited variety of tiles, and skilful superimposing of vagueness has similar advantages over the fitting together of precise technical terms.[38]

Vagueness has another theoretical advantage in coping with what Quine calls linearity of discourse. Sometimes it so happens, particularly in the context of polar concepts, that understanding of some concept, say, B depends on understanding of a different concept A. But the nature of A may be such that A cannot be properly understood without prior understanding of certain features of B. Here vagueness comes handy. First A is stated vaguely and B is tentatively explained, then one can once again take up A and have fairly precise understanding of it. Thus one can avoid the tedious task of unlearning precise but false preliminary characterizations of A.

Besides, vagueness of a sentential component does not always affect the truth value of that sentence. Only sentences whose truth values depend on the penumbra of a vague word turn out to be problematic.

Popper has warned us succinctly that 'precision for its own sake' is not a virtue but an obsession which should not be cultivated. He has said in his *Autobiography:*

> I do not suggest, of course, that an increase in the precision of, say, a prediction, or even of a formulation, may not sometimes be highly desirable. What I do suggest is that it is always undesirable to make an effort to increase precision for its own sake—especially linguistic

> precision—since this usually leads to loss of clarity . . . one should never try to be more precise than the problem situation demands . . . an increase in precision or exactness has only a pragmatic value as a means to some definite end.[39]

We shall, therefore, try to take vagueness in our stride. In the long run we might have to alter our logico-semantic framework. But we shall not be going in for an alternative logic unless a step in that direction becomes absolutely necessary for explaining the general nature of vagueness and its role in human communication as well as for solving the sorites paradox.

## NOTES AND REFERENCES

1. L. Wittgenstein (1953), p. 88.
2. C.S. Peirce (1902).
3. B. Russell (1923).
4. C.S. Peirce (1902), p. 248.
5. The term was coined by Russell in 'Vagueness' (1923).
6. Max Black (1954), p. 37.
7. B. Russell (1923), p. 87.
8. Crispin Wright (1975), p. 334.
9. Ibid., p. 337.
10. B. Russell (1923), p. 89.
11. Max Black (1954), p. 29.
12. R.M. Sainsbury (1988), p. 27.
13. W.P. Alston (1964).
14. S. Termini (1984), p. 205.
15. Max Black (1954).
16. Ibid., pp. 52–57.
17. We are not including purely syncategorematic expressions and articles in isolation within the ambit of our discourse.
18. B. Russell (1923).
19. Ibid., p. 87.
20. H. Khatchadourian (1962), pp. 138–52.
21. Please see note 32.
22. The hint of such a distinction can be found in *Paradoxes* by R.M. Sainsbury (1988), p. 38.
23. The example has been used by George Lakoff (1973), p. 459.
24. V.C. Chappell (1964), pp. 19–20.
25. W.V.O. Quine (1960), p. 126.
26. Max Black (1954), p. 42.
27. L. Wittgenstein (1953), p. 60.

28. G. Pitcher (1964), has analyzed Wittgenstein's notion of game in this manner.
29. John Hospers (1977), p. 71.
30. W.P. Alston (1964), pp. 90–95.
31. F. Waismann (1953), pp. 119–20.
32. Ibid., p. 38.

    Waismann drew a subtle distinction between vagueness and open-texture. According to him, 'A word which is actually used in a fluctuating way (such as 'heap' or 'pink') is said to be vague; a term like 'gold', though its actual use may not be vague, is non-exhaustive or of an open-texture in that we can never fill up all the possible gaps through which a doubt may seep in'. Open texture, then, is something like possibility of vagueness.

    In our terminology *essentially* vague expressions are actually vague whereas *inessentially* vague expressions are merely open-textured.
33. Russell in his Introduction to the *Tractatus*, L. Wittgenstein (1961) G. Frege (1952); L. Wittgenstein (1953).
34. L. Wittgenstein (1953), p. 88.
35. Ibid., p. 71.
36. Ibid., p. 101.
37. W.P. Alston (1964), p. 86.
38. Quine (1960) quotes on p. 127 from I.A. Richards (1936), p. 48.
39. *The Philosophy of Karl Popper*, edited by P.A. Schilpp (1974), p. 17.

CHAPTER 2

# Vagueness, Observation and Coherence

## 2.1 OBSERVATION AND VAGUENESS

The remark that observational terms are vague has almost become platitudinous. We saw in the previous chapter that difference of opinion regarding the nature, scope, foundation and status of vagueness has not made any difference to this particular point. Russell adduced physiological and psychological reasons for vagueness of observational terms. Waismann found the source of vagueness in the 'open texture' of observational expressions.

Yet, when we are faced with the question what an observational term is, we ponder for some time. For observational/theoretical dichotomy, as popularized by Carnap, has become obsolete today, and almost all attempts at defining an observational term have met with counter-examples. So, before enquiring whether observational terms are necessarily vague and whether observational terms alone are vague, let us first settle the sense of 'observational term' relevant to the present context.

The first cue in this regard may be taken from Carnap though it is not the case that I find Carnap's characterization of observationality adequate. But Carnap had set the stage for this sort of discussion and if I do not point out why I dissent from Carnap, readers may unconsciously impose Carnap's views on me and the result will be an avoidable confusion.[1]

Carnap has not given any formal definition but has listed some important features of observational terms which are usually manifested in some well-known examples of observational predicates. As he puts it,

The terms of Vo (i.e. the observation vocabulary) are

> predicates designating observable properties of events or things (e.g. 'blue', 'hot', 'large', etc.) or observable relations between them (e.g. 'X is warmer than Y', 'X is contiguous to Y', etc.).[2]

So 'blue', 'hot', 'large' are considered typical examples of observation terms by Carnap all of which are, we have seen, vague in our sense of the term.

In 'Testability and Meaning' Carnap points out that an observational term must not only correspond to an observational quality but the observer must be able to determine whether the quality is present or not in a relatively short time and with a high degree of confirmation.

These characterizations are not found very effective. For we are always in a quandary if we are to answer questions like: how short is relatively short time, what will count as high degree of conformation and so on.

Carnap defined the characteristics of observational terms in contradistinction to theoretical terms. That is why he emphasized the following points:

(*a*) Observational terms can in principle refer to only observable things and properties.
(*b*) Observational terms are prior to theoretical terms both from the points of view of origin and of verification.
(*c*) Unobservables are to be explained by theoretical terms.

A good many philosophers, however, are not willing to drive a wedge between observational and theoretical. For, to them pure observation is a myth; observation is always theory-laden. They, therefore, contest Carnap's view. The sum and substance of their argument is: we cannot reasonably draw any line between what is observational and what is theoretical. While we observe an object, we do not take in all its features. To which features of an object our observation will be directed depends on what theory we have at the back of our minds. Besides, we can easily refer to and understand unobservables without recourse to any theoretical term. For example, even a pre-school child can easily comprehend a story about 'people too little to see' and the expression does not contain a single theoretical term.[3] On the other hand, an almost unanimously accepted observational term like 'red' refers to something unobservable in one of its very important senses. If by 'red' is meant red *corpuscles* or *light wave of a particular frequency* then 'red' ceases to be an observation term. For neither *corpuscles* nor *light waves* are observable.

If these philosophers are right, then what do we mean by saying that *observational* terms are vague? We may try to answer the question following Crispin Wright. And we should remember what Wright maintains in respect of colour predicates is easily extendable to other observational terms. Wright writes:

> colour predicates, it is plausible to suppose, are in the following sense purely observational: if one can tell at all what colour something is, one can tell just by looking at it. The look of an object described its colour, as the feeling of an object decided its texture or the sound of a note its pitch.[4]

So, a predicate is observational if it is determined *solely* by observation. It is usually thought that we cannot be mistaken about what we come to know through direct observation. Wright does neither emphasize nor contest this point. But the point to which he wants to draw our attention is that if there is any error in determining whether an observational predicate is correctly applying to a thing then that error can be rectified and must be rectified by observation alone. Thus, if we erroneously say that a shade is orange while it is actually red, our error is to be rectified just by looking at the shade again and not by measuring the frequency of the corresponding light wave by a spectrophotometer.

There is another cluster of predicates, e.g. 'heap', 'old', 'young', 'small', 'bald', 'tall', etc., which are not generally considered observational like 'red', 'sweet', 'fragrant', 'smooth' or 'loud'. In the case of the first cluster, it has often been doubted, some non-observational elements, metrical or inferential or both, are tacitly involved. But this difficulty can be circumvented. Each predicate of the first cluster can be given a non-metrical reading. And if one starts questioning how much in our observation we actually observe and how much we infer, one will be in deep trouble. The person will probably end up with pure myth of bare observation. Keeping these things in mind, if we redefine 'observational predicates' as those that characterize a thing in exactly the same way as it appears 'to an ordinary observer on casual observation'[5] without the aid of any instrument, metric scale or counting system, then predicates belonging to both the clusters may be called observational. Yet, to avoid unnecessary confusions and misconceptions we propose to call the first cluster of predicates *semi-observational* and the second cluster *purely observational*.

Crispin Wright has repeatedly mentioned that one important feature shared in common by semi-observational and purely observational predicates is that they are to be learned ostensively. This remark has caused genuine puzzlement to all who take 'ostensive definition' in a non-Wittgensteinian sense. To Wittgenstein ostensive learning does not merely comprise of grasping the meaning of words by being shown objects and hearing their names pronounced but it involves the mastery of the word's general use.[6] Being an object of ostensive learning when understood in this sense applies to 'red' and 'heap' with equal facility.

This way of viewing an observational predicate, it is evident, will rule out 'red' in the physicist's sense to be observational. Only 'red' as ostensively introduced will qualify as observational. Similarly 'tall' when expressed in terms of centimetres or 'heap' in terms of grain count will disqualify.

But we cannot and should not overlook a special problem concerning colour predicates.[7] Just now we have summarily discarded the scientists' sense of 'red', but not without compunction. We have been told many times by the experts that the red colour that we see is nothing but a light wave of a specific frequency. The saying has become so well-entrenched in our web of belief that 'red' is usually predicated of a thing if it conforms either to the ostensive definition or to the physicist's definition. We cannot even always decide which of the two senses is basic. The balance swings one way or the other depending on our purpose at hand.

None of these considerations, however, compels us to admit that the physicist's 'red' is observational too. For, it is not only the case that a light wave is unobservable, but also there is no guarantee that a light wave of the specified range will have universal concomitance with observed red. That these two reds do not always go together becomes evident from the colour perception of a colour-blind person.

C.D. Broad contends that 'being red' is an ambiguous predicate. Broad's thesis is corroborated by the philosopher's distinction between 'phenomenal red' and 'physical red'. While 'phenomenal red' is undoubtedly observational, 'physical red' is not. The physical counterpart of the red-as-it-appears to us can never be an object of unaided observation.

But in colour perceptions of normal human observers physical red and phenomenal red are usually found to be correlated. The question may be raised: what happens if they are discrepant? How do we decide which of the two senses we should back in case there is a conflict between them? Is any of the above senses of 'red' more basic than the other? The general tendency is to consider the observational red to be more basic than the physical red but there is no reason why the converse should not be accepted if the situation is viewed from a different perspective.

Let us consider an imaginary situation.[8] Let us suppose that in a particular community everybody calls a particular shade 'red' but the light wave corresponding to that shade does not fall within the frequency range specified for red colour by the scientists. In such a situation what should be our attitude? Should we consider community assent to be sacrosanct or should we go by scientific measurement? The thumb rule is to specify the purpose for which the word is being used and in no time we shall be able to determine the appropriate sense of 'red'.

Let us elaborate our example of the imaginary community. Suppose, in the above-said community every participant is to wear a red armband in a particular meeting. The armbands which look red to every normal observer will meet the requirement of this particular situation irrespective of whether or not that particular shade of red conforms to the physicist's criterion. But suppose again that someone from that community wants to calibrate an instrument or to conduct a sensitivity test, then the former exercise will not be adequate. Here he will have to rely on the reading of the instruments measuring wavelengths, i.e. he has to use 'red' in the physicist's sense.

We must therefore admit that some situations demand that 'being red' should be read in a non-observational way. And we shall see later that non-observational reading of a colour-predicate does not guarantee immunity for vagueness or incoherence.

Observational terms, we have found in the last chapter, are vague because there are situations where it is not possible to determine whether the terms apply or not. This, we have said, is due to the fact that a vague expression lacks sharp boundary. Now we shall see that vagueness of observational terms follows directly from our definition of observationality.

Observational terms of our language are applied depending on our unaided observation. But there are certain limits to human power of observation and sensory discrimination. Too minute differences amongst two things cannot be detected by naked observation. Consequently two things, the difference amongst which lies below the threshold of our perception, appear indistinguishable even though there remain some unnoticed physical differences. But as the predicates under consideration are observational, non-discriminable physical differences do not affect their applicability. Not only that, applicability of such predicates should be tolerant to discernible marginal changes too. For example, if two collections of pyramidal shape marginally vary with respect to size, we call both of them heaps. Similarly slight difference in quantity of hairs of two persons does not make any difference to the applicability of the predicate 'bald'; if one of them is called 'bald', the other should also have the same appellation. This character of remaining unaffected in face of small variations was called 'tolerance-susceptibility'. It is important that we grant tolerance with respect to marginal changes to all observational terms. For, observational terms are known ostensively and we could never have known or used such expressions if too subtle differences were to be taken into account either perceptually or by way of remembering. Since observational predicates are tolerant, we cannot draw any sharp line of demarcation between cases where they apply and cases where they fail to apply. So, it is the tolerance susceptible nature of observational predicates that makes them vague. Non-observational predicates do not possess this feature. If we set a lower limit to the number of grains collected in a heap, say 100 grains, and resort to counting, then we have a precise cut-off point. Any collection of a particular shape containing 100 grains or more will be a heap. Moreover, though a collection of the specified shape containing 100 grains is a heap, a collection of the similar shape containing 99 grains will not be a heap even if these two collections appear indistinguishable in size to an ordinary observer on casual observation. But then 'heap' will be neither observational, nor tolerant, nor vague.

An objection might be anticipated at this point. If observation is the sole determinant of the applicability of a predicate like 'heap', then why should its applicability be affected by its tolerant nature? Why cannot we stop calling a collection heap the moment it ceases to 'look heap-y'? Actually in our everyday life we go on stipulating such cut-off points in an *ad hoc* manner and that does not create any problem in communicating with observational expressions. This is true. But the problem is, can we really be sure in the case of a *marginal heap* whether it 'looks heap-y' or not? If there is one such case that would serve as a counter-instance to the generalization: whatever does not 'look heap-y' is not a heap. And it is very often indeterminate whether something is looking heap-y or not.

This then explains why the observational terms are vague.

Though it is a general belief that observational predicates of our language referring to phenomenal properties are worst affected by vagueness, predicates referring to physical properties are also equally susceptible to vagueness. Rohit Parikh[9] very forcefully argues that paradoxes related to vagueness 'do not arise from the fact that we are restricting ourselves to unaided vision. They will also occur if we consider a physicist who is allowed the use of instruments, only he will be dealing with smaller differences'.[10] The physicists will unhesitatingly support Parikh's contention and will point out that no measurement is precise and that no mathematical formula used as a picture of reality can be regarded as a precise picture.

But we have pointed out in Chapter One that all imprecision do not amount to vagueness. So we have to examine carefully Parikh's thesis that predicates corresponding to physical qualities are also vague.

Parikh has taken the instance of physical colour to substantiate his thesis. According to the physicists, the physical counterparts of our perceived colours are wavelengths usually measured in micro-millimetres. The wavelengths of pure spectrum colours under laboratory conditions can be measured almost accurately. Then the difference between two pure spectrum colours depend on the difference between two wavelengths. But usually most objects reflect light of many different wavelengths though not in equal proportions. A red object, for example, reflects more red light but also some blue, some yellow and some green lights. So it is usual practice among physicists to consider the physical colour of an object a function $f$ from the visible spectrum into the set $[0, 1]$, the value of $f$ at a wavelength $x$ being the proportion of incident light of wavelength $x$ which is reflected by the object in question. So the space constituted by physical colours is an infinite dimensional space. But our visual colour space is only three dimensional for most colours can be obtained by an adequate mixture of three primary colours. The space corresponding to a pure spectrum colour is uni-dimensional and such a colour is obtainable only under laboratory conditions. Yet for simplicity's sake we shall substantiate our point by pure spectrum colours.

Let us take for instance the pure spectrum colour red. There are infinite number of shades of red corresponding to which there are infinite number of wavelengths of a specified range. Let us grant for the time being that any object reflecting wavelength between 560 nm and 700 nm be called red. Now, even if we can fix a certain wavelength to be a particular shade of physical red, we shall never be able to measure precisely the said wavelength, not even with a very sensitive spectrophotometer. That is why our theories of measurement always allow for some amount of deviation. Let us suppose that a particular shade of physical red measures $y$ units. If the measuring meter records $y \pm .5$ units as the value of the same shade subsequently, we might consider the first measurement erroneous. But if the subsequent reading of the shade turns out to be $y \pm .2$ then the two readings may be considered not unequal. Once we allow this deviation, the floodgate will be opened. In case of expressions corresponding to observational quality the most important question was how much tolerance should be allowed? Here the analogous question will be how much deviation in measurement should be allowed? Should we call an object reflecting wavelength measuring 559.8 nm red? If yes, then why not 559.6 nm and so on? Therefore, in such cases we shall never know the precise limit of application of 'physical red'. Thus 'physical red' is just as troublesome as 'phenomenal red' is. One might solve this problem by fixing the limit of deviation. Supposing $\pm .2$ is the limit, no wavelength measuring less than 559.8 nm or greater than 700.2 nm should be considered red. Admission of such a strict cut-off point might have solved our problem if the colour spectrum were not a continuum. But the colour spectrum being a continuum we cannot legitimately draw a sharp boundary line without giving up the distinction between 'discrete' and 'continuous'. The physicists do uphold the said distinction. Hence we would like to maintain with Parikh that vagueness also affects predicates corresponding to physical properties whenever the physicists attempt to correlate these properties with numbers.

## 2.2 OBSERVATION AND INCOHERENCE

Now that we know what an observational term is and why vagueness follows from observationality, we must try to find out why vague expressions lead to incoherence in our language. To start with we shall take once again 'being red' as an example of a vague observational term and whatever we are establishing in connection with 'being red' will be applicable to 'being tall', 'being bald', etc.

To make the paradoxical nature of observational terms and the consequent incoherence of language evident we are going to state two reasonable maxims depending on our intuitive notion of observationality.

> MO : If an observational property corresponding to an observational predicate P is observable through some perceptual device d, then it is inconceivable that an observer by exercising *d* comes to take an item O to be what P says something to be, while O is not what P would say it to be, even though no abnormality is involved in the perceiver or in the accompanying circumstances.[11]

This general formulation of the first maxim of observationality is slightly awkward. Its instantiation in terms of visual perception of red can be formulated quite simply. In plain words it would mean: if the observational property red is visually perceptible then it is inconceivable that an observer holds an object to be red depending on his visual perception while the object is not red, even though no abnormality is present either in the observer or in the accompanying circumstances. That is, when a normal observer under suitable conditions calls an object red just by the look of it, then the object is red.

The second maxim of observationality will take the following form:

> MO1: If two objects a and b are indistinguishable in respect of a feature that alone matters for the application of an observational predicate, say P, and if a is P, then b is P too.[12]

That is, if two objects a and b are indistinguishable in respect of colour and the predicate red is applicable to a, then it is also applicable to b. The tenability of MO1 is too obvious in the context of purely observational predicates. The applicability of purely observational predicate is determined solely by the use of the senses and a casual observer is its final arbiter. So when a casual observer applies a purely observational predicate relying on his sense organs to an object observationally indistinguishable from another object in respect of a feature relative to the said predicate, he should apply the predicate to the second object too.

But the tenability of the second maxim may not be that obvious in case of semi-observational predicates. Yet the maxim must hold. To quote Wright:

> It would be a poor joke on the recipient of an ostensive definition if the defined expression applies selectively among situations indistinguishable from one which was originally displayed to him as a paradigm.[13]

We shall now see how following these two apparently innocent maxims we arrive at inconsistency.

The first maxim of observationality highlights the claim that observational predicates are applicable on the basis of observation and observation alone. The second maxim follows from this claim. If an observational predicate applies to an object, then it applies to another object indistinguishable from the former with respect to the relevant property. If we are to apply or withhold a predicate depending on some unobservable difference, then observation would not provide the adequate basis for the application of an observational predicate and thus the claim upheld by the first maxim will be undetermined. The two maxims of observationality are, therefore, compatible with one another.

But when some visually indistinguishable objects are arranged in an ordered series, sometimes we do justifiably apply some predicate to the first member of the series but withhold the same predicate from the last member or the last few members. Let us assume that we are presented with a number of colour samples $A_1 \ldots A_n$, and the first sample $A_1$ is red and looks red. The samples $A_2$ through $A_n$ are each indistinguishable from the immediately preceding sample, yet $A_n$ is and looks not red. So when objects are arranged in a chain, we find that the two maxims of observationality appear to clash and give rise to inconsistency.

The easiest way out of this predicament is either to blame the maxims or to conclude that the predicate under consideration is not really observational. The maxims cannot be given up because they conform to our intuitive understanding of observationality. Nor can we maintain that predicates like 'is red', 'looks red', etc. are not observational. Our problem, therefore, boils down to this: if the maxims are acceptable and the given predicate is observational, then how are we to avoid inconsistency? The answer according to Dummett is that we cannot. Let us therefore, see why Dummett thinks that observational predicates are bound to introduce incoherence in a language.

## 2.3 DUMMETT ON INCOHERENCE IN LANGUAGE

Dummett exposes incoherence in language by specifying the extension of any vague predicate which is observational in nature. The extension of any vague predicate, says Dummett, following a strict finitist, is an ordered series of a peculiar nature. Let us try to understand Dummett's argument step by step. Consider a series of homogeneously coloured strips where each contiguous members are so similar that they form a continuous band of colour ranging from red to orange. Let this series be named R and the shades $R_1$ to $R_n$. $R_1$ as presented to us is red and is also indistinguishable from $R_2$. So $R_2$ is red.

Again $R_2$ is indistinguishable from $R_3$ and $R_3$ is red . . . so is $R_{n-1}$ is indistinguishable from $R_n$. Then by MO1, $R_n$ is red. But $R_n$ just by the look of it, is different from $R_1$ and looks orange. Then by MO, $R_n$ is and looks orange. Thus $R_n$, we should say, is and looks both red and orange and is therefore inconsistent. The series R displays this inconsistency because it is an ordered totality which is both weakly finite and weakly infinite. (A detailed analysis of such totalities will be given in later chapters. For the time being I shall mention their definitions only. A weakly infinite totality has a well-ordering with no last member and the totality of some finite ordinal n is weakly finite where there is no nth member.) Such a totality, maintains Dummett, cannot but be inconsistent. Let us reconsider the series R. Suppose we have put one dot on each strip of R. Now, R is weakly infinite for every dot appearing in the red background has a successor dot to the right of it which also appears in the red background. But this totality is also weakly finite for though we are not aware of the last red shade or the exact cross-over point between red and orange yet not all dots are on the red background since red shades gradually merge with shades of orange.

The peculiar nature of the totality of this type corresponding to a vague term is actually responsible for incoherence of language. The series is such that transition from one shade to the next shade is not observable. But colour predicates being observational predicates are guided by the maxim MO1. So any shade which is not distinguishable from the next cannot possess different properties. That is, if one is red, the other is red too. So the difference between two shades of the series, if there is any, is not discriminable by our sense organs. MO1 demands that such non-discriminable difference be transitive. But the series at hand is also weakly finite. That means, the nth term falls outside the red segment. So transitivity of non-discriminable difference comes to an end, or in other words, non-discriminable difference between two shades becomes *non-transitive* somewhere along the series thus engendering inconsistency. That is why Dummett writes:

> Hence it appears to follow that the use of any predicate which is taken as governed by such a principle is potentially inconsistent.[14]

One may wonder what does Dummett actually mean by consistency? He himself gives the following answer.

> 'Consistent' here means that it would be impossible to force someone, by appeal to rules of use that he acknowledged as correct, to contradict himself over whether the predicate applied to a given object.[15]

But very often we are compelled to admit by following the maxims of observationality that an object which is red is also orange (i.e. not red) since we do not know where the relation of indistinguishability becomes non-transitive, i.e. where red ends and orange begins.

Dummett's notion of consistency as mentioned above can be directly linked with his general notion of systematization.[16] Dummett considers the practice of using a sentence unacceptable if it is impossible to systematize it. The use of any observational sentence has at least two different aspects. One aspect 'lies in the properties we have acquired to assent to and dissent from them under certain types of stimuli, another lies in the possibility of deducing them by means of non-observational statements'. If our language as a whole is to be coherent, there must be harmony between these two aspects. But a vague observational sentence fails to fulfil this condition. It is a part of our acquired propensity that we call an object red, if it appears red to us just by looking at it. But when we try to apply the predicate 'red' depending on the transitivity of the relation of indistinguishability, it comes into conflict with the result of our perception and thus violates Dummett's dictum: 'it must not be possible to deduce observation statements from which the perceptual stimuli dissent.'

Dummett, therefore, concludes in 'Wang's Paradox' that the whole notion of phenomenal quality is in jeopardy. It is better to accept that there are no phenomenal properties. There are only physical properties of things.

This conclusion of Dummett, however, does not help us in the least to understand how we do communicate by using such inconsistent observational predicates.

Though this intrinsic inconsistency is a special feature of observational terms, Dummett has shown that any and every observational expression is not endowed with this feature. A relational expression like 'x is discriminably different from y' or 'x is more red than y' though observational is not inconsistent. Even 'red' ceases to be vague if its application depends on observational comparison. If application of 'red' is guided by a comparison with a colour chart, as upheld by Wittgenstein in *Philosophical Investigations*, then it can also have a definite and consistent use. In that case, 'red' will not be observational in the normal sense. Besides, there are some practical difficulties if we are to determine a colour not just by looking at it but also by making a comparison with a handy prototype.

Could we successfully evade the intrinsic inconsistency of an observational predicate by showing that its extension is not a series which is both weakly finite and weakly infinite? Let us seriously consider the possibility. Suppose there are four shades in a graded colour series R such that $R_2$ as presented is indistinguishable from $R_1$, $R_3$ as presented is indistinguishable from $R_2$ but $R_4$ as presented is clearly distinguishable from $R_1$. This series, characterized by non-transitive non-discriminable differences, is definitely weakly finite. But this series cannot be weakly infinite simply because there is a last red strip and that is $R_3$. It follows, therefore, 'red' the extension of which is the series R can no longer be said to be vague for the series satisfying the predicate 'red' admits of a sharp dividing line.

Inconsistency of observational predicates can be removed only at the cost of their phenomenality. It might be argued that though $R_2$ appears to be indistinguishable from $R_1$, $R_3$ from $R_2$ and $R_1$, yet all of them must have been different otherwise $R_4$ could not have been different from $R_1$. This sort of argument cannot be put forward in case of phenomenal predicates. For in this case indistinguishability and identity coincide. So either two phenomenal predicates which appear indistinguishable are really indistinguishable or none of them is phenomenal. An inevitable consequence of it is that either we learn to live with inconsistency or have to manage without strictly phenomenal predicates.

## 2.4 CRISPIN WRIGHT ON INCOHERENCE

Crispin Wright singles out tolerant nature of observational terms as the root of incoherence in language. Wright thinks that this species-liability to tolerance is a kind of original sin having its base in the very mode of introduction of observational predicates. Wright has presented all his arguments in the background of language learning and use of language. Therefore, if we are interested in understanding how tolerance susceptibility of an observational predicate paves the way for incoherence, we have to discuss Wright's theory about 'the governing view of language' in considerable detail.

Wright's thesis has two distinct parts. The first part establishes that language is governed by a set of rules which determine correct use of expressions. The second part is concerned with the correct methodology of discovering 'the substantial rules'[17] for the use of language. The method of discovering such rules, insists Wright, must reflect the mode of understanding of expressions by the native users of language including the speakers' known limitations of memory or perceptual acuity. Since these rules guide and justify the use of expressions in suitable contexts, these should bring out the special features of expressions so that even a novice learner of the language can use those expressions suitably. The substantial rules for the use of predicates of a language should enable us to match the predicates with the corresponding properties of objects. Now, the special feature of observational predicates which distinguish them from non-observational ones, we have seen, is tolerance to marginal changes due to lack of sharp boundary. So the substantial rules governing the use of observational predicates must reflect this feature. But how are we to discover such rules? Just by consulting intuitions and working knowledge of the native users of language regarding the expression in question. But if we as users of language try to determine the meaning/use of vague observational terms (especially borderline application of such words) by appealing to our reflection, memory, intuition about the senses of these words, paradoxical consequences are bound to follow. Since observational expressions are guided by strict tolerance rules like, if one man is bald and the second man has just a little more hair than the first, then the second man is bald too; and as marginal change lying below the threshold of perception does not affect the applicability of such expressions, by repeated application of the tolerance principle we shall reach a paradoxical conclusion like all men are bald. Thus tolerance—susceptibility of observational predicates is the sure source of incoherence in language.

One may ask, if tolerance to marginal changes is an intrinsic feature of observational terms and observational terms necessarily lead to incoherence, why can't our language be purged of such faulty expressions? Simply because without observational predicates the gap between language and the world can never be bridged. Besides, while learning a language we cannot go on understanding an expression in terms of another for ever. Ultimately we have to come down to some terms which defy all our attempts at linguistic definition but can only be defined ostensively. That is, these observational expressions are such that one can learn them only if one is actually shown instances of their application and on which depends the whole corpus of understanding and learning a language. So a language without observational terms is thoroughly inadequate.

It might not still be clear, if observational expressions are known ostensively, then how can they at all give rise to the much discussed paradoxical situation? For an ostensive definition of an expression always draws our attention to some features in our experience that warrant the application of the expression. So there should not be any anomaly in the use of ostensively defined expressions. Wright was fully aware of this problem. His explanation of the situation runs as follows. It is true that an ostensive definition issues a licence to apply an expression to any situation relevantly matching that which the definition uses but that should not be taken as a command to apply the expression to a situation which does not match the original situation, but merely matches an intermediate situation indistinguishable from both. So he writes:

> If we think of an ostensive definition as a command: 'Apply F to situations like this', the command obviously does not apply to situations which are not 'like this' but merely like something like this. This is so whether the required resemblance is conceived as indistinguishability or as some less exact likeness.[18]

But as observational expressions are tolerance susceptible we cannot but apply these expressions to cases which appear indistinguishable from the paradigm or which marginally differ from the paradigm. Hence observational expressions lead to inconsistency notwithstanding their ostensive definability.

> . . . there is a clear, general connection between observationality and ostensive definition. If there is in the conditions of correct application of a predicate nothing which is incapable of ostensive communication, then the predicate must apply to both, if to either, of any pair of indistinguishable objects. But it seems manifest that adjectives of colour, and many others, do precisely not involve any such further condition of correct application; on the contrary, ostensive training would appear fully determinant of their meaning—or, if it is not, it is the only training which we get.[19]

Another question that puzzles us very often is: if observational expressions are really inconsistent then how is it that we can communicate by using them? It is found that people in a community largely agree in their application of such predicates.

Dummett thinks the reason of our pragmatic success lies in the fact that in our everyday life we usually do not push the non-discriminable differences beyond the limits of transitivity. Wright, on the other hand, thinks that our successful communication results from our adopting a behaviouristic methodology. Actually speaking, in the real-life-situation we do not follow *the governing view.* Wright makes his point clear by introducing the analogy of a game situation. A game with inconsistent rules can be played to a conclusion by members of a community if the players agree to an admissible move whenever there is some possibility of an impasse. This sort of agreement is feasible, for the set of rules, though inconsistent, is applicable partially. Similar is the case of 'red' like predicates. These terms can be used in the same sense within a particular community. Just as for the successful conclusion of the game it is not required that there should be some consistent rules which the players must master, similarly it is not required for successful communication with vague words that explicitly formulated strict semantic rules governing their usage should be mastered by the users. Mere implicit knowledge of the rules serves the purpose. Moreover, mastery of the so-called inconsistent rules does not guarantee proper use of problematic expressions. A parallel of this in the game situation would be: a person may have mastered the inconsistent rules of the game yet he may not be able to participate in the game because he is not sure what sort of electic application of the rules his opponent is likely to make and how he is going to preempt the moves of his opponent. For the agreement on a move has been purely *ad hoc.*

If all our linguistic usages were guided by semantic rules, then we could never explain how a foreigner can possibly learn the use of an observational predicate of an alien tongue. For semantic rules are supposed to state the correct use of expressions but there is no such rule that can provide any clue as to how to use an expression in face of inconsistency. Even if members within a community can somehow agree to implement an inconsistent set of instructions, an outsider will never have any inkling of such an agreement and therefore should not be able to follow them. But the foreigners can learn and understand our use of observational terms. So concludes Wright:

> The methodological approach to these (vague observational) expressions at any rate, must be purely behaviouristic and anti-reflective, if a general theory of meaning is to be possible at all.[20]

Here Wright's emphasis is on the qualifier *purely*. A behaviouristic approach, if not anti-reflective at the same time, cannot check the possibility of the sorites type paradox. Our analysis of the maxims of observationality has made this obvious that reflective approach to observational expressions always tugs us towards inconsistency.

Successful adoption of behaviouristic approach presupposes community agreement. And if this approach is to account for understanding and use of observational terms by foreigners as well, 'the community agreement' has got to be interpreted in a much wider sense than the one usually admitted by Wright. As McDowell points out following Wittgenstein, the agreement that is needed here is not agreement of opinion but agreement in form of life.[21]

In his 1987 paper Wright explains elaborately what he means by a purely behaviouristic methodology and how adoption of such a method helps in avoiding inconsistency. According to Wright, it is a legacy of the governing view to think that linguistic competence with respect to 'looks red' and its ilk consists in possessing implicit knowledge of some semantic rule. But mastering of observational predicates like 'looks red' does not require any such rule. Nor can there be a semantic rule concerning an observational predicate where responses of a subject do not play any essential role. Rather a subject is said to understand an observational predicate, e.g. 'looks red' if when presented with something having the property red in conjunction with the utterance 'looks red' he assents to it provided his perceptual faculties are normal, his cognitive capacity is in order, he is in a position to apprehend the object possessing the said property clearly and he is sufficiently attentive. If all these provisos are met then 'x looks red' is true if the subject assents to 'x looks red'. This is what is meant by a purely behaviouristic approach. If somebody still wishes to think in terms of semantic rules, the following is Wright's advice:

> The rules to which competent use of 'looks red' conforms . . . are not rules knowledge of whose content, at some deep level, makes competence possible, rather their content is given by the course assumed by competent use.

Let us now reconsider the sorites situation. Suppose a group of subjects are agreed that 'looks red' applies to the first colour strip in a sorites series when all the above said provisos are fulfilled. But as they proceed along the series at some point, which is also indistinguishable from the immediately preceding strip, the subjects failed to respond unanimously. Given that all the provisos are still met there should not arise any problem if one continues to stick to the purely behaviouristic methodology. For then it can be admitted without any qualm that borderline cases are exactly cases about which competent subjects are allowed to differ and consequently it will be considered legitimate to doubt whether 'looks red' should be applied to that particular strip at all. Hence to one of an indistinguishable pair an observational predicate can be applied whereas the same can be withheld from the other without leading to inconsistency.

Such responses on the part of the subjects are totally unprincipled, therefore, purely behaviouristic but no less appropriate for that matter.

## 2.5 CHARGES REPEALED

There are different ways of countering the incoherence in language view upheld by Dummett and Wright. One may refute the view by maintaining that there is no *observational expression* in our language in the sense in which Dummett and Wright use the term. The second way is to show that observational expressions do not really lead to incoherence. Travis criticizes the Dummett-Wright thesis on both the grounds. Williamson[22] and Burns follow the second line of attack.

Let us recount Travis' contention very briefly. According to Travis, there is no observational term in our language the applicability of which is determined solely by observation and our language cannot be inconsistent due to the reason pointed out by Dummett. Travis tries to drive this point home with the help of a unanimously accepted observational predicate 'looks red'. To avoid unnecessary complications Travis wants us to assume for the time being that our power of sensory discrimination of colour is very limited and we can discern only three samples of colour, A, B, and C and we can arrange them in a series in the order mentioned just by the look of them. A, the first sample, looks distinctly red and C, the last sample looks distinctly orange when viewed on their own. The middle sample B is such that it looks indistinguishable in colour from A when compared with A but looks indistinguishable in colour from C when held next to C. Now the question is, how does B look? Since A and B are indistinguishable in colour and A looks red, we have very strong reason to say that B looks red. But, *ex hypothesi* B is indistinguishable from C and C distinctly looks orange. So when we compare the colour of B with the colour of C we have an equally strong reason to uphold that B looks orange. So the question: what colour B looks, admits of two solutions which are *prima facie* contradictory. 'What happens when we hold B next to A gives us reason to say B looks red; what happens when we hold it next to C gives us reason to say B does not look red.'[23]

Travis claims to establish two points by analyzing the above example. First, 'looks red' is not an observational predicate in the sense upheld by Dummett and Wright, not at least in cases like B. For we do not determine how B looks just by noticing its colour but by attending to some argument. Second, the predicate 'looks red' is not contradictory. We have contradicted ourselves by fixing the terms of the given example in a peculiar manner. In fact there will be no contradiction if we emphasize the fact that B looks red in respect of A and B looks not red in respect of C. A thing may have different properties in relation to different things So, 'looks red' would have been contradictory if application of the predicate had entailed that B looks red and looks not-red with respect to the same thing.

Moreover, points out Travis, we cannot remove our doubts regarding the application of an observational term in a borderline case merely by observation. In fact, when we are unsure about the nature of a given shade, we do not gain much just by looking harder at the given shade. To resolve our doubt we actually have to recourse to reasoning of the following type. I am unsure about the colour of B. But B matches A when I hold it next to A. I know A to be red, therefore, B is red. So to determine what the nature of a given shade is and how to characterize it, especially in a doubtful case, we have to rely on our reasoning, our judgement and not merely on our observation.

Besides, our problem with graded colour series is not really generated by observation. The two maxims of observationality do not come into conflict unless we reason with an additional premiss: red and orange are mutually opposed. It is, therefore, Travis' considered opinion that inconsistencies lie not in language but in our methods of judging. By exercising good judgement inconsistencies can be made ineffective.

I do not agree with Travis' contention that there is something wrong or unusual with the sense of 'observational' as understood by Dummett and Wright. For this is how we understand the term 'observational' ordinarily. Travis' difficulty results from the manner in which he has contrived his example. Not only that, the maxims of observationality which embody the intuitive understanding of 'observational' appear reasonable. Surely, we are to determine whether an observational term applies or not solely by observation and if two objects appear indiscernible by mere observation then the same observational predicate should be assertable about them. The so-called additional premiss on which Travis puts the blame is not really non-observational. That red and orange are not the same follows directly from our observation. Just by looking at a red shade and an orange shade we know that they are different from each other, we do not have to go beyond observation for this. Moreover this is the part of our ostensive learning of 'red' and 'orange' that we know them to be opposed. This charge of Travis at best applies to 'strictly phenomenal predicates'.

Though the way Travis has challenged the point that observational predicates are sure to lead to inconsistency is not very effective, the spirit underlying it is nevertheless correct. Unless one applies the second maxim of observationality (MO1) recursively or treats the relation of indistinguishability as transitive, there is no problem at all. And if we remain confined within the realm of phenomenal colours, then the colour of an object should be determined by its look. There is no chance of applying a predicate to an object and withholding it from another object indistinguishable from the first unless we invoke the logical principle of transitivity/non-transitivity of indistinguishability. Dummett also concedes this point. But then we need not reject the whole notion of phenomenal properties. Timothy Williamson has reinstated the phenomenal properties by his semantic analysis of observational predicates and the relation of indistinguishability.

Williamson draws our attention to two readings of observational predicates, non-intentional and intentional. A predicate F is said to be *non-intentionally observational* if (*a*) when something is F it can be observed to be F and (*b*) when something is not F it can be observed not to be F. F is, on the other hand, *intentionally observational* if (*a*) when something is F as presented in a certain way it can be observed to be F as presented in that way and (*b*) when something is not F presented in a certain way it can be observed not to be F as presented in that way. In fact non-intentional and intentional readings of observational predicates coincide with their *de re* and the *de dicto* readings. Like an observational predicate the relation of indistinguishability may also have two readings: (i) non-intentional and (ii) intentional. The first holds amongst objects of discrimination *per se* and the second holds amongst objects of discrimination *as presented.*

Williamson then proceeds to show that non-intentional observational predicates do not generate any inconsistency. If a pair of objects are non-intentionally indistinguishable then if the first possesses a non-intentionally observational property p, then the second cannot but possess p. For *de re* indistinguishability is the same as identity. But intentionally observational predicates are susceptible to inconsistency. For intentional indistinguishability is non-transitive and does not reduce to identity. So it is possible to construct a series of experiences each indistinguishable intentionally in respect of its phenomenal character from the next yet its first member may have a painful character and its last member a painless one.

Thus by following Williamson we can counter Dummett's thesis. We need not give up the notion of phenomenal properties, nor do we need to banish phenomenal predicates from our language. Phenomenal predicates, at least in their *de re* reading are free from inconsistency. Only on *de dicto* reading phenomenal predicates may lead to sorites paradox. But we shall see later that the sorites paradox is solvable.

Another way of handling inconsistency is by stipulating arbitrary border lines. This move is not totally unjustified either. When we are shown consecutively strips of red colour which are indistinguishable from one another but gradually merge with strips of orange, at some point of time we do say that the strip shown is neither red or orange, and after some time we say that the strip in display is more orange than red and finally we do identify the colour of a strip as orange. So depending on such experience, we can draw a line at the point where we last predicated 'red'. And it is possible to draw another line where we first assert the colour of the strip to be orange. Thus domains of application of 'red', 'neither red nor orange' and 'orange' become specifically demarcated. Consequently both vagueness and inconsistency are removed. This is no doubt a very effective way of bypassing incoherence but goes against our understanding of vagueness. This approach presumes that border line instances can be sharply demarcated from positive and negative instances of 'red'. But a predicate, the penumbral zone of which is sharply defined, cannot be a vague predicate. A move that restores coherence by eliminating vague predicates from language is not an acceptable move.

Before we discuss another strategy to avoid incoherence in language let us try to trace the root of the trouble once again step by step. The applicability of vague observational predicates is to be determined by our observation. Our limited capacity of observation compels us to grant tolerance to observational terms. At the same time we have a feeling that tolerance should not be pushed too far. But we do not know where to stop. For an arbitrary stopping point will rob the vague observational terms of their essence. So we stick to the strict tolerance rule like,

> If A is tall and B's height is indistinguishable from that of A to a casual observer, then B is tall too.

Here, of course, we presuppose more or less fixed discrimination thresholds. Then we go on applying the tolerance rule. Indistinguishability, however, is a non-transitive relation. So after some time the principle of tolerance comes into conflict with the first maxim of observationality and inconsistency ensues. The crux of the problem lies in the fact that in an array elements appear indistinguishable up to a point, then all of a sudden at the next point the difference becomes conspicuous. Our reason tells us that it is due to the cumulative effect of non-discriminable differences that we suddenly become aware of the difference. Hence, it is only when things are arranged in a chain following a natural ordering, apparently non-discriminable differences add up to noticeable distinction. This phenomenon is puzzling because it hurts our intuition. It is our firm conviction that things which are indistinguishable in some respect can never give rise to distinction in that respect, *all other conditions remaining the same*; just as things equal to each other cannot lead to inequality.

This proviso of *all other conditions remaining the same* is a very important one. The applicability of the strict tolerance rule is subject to this proviso. Incoherence results, points out Linda Burns, when we ignore this *ceteris paribus* condition. The strict tolerance principle involving 'indistinguishability' becomes suspect where there is detectable difference amongst two indistinguishable objects in some relevant respect. Burns rightly observes that the principle of strict tolerance presupposes that the objects we are comparing vary only in one factor, every other factor remains the same. For example, while discussing the paradox of the heap we take it for granted that two collections differ only in number of elements, not in shape or in any other factor. This *ceteris paribus* condition can never be fulfilled outside a laboratory. So while applying the principle of tolerance we must take into consideration the 'relevant variations'. Burns explains the notion of 'relevant variation' with the help of the example given below.

Let S be a series having $S_1$ and $S_n$ as its end points. Let $S_i$ be indiscernible from $S_{i-1}$ with respect to ø and $S_{i-1}$ be indiscernible from $S_1$ with respect to ø. $S_i$, however, is just discernible from $S_1$ with respect to ø. So, though $S_i$ and $S_{i-1}$ are contiguous and indistinguishable from each other with respect to ø, they differ with respect to their indiscernibility from $S_1$. We can, therefore, very legitimately ascribe one predicate to $S_i$ and desist from ascribing the same to $S_{i-1}$. This is how Burns proposes to avoid incoherence. Her suggested remedy to the malady of observational predicates is to apply the principle of tolerance loosely.

> If indiscernibility is to matter at all in determining a thing's colour it must do so according to loose rules. For 'red' we will have: If one thing is red, and a second indistinguishable from it in colour, then provided there are no other relevant differences between the two, the second is red also.[24]

When loosely interpreted the principle of tolerance can serve as the substantial semantic rule.

Burn's move is undoubtedly in the right direction, yet it is not wholly satisfactory. The moment any two elements display just discernible difference among them in respect of certain ø, we do not desist from ascribing the observational predicate ø to the second.[25] Suppose in the series R, we could observe that $R_7$ is of slightly lighter shade than of $R_1$, but we do not cease to call $R_7$ 'red' immediately. Rather in such cases we go on applying a different version of the tolerance principle.

> If A is P (where P is an observational predicate) and B is just discernible from A in relevant respects, B is P too.

It is obvious that this version of tolerance too will clash with MO very soon. The outstanding problem that remains here is : how much dissimilarity from A, B has to possess to distinguish itself as not-red while A is red?

The most plausible way out will be to assign degree of membership to the elements belonging to a series of the above type. So when $R_7$ is just discernible from $R_1$, and $R_1$ is paradigmatically red, we shall call $R_7$ red too, only red to a lesser degree than $R_1$. Assignment of degree will enable us to answer the above question. Not only that, as degree of membership of a concept will be continuously graded, it will take care of cases where indistinguishability turns out to be non-transitive. So I presume, I am now free to spell out this proposal with the help of a suitable example, say, 'tall'.

Let us consider a group of men arranged in a row strictly in accordance with their discerning height. Though no two neighbours are ever found unequal in height by a casual observer yet there may be just noticeable difference in height amongst non-adjacent members. Let us also suppose that the man standing at the head of the row is really tall and we cannot visually detect any difference in heights of men till we reach the seventh man in the row. We definitely find the seventh man tall but slightly less tall than the first man. So just *on the basis of this observation* we can assign to each man some grade or degree of tallness. We would like to say that the first man is our paradigm of tallness in this case but the seventh man is tall, say, to the degree 0.9. In this manner when we reach the middle of the row we might come across a man whose height is such that he is tall, say, to the degree .52. Now if somebody asks us whether this man is tall or not we may not be ready to answer him with a clear 'yes' or 'no'. It would be perfectly sensible to say that the man in question is neither tall nor short. But if a man standing towards the end of the row is tall to the degree 0.2, he will be judged rather short by us. There is no inconsistency involved in these assertions, consequently there will be no incoherence either. Thus just by relativizing the principle of tolerance and by redefining indistinguishability in terms of a weak equivalence relation which is reflexive, symmetric but non-transitive, we can successfully evade incoherence, and can even hope to formulate semantic rules.

This interpretation of observational expression, of course, has some underlying presuppositions.

(i) Instances exemplifying an observational predicate can always be arranged in an ordered series.
(ii) An observational predicate can be asserted of a subject to greater or lesser extent, it is not a clear-cut 'yes' or 'no' affair.
(iii) Assignment of degree to an observational expression does not rob it of its essence.
(iv) There is an important ordinary use of 'indistinguishability' which enjoins its conception in terms of reflexivity, symmetry and non-transitivity perfectly plausible.

All these presuppositions are debatable and are in need of justification. We shall try our best to justify them in course of our presentation of the logic of vague sentences.

## NOTES AND REFERENCES

1. Rudolf Carnap (1956).
2. Rudolf Carnap (1965).
3. Hilary Putnam (1979).
4. Crispin Wright (1975).
5. Linda Burns (1986).
6. L. Wittgenstein (1958).
7. In fact this problem has parallels in metrical representations of almost all sense-datum predicates.
8. The example is an adaptation of Charles Travis (1985).
9. Rohit Parikh (1983).
10. Ibid., p. 242.
11. This is an edited version of Travis' formulation of the *maxim of observationality* following Crispin Wright.
12. MO1 is taken from Dummett's maxim as stated in 'Wang's Paradox'.
13. Wright (1975), p. 341.
14. Dummett (1970), p. 264.
15. Ibid., p. 261.
16. Dummett (1973), pp. 220–21.
17. For a detailed account of the substantial rules see Wright (1975), Burns (1986).
18. Wright (1975), p. 342.
19. Ibid., p. 343.
20. Wright (1976), p. 247.
21. John McDowell (1984).
22. Timothy Williamson (1990).
23. Travis (1985), p. 356.
24. Burns (1986), pp. 506–7.
25. Burns was aware of this problem. So she has added in note 11, 'How great must the similarity be between two things if we are to classify them as falling under the same observational predicate? There is no answer to this except the uninteresting one that resemblances and differences between things are large enough to matter in this way when they are large enough to be noticed and taken to matter to the applicability of the predicate by most observers . . . . In many cases small observable differences do not matter: Why do they matter when they do has no philosophically interesting general explanation other than that they add up to a difference large enough to oblige a different classification.'

CHAPTER 3

# Vague Objects and Vague Identity

## 3.1 PREAMBLE

In the *Introduction* of this work, we proposed to confine our discussion to vagueness in language. Now our venture in the realm of vague objects might be viewed as over-stepping of that self-imposed boundary. But our discussion on vagueness will remain incomplete if we do not seriously consider the question: what is the source of vagueness in language? Is the world itself vague, and vagueness in language reflects the vague nature of reality? Or, is it the case that vagueness is a peculiar feature of human description? Philosophers widely differ among themselves on this issue. Russell,[1] for instance, maintains that those who think that things are vague because some words are vague commit the 'fallacy of verbalism'. He is of the opinion that only our ways of looking at things, our descriptions of reality are vague, but reality itself is not. 'Vagueness and precision alike', wrote Russell, 'are characteristics which can only belong to a representation, of which language is an example.'[2] Dummett's view is still more conservative; he upheld that 'the notion that things might actually be vague, as well as being vaguely described, is not properly intelligible.'[3] Notwithstanding these stalwarts and their opinion, there are people who go on believing that vagueness of language sometimes does stem from vagueness of objects. That is, there can be vague objects and a discussion into the nature of vague objects is neither unintelligible, nor incoherent nor ludicrous. Though I must admit that believers in vagueness-in-reality are a minority in the philosophical community.

## 3.2 VAGUE OBJECTS

There are some *prima facie* good examples of vague objects.

(i) Mountains may be considered vague objects for they have no sharp boundaries. Of course, when we look at a distant mountain, it so appears that the mountain has gone straight up from a particular place and we can easily demarcate the plain land that lies at the base of the mountain from the mountain itself. But truly speaking, we can never be certain regarding where the mountain ends and the plain begins.

(ii) The sun may be said to be another example of vague object for the sun has no distinct surface. So any statement relating to the measurement of its radius or diameter will be indeterminate.[4]

(iii) Another very widely used example is Theseus' ship.[5] As far as Hobbes' story goes Theseus' ship arrived late in 399 B.C. at the port of Pireus. Its late arrival delayed Socrates' drinking of the hemlock. Let us also suppose that the ship was caught in a storm and some vital part of the ship got damaged and it became unseaworthy. So it was decided that the ship be repaired. Accordingly some new planks were substituted for the rotten planks and the discarded ones were preserved. Let us further assume that over the years Theseus' ship was gradually repaired with new spars, while the old spars were simultaneously collected and reassembled to construct the original ship. But do we really have the original ship? Which of the two ships should be taken as Theseus' ship now? Even before the construction of the second ship one could ask how much of replacement can Theseus' ship withstand before it loses its identity? In such cases 'it may be said that there must be relatively late stages in the story of the single enduring entity at which it is indeterminate whether the original entity has survived.'[6]

Thus we may go on citing instances of vague objects. But that is not necessary. These three examples are representative enough of different types of objectual vagueness that we want to point out.

We talked about mountains in our first example. Now a mountain possessing fuzzy boundaries is said to be compositionally vague if and only if we fail to divide the matter composing a mountain, say Mount Everest, from the matter outside it.[7] That is, there are objects in Nepal about which there is no fact of the matter whether they are parts, non-parts or borderline parts of Mount Everest. So we shall be defining compositionally vague as follows.

> An object x is compositionally vague iff x is such that for some y it is indeterminate whether y is a part of x.[8]

The sun is also a compositionally vague object. When we say that

> The sun has a diameter of exactly $1.39 \times 10^9$ metres.[9]

the sentence is undoubtedly vague. Its vagueness is due to the compositional vagueness of the sun. The property of having a diameter of exactly $1.39 \times 10^9$ metres is a sharp property but it neither definitely applies to the sun nor definitely fails to apply. Keeping in view such cases we have to revise the commonly accepted definition of a vague property that a vague property neither definitely applies nor definitely fails to apply to an object. The amended definition will be:

> A property is vague iff there is an object such that (i) the property neither definitely applies nor definitely fails to apply to it, and (ii) the object about which the property has been asserted is vague.[10]

Thesues' ship instantiates both (a) temporal vagueness and (b) individuative vagueness.[11] We are giving below the definitions of these two types of vagueness.

(a) x is temporally vague iff x is such that for some time y, it is indeterminate whether x exists at y.

(b) x is individuatively vague iff x is such that for some y, it is indeterminate whether y = x.

So Theseus' ship is temporally vague for it is indeterminate whether it exists at y, where y is the time of replacing. the 40th new spar. Theseus' ship is individuatively vague too. If we take y to be the ship from which already fifty planks have been replaced, then it is indeterminate whether y is the same as the original ship of Theseus. It is obvious that there is a close connection between temporal vagueness and indivituative vagueness.

Now we are in a position to give a generalized definition of a vague concrete object following Rolf. A non-empty subset of four-dimensional space-time is said to be an object base. An object is said to be a pair set of object bases, x = {y, z}, where $y \subseteq z$. We put Max (x) = z and Min (x) = y, x is said to be vague iff Min (x) is a proper subset of Max (x). The doubtful region of x is the set {Max (x) – Min (x)}. The doubtful region of x is an object if {Max (x) – Min (x)} is non-empty.

Let me try to represent this definition diagrammatically.

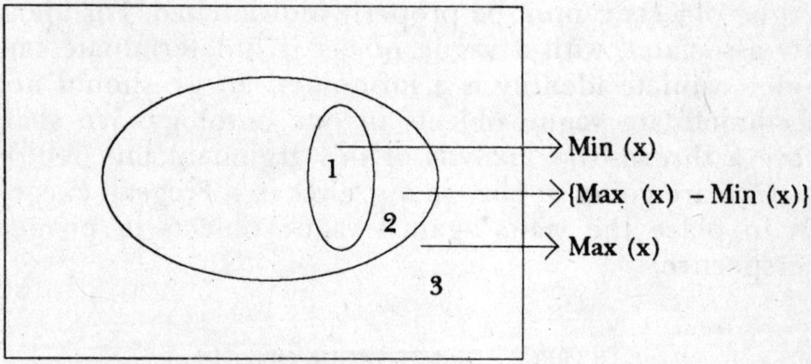


Diagram of a vague object

It is clear from the diagram that the region 1 or Min (x) is the core of the vague object and the region 2 or {Max (x) – Min (x)} is the penumbral region. So the space-time points that will definitely belong to the vague object x will fall in the region 1, space-time points which are definitely not in x will fall in the region 3. The region 2, {Max (x) – Min (x)}, contains those space-time points which are neither definitely inside x nor definitely outside x. Rolf also maintains that if x is non-fuzzy Max (x) and Min (x) will coincide. That means there will be no penumbral region and it will always be determinate whether some space-time points fall within the object base or outside.

Our diagram is a bit inaccurate. We shall have to remember that the demarcation between the core and the penumbra as well as the penumbra and the outside limit of a vague object is not sharp. So in case of a vague object we shall always be in doubt whether certain space-time points are parts or non-parts or borderline parts of the object.

I have already mentioned that the majority of philosophers are against admitting such vague objects. The grounds they have offered for their rejection are many. But the most used argument against vague objects is this: Vague objects cannot be properly individuated. For identity associated with a vague object is indeterminate but indeterminate identity is a misnomer. So we should not accommodate vague objects in our ontology. We shall have a thread-bare analysis of this argument but before that we are going to engage ourselves in a Fregean exegesis to place the views against vague objects in proper perspective.

### 3.3 FREGE AGAINST VAGUE OBJECTS

No discussion on objects taken up in the post-Fregean period should fail to consider Frege's view seriously for Gottlob Frege has really added a new dimension to the notion of object. Not only that, he is the first among the philosophical giants who explicitly opposed the thesis of 'vagueness-in-reality'. Frege was one of the enthusiastic adherents of the view that the nature of reality is determinate, no part of it is vague. Only some expressions of natural language which we use to designate or express the items of the world are vague. Frege had been very much vocal against the theory of there being any vague concept throughout his life. He did not offer any explicit argument against admissibility of vague objects. But the latter thesis follows from the former. 'Object' and 'concept' are used here in a very technical sense and not in the ordinary sense of the word.

Frege, we have noted, did not have much respect for natural language, for its grammar is loosely structured and it abounds in vague expression and ambiguous sentences. Natural language is, therefore, totally unsuitable as a medium of precise thoughts. Now, vague expressions that occur in a natural language can have as their referents either some concepts or some objects. An object, according to Frege, is the objective correlate of a singular term, a thing of which something can be predicated but which can never be the whole reference of a predicate. A concept, on the other hand, is that what can be predicated of an object. A concept is a referent of a predicate, not its sense, and is thus correlative to 'function' and 'relation'. Following Michael Dummett we can, therefore, maintain that Fregean 'concepts' come very close to what we call 'properties' and not to ideas or notions which they have ordinarily come to mean. The predicative expression of a language is incomplete and can never be exhibited in isolation.

In *posthumous writings* of Frege we find a categorical assertion to the effect that there cannot be any vague concept. He writes:

> Every concept must have sharp boundaries so that it is determined for every object whether it falls under the concept or not.[12]

He compares a concept to an area and says that an area with vague boundaries cannot be called an area at all. If we try to explain this thesis of Frege with Frege's own examples, then we shall find that Frege himself has very often confused vagueness of a concept with the incomplete definition of a predicate or of a functional expression. The cause of such confusion is not very difficult to find. According to Frege, both the sentences containing an incompletely defined predicate and the sentences containing a predicate standing for a vague concept are meaningless, i.e. neither true nor false. Now, what is an incompletely defined predicate? It is a predicate which is not defined for every argument. Consider, for example, 'x is male' or 'x is scrupulous' or 'x is scalene'. 'x is male' is defined only for organisms, 'x is scrupulous' is defined for adult population and undefined for babies and 'x is scalene' is defined only for triangles. Frege thinks that these predicates do not really have any reference at all. For they stand for concepts whose boundaries are not uniformly determinate, and a concept with indeterminate boundaries, a concept about which we cannot tell surely whether certain objects fall under it or not—is no concept at all.

If we carefully read the above remarks we shall understand that they really apply to vague concepts and not to concepts with incompletely defined or restricted boundaries. For in the latter case the boundaries are quite sharp—at least in principle completely specifiable and where an object does not fall within its domain of definition we need not raise the question whether or not the object falls under the concept, but 'in the case of a vague concept, the question arises all right, even in cases in which there is no answer.'[13]

Frege's reluctance to admit a vague concept might puzzle us. We may fail to understand why an incompletely defined predicate or a vague predicate cannot have any reference at all? Why should a concept with blurred edges fail to qualify as a concept? Michael Dummett had offered us a Fregean solution to the puzzle.

Let us grant for argument's sake that vague predicates also have referents. But the reference of such expressions can at best be some incompletely specified concepts. As we all know, the referent of any expression is extralinguistic in nature, it is a thing in the world. And it is one of Frege's deep rooted beliefs that the real world does not contain anything that is intrinsically incompletely specified. Hence a vague predicate cannot have any referent.

Moreover, if a referent of some expression is incompletely specified, then that expression may have more than one referent, i.e. all things that fit the incomplete specification qualify as referents of that expression. Frege does not admit that any referring expression can have more than one referent and that is why he upholds that an incompletely defined predicate does not have any reference at all.

It is true that whenever we use such an expression in a sentence, the resulting sentence does not always lack truth value. The expression will have definite truth value if we use the name of some object from the defined domain in its argument place. But if the argument place is filled up by a variable bound by a quantifier, the sentence will lack a determinate truth value. For, how can we determine the truth value of a quantified sentence if some instances of it lack determinate truth value? Hence to avoid this difficulty Frege offers his *doctrine of complete definition*—the thesis that every predicate, relational expression, or functional expression, must be defined for every object. Though natural language over-produces incompletely defined predicates, it was Frege's belief that a properly constructed language like *Begriffsschrift* can be kept totally free from them.

Completely defined predicates are a necessity in Frege's philosophy for another reason too. Frege subscribes to the thesis of homogeneity of objects. He assumes that there is one single unsorted domain and that is the domain of all objects. Any restriction that he wants to impose on such a homogeneous domain comes from the appropriate concepts. So if the concepts are incompletely defined, no restriction can ever be introduced into the domain of objects. Consequently, no domain for any variable can ever be fixed and there is every chance of this theory being vitiated by the set-theoretic paradoxes. In absence of any theory of types, therefore, Frege cannot afford to accommodate any incompletely specified predicate.

Another equally important argument against vague concepts can be reconstructed from some pithy comments of Frege on the criterion of identity of a thing. Frege's formulation of the criterion is given below.

> We say that an object *a* is equal to an object *b* if *a* falls under every concept under which *b* falls and conversely.[14]

Thus formulated, Fregean criterion of identity of objects demands an inquiry into the criterion of identity for concepts. Otherwise, it is not possible to determine whether the objects *a* and *b* fall under the same concepts or not. But here we shall face some problems. For Frege has declared that the relation of identity can hold only between objects and not between concepts. Nevertheless, he thinks that there is an analogous relation of equivalence for concepts though this is a second level relation. But how are we to grasp that relation?

> We obtain something corresponding to this for concepts if we switch the roles of concept and object. . . . The relation (an analogue of identity relation) holds between the concept $\phi$ and the concept $\chi$, if every object that falls under $\phi$ also falls under $\chi$ and conversely.[15]

As an example of concept equivalence we may cite the following. For every argument the function $x^2 = 1$ has the same (truth) value as the function $(x + 1)^2 = 2\ (x + 1)$, i.e. every object falling under the concept less by 1 than a number whose square is equal to its double falls under the concept square root of 1 and conversely.

Here, it may appear, Frege has definitely entwined himself in a tangle for his criterion of identity of objects presupposes his criterion of identity of concepts and vice versa. Even if we ignore the comment that there cannot be any relation of identity that holds between two concepts and therefore two concepts cannot be strictly identical, at least not in the sense in which two objects can be, and think that the analogous relation of equivalence will be a surrogate of identity, we have to find a way to break the circle. Or else, how can Frege claim that a concept is not vague, in fact, cannot be vague?

Someone might try to solve this difficulty by suggesting that Frege's is a sort of holistic theory of objects and concepts. The nature of objects and concepts are such that they are interdefinable and one cannot be understood without understanding the other. In fact, in the basic level of various branches of philosophy there are such related concepts. Take, for example, the notions of conjunction and disjunction. These notions are interdefinable and understanding of any one of them requires simultaneous grasping of both the notions. Nobody, for that matter, brings any charge of circularity against these definitions. Similar are the Fregean notions of objects and concepts. Besides, Frege's realistic commitment to both objects and concepts makes the circularity quite harmless.

Frege has offered a logical argument too against vague objects. Frege's adherence to the bivalent logic and his unshakable faith in the law of excluded middle also demand that no concept be vague. To quote from Frege,

> Every concept must have sharp boundaries so that it is determined for every object whether it falls under the concept or not. Were this not so, there would be a third case besides just the two cases 'a falls under the concept F' and 'a does not fall under the concept F'—namely the case where that is undecided.[16]

One of the grave consequences of admitting vague concepts is to fall prey to the sorites paradox.

> The fallacy known as 'Sorites' depends on something (e.g. a heap) being treated as a concept which cannot be acknowledge as such by logic because it is not properly circumscribed.[17]

Hence Frege goes on to add, if

> . . . truth is the goal of logic . . . we have to throw aside proper names that do not designate or name an object, though they have a sense, we have to throw aside con-

> cept words that do not have a meaning. These are not such as, say, contain a contradiction—for there is nothing at all wrong in a concept's being empty—but such as have vague boundaries.[18]

It is evident that commitment to metaphysical and logical realism will stand in Frege's way of admitting any vague object. As he himself has not offered any such argument, let us construct an argument against the possibility of vague objects remaining within the Fregean framework.

Let us suppose for argument's sake that vague objects exist. Now, since there is no entity without identity, to exist vague objects too must fulfil their identity condition. But a vague object *a* will be identical with another vague object *b* if *a* falls under every concept under which *b* falls and conversely. That means *a* and *b* must fall under the same concepts. Let *F* be any arbitrary concept under which *a* and *b* fall. We must be in a position to say under what condition *F* is equivalent to a concept *G*. How is the equivalence of concepts determined? We already know that two concepts *F* will be equivalent if every object that falls under *F* also falls under *G* and conversely. But by hypothesis the objects are vague. So we are not in a position to state even in principle whether the equivalence condition holds for the concept F or not. Thus identity condition for vague objects cannot be fulfilled. Therefore we cannot be committed to vague objects in our ontology.

Moreover, if there is no vague concept then there cannot be any vague object either, not within Frege's scheme. For in that case, the criterion of identity for every object will be determinately specified.

### 3.4 INDETERMINATE IDENTITY

Even a cursory reading of the previous section will make it transparent that Frege's criterion of identity for objects is nothing but a reformulation of Leibniz's law of *Identity of Indiscernibles.* This law also forms the basis of a number of important arguments against the possibility of indeterminate identity, for example, those of Gareth Evans,[19] Nathan Salmon[20] and David Wiggins.[21] In this section we shall be presenting these arguments in the above-mentioned order and assess their merit.

Evans' one page article entitled 'can there be vague objects?' is easily comparable with Gettier's brief article containing his counter-example to the JTB thesis of knowledge in respect of multiplicity of responses evoked, intensity of sentiments aroused and enormity of commotions created. Since Evans' commentators could not agree among themselves on the very structure of the argument, nor on its proper interpretation, we shall proceed by quoting almost the entire argument instead of paraphrasing it. If we go by the letter of Evans' reductio argument then it is possible to uphold that Evans wants to refute the idea that an identity statement a = b may be indeterminate because one or both of a and b might refer to vague object/objects. As the fate of vague objects is essentially linked with the possibility of indeterminate identity, Evans concludes that vague objects cannot exist since identity cannot be indeterminate. Evans' argument runs as follows:

> Let *a* and *b* be singular terms such that the sentence 'a = b' is of indeterminate truth value, and let us allow for the expression of the idea of indeterminacy by the sentential operator, '$\nabla$'. Then we have
>
> (1) $\nabla (a = b)$
>
> (supposition for reductio)
>
> (I) reports a fact about b which we express by ascribing to *b* the property $\hat{x}\ [\nabla (x = a)]$.
>
> (2) $\hat{x}\ [\nabla (x = a)]b$.
>
> (*b* has the property of being such that it is indeterminate whether it belongs to the class of objects identical to *a*)
>
> But we have

(3) $\sim \nabla (a = a)$
(since everything is determinately identical with itself)

and hence:

(4) $\sim \hat{x} [\nabla (x = a)]a$.

But by Leibniz's law we may derive from (2) and (4)

(5) $\sim (a = b)$

contradicting the assumption with which we began, that the identity statement 'a = b' is of indeterminate truth value.[22]

Evans realized that (5) is not a straightforward contradiction of (1). So he supplements his *reductio* argument with the following observation:

> If 'indefinitely' [i.e. '$\nabla$'] and its dual 'definitely' ('$\Delta$') generate a modal logic as strong as $S_5$, (1)—(4) and, presumably Leibniz's Law, may each be strengthened with a 'definitely' prefix, enabling us to derive (5') $\Delta \sim (a = b)$ which is straightforwardly inconsistent with (1).

Evans' argument is apparently simple and straightforward but is anomalous. The main problem lies in the fact that it is not a formal derivation in a well-defined language using well-defined rules. So we shall point out the anomalies in it from several points of view.

Evans has introduced a new operator '$\nabla$' but has not been specific enough about its interpretation. From his explicit statement we get this much of a clue that '$\nabla$' expresses indeterminacy and we are supposed to prefix it to a sentence which has an indeterminate truth value. But while supplementing his argument towards the end of his note he has presented another operator '$\Delta$' to mean 'definitely' and wants us to consider '$\Delta$' to be the dual of '$\nabla$' in the analogue of the modal operators 'L' and 'M'. These two interpretations of $\nabla$ are so different that we cannot but raise the question: which of the above senses Evans actually had in mind when he introduced these operators? We should therefore make a few enlightened guesses.

1. If ∇ is taken to be a modal operator then it is more in conformity with epistemological vagueness than with vagueness-in-reality. For a sentence to which ∇ can be prefixed is either true or false in any designated world, say, $w^*$. In order to prefix ∇ to a sentence, p, we have to consider first whether the given sentence p is true or false in a world accessible to $w^*$. Then and then alone we can test the truth value of ∇ p at $w^*$. Due to inadequate information or for lack of perspicuity of the form of the given sentence, we may not be able to determine whether p is true or not. So p, under the circumstances, deserves the prefix ∇. But by hypothesis p is either true or false in the designated world. So, indeterminacy here cannot be due to the vagueness of the world.

2. A truth value interpretation may mean any of the following:

(a) Indeterminacy may be purely epistemic. 'A sentence is neither true nor false' will mean in this context that though the sentence is actually either true or false, it is not known to be true or false.

(b) '∇' may mean 'it is neither definitely true nor definitely false'. This interpretation presupposes a distinction between some sentence's being true and its being definitely true. If we agree to make such a distinction then we may be led to a degree of truth interpretation where 'indeterminacy' will mean that a sentence could be true to some degree without being definitely or completely true.

(c) Prefixing ∇ to a sentence, again, may signify that the sentence has a truth value other than T (truth) and F (falsity). Indeterminacy, whatever be its nature, be it a third truth value or a truth value gap, is due to the vague nature of reality.

Since Evans was interested in exploring the possibility that 'the world might actually be vague', as well as being vaguely described, and as he was also loyal to classical logic, 2(c) appears to be the most acceptable interpretation of $\nabla$.

But the truth value interpretation of indeterminacy will take the sting out of the *reductio* argument; the conclusion (5) will not contradict the first premiss (1). In three-valued systems, as we all know, there are two types of negation—strong and weak, the truth table definition of them is given below:

| p | $N^w p$ | $N^s p$ |
|---|---|---|
| T | F | F |
| I | T | I |
| F | T | T |

On the weak interpretation of negation (5) will not contradict (1) rather (1) will entail (5). For, ~ (a = b) is true when (a = b) is either false or indeterminate and (1) says that (a = b) is indeterminate.

If, on the other hand, the strong interpretation of negation is adopted then (5) contradicts (1). For on this interpretation if ~ (a = b) is true, then (a = b) has to be false and (a = b) in (1), being neither true nor false, cannot be false.[23]

But there is no justification for accepting the strong interpretation of negation and rejecting the weak one. The strong interpretation, instead of backing the *reductio* argument, paves the way for another objection. That is, on the strong interpretation of negation it is not obvious whether (5) follows from (2) and (4) by Leibniz's law. Hence in absence of any compelling reason the supporters of the vague identity theory might insist on selecting the weak interpretation.

Leibniz's law is a biconditional which can be analyzed into two conditionals.

(i) Law of the Indiscernibility of Identicals:
$a = b \Rightarrow \forall E\ (Ea \leftrightarrow Eb)$

(ii) Law of the Identity of Indiscernibles:
$\forall E\ (Ea \leftrightarrow Eb) \Rightarrow a = b$

Of these two conditionals (*i*) is incontrovertible but (*ii*) is problematic. Evans has used the incontrovertible part of Leibniz's law to derive the conclusion (5) by *modus tollens.*

John Broom[24] points out that Evans' use of Leibniz's law involves a *petitio.* For Evans' interpretation of Leibniz's law precludes the possibility that it can be applied in an indefinite situation. So Broom contends that one should not deduce that 'a = b' is false from the fact that the predicate ' $\nabla$ (x = a)' is determinately true of *b* while its negation is determinately true of *a* and it is begging the question to assume that Leibniz's law warrants such a deduction. For *a* and *b* can very well be indeterminately identical even though they differ in a property.

The trend of Broom's argument is fine up to this point. But to establish his thesis that it is doubtful that *modus tollens* can be applied to the first conditional part of Leibniz's law if one is committed to a three-valued logic, and even if it is applicable the *reductio* argument becomes ineffective; Broom defines '~p' and 'p ⊃ q' in such a fashion that does not seem plausible at all. His truth table definition of '⊃' shows that it is possible to have a row where p is I, q is F but p ⊃ q is T. The basis of such a definition is Broom's conviction that under the circumstances '⊃' will be false only when the antecedent is true and the consequent is not true, i.e. false or indeterminate and in all other cases 'p ⊃ q' is true. But he defines three valued negation in the most orthodox manner as follows:

| p | ~p |
|---|---|
| T | F |
| I | I |
| F | T |

Given the above definition of negation and his conviction that 'p ⊃ q' is true only when the antecedent is true and the consequent is not true (i.e. '⊃' means ~ (p . ~ q) ) we get a table for '⊃' which does not tally with Broom's table. A comparison of the following two tables will make my contention clear.

Broom's table of '⊃'

| p\q | T | I | F |
|---|---|---|---|
| T | T | F | F |
| I | T | T | T |
| F | T | T | T |

(1)

Our table of '⊃' based on Broom's presupposition

| p\q | T | I | F |
|---|---|---|---|
| T | T | I | F |
| I | T | I | I |
| F | T | T | T |

(2)

Broom's definition of '⊃' is the same as Bochvar's definition of '⊃' in $B_3^E$. But in $B_3^E$ negation is defined as:

| p | ¬p |
|---|---|
| T | F |
| I | F |
| F | T |

The second table is actually the definition of '⊃' in $K_3^S$ i.e. Kleene's Strong 3-valued system.

It is unfortunate that Broom could not establish his point against Evans due to his faulty table of '⊃' resulting from his confusion between the object-language symbol '⊃' and the metalinguistic 'If then'. Bruce Johnsen[25] shows that adoption of Kleene's Strong Tables for '¬' and '⊃' will warrant application of modus tollens as intended by Evans provided Leibniz's law can be given a suitable interpretation in face of indeterminacy. But Leibniz's law, in none of its suitable versions, seems appropriate for applying modus tollens and deducing Evans' conclusion when identity of the objects in question is indeterminate. So Johnsen concludes that doubt concerning Leibniz's law 'is the logical result of any adequate enquiry into the nature of the problem of vagueness itself.'[26]

Having thus shown the main *reductio* argument to be ineffective, let us now pass on to Evans' supplementary comment. To derive a straightforward inconsistency of (5) with (1), he introduces '∆', a dual of '∇' and prefixes steps (1) to (4) as well as Leibniz's law with $\Delta$ and thus derives (5') which directly contradicts (1). But to achieve this direct inconsistency Evans has to posit three equivalences:

(i) $\nabla p \equiv \sim \Delta \sim p$
(ii) $\Delta p \equiv \sim \nabla \sim p$
(iii) $\Delta p \equiv \sim \nabla p$ (implicitly assumed in (3))

From (ii) and (iii) follows (iv) $\Delta p \equiv \Delta \sim p$, i.e, 'definitely p' is equivalent with 'definitely ~ p'. At first glance (iv) may appear counter-intuitive. But we can offer a truth table to satisfy all these conditions together depending on the intuitive understanding of 'definitely' and 'indefinitely'.

| p | ~p | Δp | ∇p | ~Δp | ~∇p | Δ~p | ∇~p | ~Δ~p | ~∇~p |
|---|---|---|---|---|---|---|---|---|---|
| T | F | T | F | F | T | T | F | F | T |
| I | I | F | T | T | F | F | T | T | F |
| F | T | T | F | F | T | T | F | F | T |

Therefore,

$$\Delta p \equiv \sim \nabla p \equiv \Delta \sim p \equiv \sim \nabla \sim p$$
$$\nabla p \equiv \sim \Delta p \equiv \nabla \sim p \equiv \sim \Delta \sim p$$

One feature of '∇' that becomes evident from the above table is that '∇' is basically a two-valued operator. We shall come back to this point later.

We are yet to decide on the appropriate reading of '∇'. Lewis[27] and Over[28] suggest that '∇' should be read as 'It is indefinite whether'. Since 'Δ' is the dual of '∇', 'Δ' should amount to 'it is not indefinite whether not'. By introducing this interpretation in (iv) we get,

'It is not indefinite whether not p'
≡ 'It is not indefinite whether not not p'
≡ 'It is definite whether p'

Hence the apparent inconsistency between (i) and (ii) on the one hand and (iii) on the other is resolved.

A difficulty that still remains here is that '∇' and 'Δ' when taken as analogues of 'M' and 'L' fail to generate a modal system as strong as $S_5$. This goes contrary to Evans' claim. For neither (iii'), the weakened modal counterpart of (iii): $Lp \rightarrow \sim Mp$ nor (iv'), the weakened modal counterpart of (iv): $Lp \rightarrow L \sim p$ can be theorems of $S_5$. Moreover to deduce (5') from the reformulated premises and Leibniz's Law, Evans has to depend on the formula,

$$\Delta (x \rightarrow y) \rightarrow (\Delta x \rightarrow \Delta y)$$

which would not hold in $S_5$, if 'Δ' is read in the above manner.

Evans reformulates (1), i.e. $\nabla p$ as (i') $\Delta \nabla p$. That means, according to Evans, $\nabla p \rightarrow \Delta \nabla p$ should hold. The modal counterpart of it is the characteristic $S_5$ Axiom 8: $Mp \rightarrow LMp$. But $\nabla p \rightarrow \Delta \nabla p$ cannot always be true in vague logic. The counterpart of the $S_5$ Axiom 8 will hold only if Evans rejects the possibility of higher order vagueness. That Evans does so is evident from the above table. The basic two-valued nature of the indeterminacy operator leads us to doubt that Evans ever took vagueness seriously. If one denies higher-order vagueness, vagueness to him becomes sharply defined; i.e. the region of neither true nor false become just another definite region, like the region of truth and the region of falsehood. But anything vague cannot have a sharp cut-off point.

On the same ground, we disagree with Pelletier[29] who uses the operator J, a two-valued operator, very effectively to present the thesis of Evans. But operators having J-like characteristic cannot really cope with indeterminacy. Such a logic is really an apology for three-valued logic.

We have not yet done away with all the objections raised in connection with the modal interpretation of '∇' and 'Δ'. Richmond Thomason[30], for example, criticized the passage from (3) to (4) in Evans' *reductio* argument. To quote Thomason:

The fallacy is analogous to the modal one that would have been committed had $\nabla$ been interpreted as 'neither necessarily true nor necessarily false'. In the modal case $\nabla$ [a = a] is equivalent to x$\nabla$ [x = a] (a) only if *a* is a 'rigid designator', so to assume the equivalence in arguing for a = b $\rightarrow \Box$ [a = b] is to beg the question. In the case of vague singular terms, ~ $\nabla$ [a = a] is equivalent to ~ x $\nabla$ [x = a] (a) only if *a* is a 'precise designator', and when Evans infers the second from the first he is assuming what he is trying to prove.[31]

To sum up the elaborate discussion on the alleged objections to and the attempted defences of Evans' argument, I would like to point out that the *reductio* argument goes through only under the following conditions:

(a) The singular terms 'a' and 'b' are taken as precise designators.
(b) '$\nabla$' and '$\Delta$' are interpreted as 2-valued operators.
(c) Negation is interpreted in the strong sense.
(d) '¬' and '⊃' is defined following Kleene's Strong Tables.
(e) Leibniz's law applies to indeterminate contexts.

There is, however, no compelling reason for a believer in vague objects to accept 'a', 'b' and 'c'.

Even when all these restrictions are imposed the charge of *petitio* cannot be avoided for there always remains some doubt regarding the valid formulation of Leibniz's law where identity is indeterminate; that is, without tacit admission of determinate identity we cannot reject indeterminate identity. Nor can '$\nabla$' and '$\Delta$' generate a modal logic as strong as $S_5$. Consequently we do not know whether a logical system containing '$\nabla$' and '$\Delta$' will be consistent, sound and complete.

We, therefore, find to our dismay that in spite of our best efforts in reconstructing Evans' argument to his total advantage, some flaws in the argument could not be avoided. Even reading between the lines of the argument was not of any help. But Evans, as pointed out by David Lewis, was no fool. So he should not be looked upon as 'a technical philosopher, out of control of his technicalities, taken in by a fallacious proof of an absurd conclusion.'[32] Lewis, therefore, tries to dispel all our misunderstandings of Evans by proposing an alternative reading of the argument. He reports a correspondence with Evans where Evans concurred with Lewis' reading and Lewis hopes that quoting the letter will 'settle the matter'. Let us, therefore, read carefully Lewis' defence of Evans' article.

Lewis points out that Evans gave us the impression that he was discussing a purported proof that there can be no such thing as a vague identity statement. But Evans could not possibly want to deny vague identity. For vague identity is possible and also intelligible. Lewis cites the example of 'Princeton = Princeton Borough'. It is indeterminate whether 'Princeton' stands for the Borough, the Borough + the surrounding Township, or one of countless somewhat larger regions.

Nevertheless in Evans' argument one can easily detect one fallacy and that is, the step from (1) to (2) is not warranted. For it depends on the following equivalence:

(1') It is vague whether . . . a . . . symbolized as $\nabla$ (. . . a . . .)

(2') It is such that it is vague whether . . . symbolized as $\hat{x}$ ($\nabla$ (. . . x . . . ) a).

But as 'a' and 'b' are non-rigid designators, this equivalence does not hold just as the following modal equivalence fails to hold in the presence of non-rigid designators.

(1") It is contingent whether the number of planets is nine (true).

(2") The number of planets is such that it is contingent whether it is nine (false).

A similar objection, we have mentioned, has been raised by Thomason, only Thomason has also used 'precise designator' to mean 'rigid designator'.

Lewis' conjecture, claimed to be duly endorsed by Evans in the said letter, is that Evans did not want to argue against vague identity. Rather Evans wanted to draw our attention to the fact that any proof amounting to the denial of vague identity is bound to involve such fallacious equivalences. But this fallacy cannot even be diagnosed if the vagueness-in-reality thesis is upheld. Only a belief in vagueness-in-description can highlight the fallacy. So Evans was really against admission of vague objects but neither against vagueness as a *façon de parler* nor against vague identity.

We shall now have to see whether what Lewis ascribes to Evans could really be Evans' motivation while he offered the original *reductio* proof against vague objects.

In the very first paragraph of his article Evans expressed his wish to find out how the assertion, objects in the world really have fuzzy boundaries, could be made intelligible. His strategy was to present a *reductio* argument against vague identity. To show that vague identity is essentially linked with vague objects Evans has to make sure that indeterminacy in identity is not due to vague descriptions involved in the terms of identity statements but is due to the vagueness of objects. So as an instance of indeterminate identity we cannot take a statement like 'The greatest ruler is the wisest ruler'[33] since vagueness of this sentence is due to vagueness of the component definite descriptions. So 'a = b' will be indeterminate in Evans' sense if either 'a' or 'b' or both refer to some vague object. Moreover, if indeterminacy is not to be due to reference-failure but due to vagueness then both 'a' and 'b' are to be taken as precise designators; then and then only it can be claimed that indeterminacy inherent in the identity statement 'a = b' stems from the vague nature of objects referred to by the terms.

'Princeton = Princeton Borough' will not qualify as a proper example of indeterminate identity. If there is any indeterminacy at all in the above example, it arises out of the ambiguity of the name given both to Princeton City and to Princeton Borough.[34] Lewis tags his supervaluational semantics onto his theory of vague identity. He, therefore, thinks that Princeton = Princeton Borough is vague and it can be precisified in various different manners. Under one sharpening or precisification 'Princeton' stands for the Borough and under another sharpening it stands for the city and so on. There is, however, every doubt that Evans would have subscribed to Lewis' supervaluational semantics and without the backing of his semantics, Lewis' defence of Evans becomes very weak.

As far as our knowledge goes, Evans was an ardent supporter of direct interpretational semantics and a homophonic theory of truth.[35] If that is the case (I mean, if Evans had not admitted that he had given up his preference for direct interpretational semantics together with a homophonic theory of truth to somebody in some letter), then Evans could not have been totally unsympathetic to vague objects if he is committed to the view that there are indeterminate identity statements which reflects *de re* vagueness. For there are vague expressions in our natural language, say for instance, 'hill'. 'Hill' will naturally refer to a hill. Now, consider a hill H which can be referred to by two names '*a*' and '*b*'. Suppose that the identity of H is indeterminate for there is no fact of the matter to determine whether some stretches of terrain belong to H or not. That is, those stretches of terrain are neither definitely parts nor definitely non-parts of H. A language the ontology of which does not accommodate vague objects will not even be able to speak about H. So Burgess rightly upholds:

> The ontology of vague language itself must be admitted to *certain vague objects* unless we were to attempt absurdly, to try to combine the view that the names *a* and *b*, above, denote directly, i.e. they each denote a single thing—with the view that it can be true, *de dicto*, that the boundaries of H are not precisely determined although the single thing which *a* and *b* both name is nevertheless precise.[36]

Burgess, therefore, counters Lewis' interpretation on the ground that as Evans was in favour of direct interpretational semantics, he had to admit vague objects theory. For precise-objects-only theory makes Evans' two great loves—direct semantics in the Fregean line and a Davidson-type homophonic theory of truth incompatible.

Even if we set aside for the time being Evans' semantic theory still we find that Lewis' interpretation of Evans cannot satisfactorily settle the matter against vague objects. Lewis senses trouble for the supporters of vague objects theory because they allegedly are of the opinion that a singular term '*a*' in an indeterminate identity statement rigidly denotes a vague object. But the proponents of vague-objects-theory need not accept that '*a*' should rigidly designate its referent; '*a*' can very well be a non-rigid designator.

A Lewisian might make the following rejoinder: 'to be is to be the value of a variable'; so if we are ontologically committed to vague objects, they must be capable of being precisely designated by some variables. Those who subscribe to the classical semantics can at best be committed to a definite realm of vague objects and to an exact number of vague objects even though the latter have fuzzy edges and so on. But

> '. . . those who want vague identity with vague objects could reject that classical view. Their domain could itself be vague or with an indefinite number of vague objects as members of it. They could have an indefinite notion of existence itself and of quantification over that domain. And finally, they might doubt the sense of claiming that a variable or any other term could be precisely assigned to exactly one, definitely unique individual to such a domain.[37]

Whether or not one accepts such vague objects and vague identity is a matter of philosophical debate and cannot simply be discarded by an argument with classical semantical presuppositions. Hence, we have to admit that Evans' argument cannot prove demonstratively what it claims to prove.

### 3.5 INDETERMINATE IDENTITY AGAIN

In this section I propose to examine two other arguments against vague objects which were developed almost on similar lines by David Wiggins and Nathan Salmon independently of Evans.

Wiggins (1986) puts forward his objection to the notion of vague objects in the form of a direct proof, albeit a conditional proof, in 'On singling out an object determinately'.

| | | |
|---|---|---|
| (i) | $a = b$ | (Hyp) |
| (ii) | $\Delta\,(a = a)$ | (Truism) |
| (iii) | $\Delta\,(a = b)$ | (i), (ii), Leibniz's law |
| (iv) | $(a = b) \rightarrow \Delta\,(a = b)$. | |

Wiggins himself has given a paraphrase of this proof.

> Suppose that *a* is *b*. Then given Leibniz's law, whatever is true of *a* is true of *b*. Now *a* is definitely *a*. So by conditional proof and the symmetry of identity, if *a* is *b*, *a* is definitely *b*. In which case there is no future in the supposition that one could say that *a* was *b* but refuse to affirm that it was definitely *b*.[38]

This conditional proof rests on the hypothesis that a = b is true. But what happens if a = b is indeterminate? Since we are trying to find out whether a = b can be indeterminate and consequently whether objects can be vague, we cannot presume that a = b is determinate, i.e. true.

Now if a = b is indeterminate, then $\Delta$ (a = b) becomes false. Then the question is, can the conclusion (iv) be true? It depends on how we interpret '$\rightarrow$' involved in (iv). If we follow Bochvar's extended 3-valued system, i.e. if we allow a conditional to be true when its antecedent is indeterminate and its consequent is false, then (iv) turns out to be true. That means the truth of the conclusion of Wiggins is consistent with the possibility of vague objects.[39]

It might be objected that when (iv) is true, one can use it as the major premiss of an argument against vague identity as well as vague objects. For, when it is not true that a is definitely b, by *modus tollens* it follows that it is not true that a = b. Then only at the risk of *petitio* we can conclude that it is false that a = b may be indeterminate. So the possibility of vague objects cannot be convincingly ruled out.

If, on the other hand, we follow the interpretation of '→' as in K then (iv) becomes indeterminate, i.e. not true. When the conclusion is not true, one of the premises must have gone awry. The question is which one? Premiss (i) has been assumed only hypothetically. We are not questioning premiss (ii) for the time being and are agreeing with Wiggins in maintaining:

> . . . even if . . . *a* were a vague object, we still ought to be able to obtain a (so to speak) perfect case of identity, provided we were careful to mate *a* with exactly the right object. And surely *a* is exactly the right object to mate with *a*.[40]

(Later on we shall mention some of the views that have questioned even the reflexivity of identity.) Then the step (iii) must have gone wrong. How? Probably Leibniz's law fails to apply. Why? Because the identity in question is indeterminate. Hence, Wiggins once again fails to demonstrate the impossibility of vague objects.

Though the direct proof mentioned above fails to eliminate the possibility of vague objects, Wiggins can establish his point with his sortal dependent notion of identity and his account of individuation of objects within the conceptual framework.

According to the conceptualist position, 'the reality is what it is and there are no lines in nature'. So no item of reality individuates itself, nor does it differentiate itself from other things. Individuation or singling out is done *entirely* by us. We use some sortal concepts to determine what are out there in reality and when we apply these sortal concepts we do pick out items of reality determinately. This process of individuation cannot be vague and objects in so far as they are sliced out cannot but be determinate. Because of such conceptualist commitment

Wiggins is interested in proving that if *a* is *b* at all, it is definitely *b*.

Wiggins, however, does not think that every sentence will remain true when prefixed with 'definitely'. For 'identity sentences may contain descriptions, and vagueness may result from these descriptions.'[41] Wiggins, therefore, does not have to do away with the notion of indeterminate identity. Wiggins can even tackle indeterminacy of $a = b$, where '*a*' and '*b*' are precise designators, without admitting vague objects, with the help of his notion of sortal dependent identity. Identity is sortal dependent, says Wiggins, when if A = B, for some sortal F (mountain, tiger, cloud, ship), A is the same F as B. So the hill H may appear to have fuzzy spatial boundaries, or it may be indeterminate whether some spatial points are parts, non-parts or borderline parts of H, yet we need not uphold for that matter that H is a vague object. It is because H is being identified by a vague sortal concept 'hill', there arises indeterminacy with respect to its identity. In *sameness and substance*, Wiggins declares boldly, the words like 'mountain' lie on the borderline between true substance terms and what might be called lump-mass terms. And,

> . . . it is not a formal, but a scientific question, however, whether a sufficiently rich theory is forthcoming to resolve the indeterminacies and possible individuative arbitrariness of putative natural kinds. . . such as mountain.[42]

Two interesting points emerge from the above discussion. (a) The success of Wiggins' project is essentially linked with admission of sortal-dependent identity and (b) to eliminate vague objects Wiggins has to admit vague concepts.

N. Salmon has offered another version of Evans' *reductio* argument but his argument is more carefully formulated and is free from many of the defects from which Evans' argument suffered. To avoid any charge of misrepresentation let me quote from *Essence and Reference*:

> Suppose that there is a pair of entities x and y . . . such

that it is vague (neither true nor false, indeterminate, there is no objective fact of the matter) whether they are one and the very same thing. Then this pair (x, y) is quite definitely *not* the same pair as (x, x), since it is determinately true that *x* is one and the very same thing as itself. It follows that *x* and *y* must be distinct. But then it is not vague whether they are identical or distinct.[43]

For convenience of discussion let me rewrite the argument separating its premises from the conclusion.

Let us suppose if possible,

(i) (x, y) is a pair such that it is indeterminate whether x is the same as y or not.
(ii) But (x, x) is a pair such that it is determinate that x is the same as x.
(iii) It is determinate that (x, x) ≠ (x, y).
(iv) It is determinate that x ≠ y.

It is obvious that Salmon's proof is also a *reductio*. To derive (iii) from (i) and (ii) Salmon has to depend tacitly on Leibniz's law. He can derive (iii) from (i) and (ii) because he thinks that the pair (x, x) possesses a property which the pair (x, y) does not possess.

Bruce Johnsen[44] argues that application of Leibniz's law here does not pose any problem since the said law applies in the metalinguistic level. In fact the whole of Salmon's argument is conducted in 2-valued metalanguage while Evans attempted to employ Leibniz's law in a 3-valued object language. But Salmon's argument to go through, it is required to presuppose that *it is always metaphysically determinate whether or not a given individual possesses the property* (*of being identical with x*) or not. Despite Salmon's reeated denials and Johnson's valiant defence, I cannot but maintain that, Salmon is begging the question here. Salmon is not being fair to the proponents of the vague-objects-and-the-indeterminate-identity-theory.

While presenting this argument Salmon anticipated two objections. First, it might be said that since 'is' of identity does not apply to the pair (x, y), it should not apply to the pair (x, x) also. Here *x* is of such a nature that it is illegitimate to apply 'is' of identity to *x*. But this objection, thinks Salmon, is absurd for every object is identical with itself.

Another common objection raised against Salmon is that he is not taking vagueness seriously. If he had, he could not have derived (x, y) ≠ (x, x) from the assumption that it is vague whether the first pair of objects stand in relation of identity but it is determinate that the second pair of objects are identical. The critic would point out that Salmon forgets that classically valid inference patterns do not apply in the presence of a vague term. Salmon refuses to admit that his argument pattern ceases to be truth-preserving here. He parries that a classical inference pattern does not become invalid whenever we use a vague term in an inference. The term 'bald', for example, has almost been unanimously admitted as vague. Yet the inference pattern

$\alpha$ has a full head of hair
∴ $\alpha$ is not bald

remains truth-preserving. He writes:

> The validity of this inference pattern ensures that in order to settle the question of whether it is true, false or indeterminate that Harry is bald, it is sufficient to take note of the fact that Harry's head is very hairy.[45]

This observation of Salmon is not acceptable to me for two reasons. First, like Evans he is also denying higher order vagueness. Second, he seems to forget a very important point about vague terms. The range of application of every vague expression can be divided into two regions (1) umbral and (2) penumbral. It is not the case that no sentence containing any vague term can be assigned a definite truth value. It is only when the expression falls within the penumbral region we fail to assign any definite truth value to the sentence containing the said vague expression. The limiting cases of vague terms are always crisp and there the classical rules of inference apply without any difficulty.

It is interesting to note that all these proofs (of Evans, Wiggins', Salmon's) stand on the assumption that self-identity is indubitable. But philosophers, especially the dialecticians, have questioned self-identity too. Even reflexivity of identity has not been treated as sacrosanct. Modern logicians[46] have constructed ingenuous arguments to show that everything is distinct from itself. Let us consider two such arguments.

(a) Identity is a binary relation. A relation always relates one thing to another thing. Since identity is a relation, there must be some distinction between the terms which it relates: 'Some kind of otherness is bound to exist between the things related'. So non-irreflexive binary relation is not at all possible.

(b) A binary relation is represented as a set of ordered pairs. Consider the relational sentence 'Narcissus loves himself'. The loving relation L can be expressed as $\langle$Narcissus, Narcissus$\rangle \in$ L. But to make the notion of ordered *pair* meaningful we must concede that there exists some kind of distinction between Narcissus and himself.

An attempt may be made to restore reflexivity of identity by appealing to a combinatorial categoryless theory of relations.[47] In such a theory the event of Brutus' killing Caesar will be identified with Brutus' being the killer of Caesar and Caesar being killed by Brutus'. So Brutus' killing of Caesar is something both of Brutus and Caesar. Even then there is a difference, the relation of Brutus-killing-Caesar holds of Brutus as the killer and of Caesar as being killed. But in the event of Brutus killing himself, the killing relation should apply to Brutus in two different ways. Hence there must be some distinction between Brutus, the killer, and Brutus, the killed.

These arguments are not very convincing. The first one to have any weight must be supplemented by some independent argument establishing that a one-term relation or a self-link relation is no relation at all. The second argument unduly emphasizes the aspect of purported otherness in the notion of ordered pair. It is true that in ordinary usage, 'pair' refers to the two distinct but matched elements, nevertheless it is not part of the technical definition of 'ordered pair' that the two members in an ordered pair must be distinct.

But reflexivity of identity in the context of a vague object really becomes suspect. We have seen that if there is genuine case of *de re* vagueness then we may not be sure whether the object referred to is a single object or more than one for there is no fact of the matter to determine whether some space-time points are definitely parts, non-parts or borderline parts of it.

Not only that, as Kripke had rightly pointed out transitivity of identity also fails to hold when the object to which identity is being ascribed is vague.

> . . . If a chip, or a molecule, of a given table had been replaced by another one, we would be content to say we have the same table. But if too many chips were different, we would seem to have a different one. . . . where the identity relation is vague, it may seem intransitive; a (chain) of apparent (identities) may yield an apparent non-identity.[48]

So an identity relation associated with a vague object can at best be an equivalence relation characterized by some sort of fuzzy reflexivity,[49] symmetry and weak transitivity. To distinguish such a relation of identity from its classical counterpart we shall call it 'approximate identity'. A believer in vague objects should, therefore, revise the classical notion of absolute identity, and if necessary, the logic associated with it.

### 3.6 THE ONTOLOGY OF VAGUE OBJECTS

Evans, Wiggins and Salmon, all three of them, formulated their arguments against indeterminate identity with a view to disproving vague objects. Of course, Lewis has pointed out that Evans was not against indeterminate identity as such but only against indeterminate identity statements arising out of *de re* vagueness. But none of them, I think, could achieve their objective. So let us reopen the issue with which we opened our discussion in this chapter. And that is, can there be vague objects or is vagueness a character of our way of describing the world? This is a tricky question, indeed. So we shall have to negotiate the ground very carefully avoiding all pitfalls.

Though Evans has failed to prove his point conclusively yet, we must admit, he has shown us how to place the issue within the framework of reference. So let Evans' assumptions be our take-off point.

The positive lessons that we have learnt in spite of the lapses of Evans are somewhat like this. If there are vague objects, then there must be indeterminate identity statements in our language containing precise singular terms or proper names and indeterminacy must ensue from the vague nature of objects referred to by the said names. That is, if 'a = b' is indeterminate and *a* and *b* are both precise, then the identity statement can be indeterminate in truth value provided there is *de re* vagueness all other sources of indeterminacy having been set aside.

Now if we grant that both believers and non-believers in vague objects admit that there are indeterminate identity statements containing precise names in our language, then whether or not one should be committed to vague objects in one's ontology will depend on what theory of reference one subscribes to. Suppose one is a supporter of direct referential theory, then a name in his language will directly latch on to an object, i.e. it will satisfy a purely semantical condition of fit. Under the circumstances it is inconceivable that a sentence like 'Snowcap' = Snowcap"' is indeterminate in truth value when Snowcap' and Snowcap" both directly and determinately designate one mountain but the mountain in question has no indeterminacy. But if, on the other hand, the mountain referred to by Snowcap' and Snowcap" is such that there are some stretches of terrain which are neither definitely parts nor non-parts of it, then the situation can be suitably explained. Admission of vague objects appear all the more necessary if one subscribes to a Tarski-type theory of truth in addition to a direct referential theory. In that case,

> It is true that Snowcap' = Snowcap" is indeterminate iff Snowcap' and Snowcap" are indeterminately identical.

And it appears that Snowcap' and Snowcap" can be identical iff the object of their reference, the mountain in question, has fuzzy boundaries/is compositionally vague.

This consequence may be avoided in either of three ways:

(a) by giving up the direct referential theory;
(b) by denying that there can be indeterminate identity sentences in our language containing precise names the indeterminacy of which is not a result of some sort of failure of reference;
(c) by rejecting the classical notion of identity.

David Lewis[50] takes the first way out. He proffers the supervaluational semantics where reference of a name is secured indirectly via precisification. When a singular term like 'Snowcap', designates a mountain, all we are to do is to precisify the predicate 'mountain' as 'mountain$^1$', 'mountain$^2$', 'mountain$^3$', . . . Such precisification will guarantee that 'mountain$^1$', 'mountain$^2$', etc. will be true of precise objects only. Consequently 'Snowcap'=Snowcap" ' will be either determinately true or determinately false.

By this move Lewis also ensures that in problem situations our language is made free of all vague expressions for all practical purposes. Thus for a supervaluational semanticist the route (a) and the route (b) will coincide. But these artificially precise meanings of predicates are not what an ordinary speaker of English understands by 'mountain'. Though Lewis' version of supervaluational semantics is compatible with no-vague-object theory, yet all supervaluationists are not against vague objects. Kit Fine[51], for example, had been quite explicit in his support for vague objects when he disapproved of philosophers who had been unduly dismissive over intrinsically vague entities.

Philosophers are probably the most reluctant to consider even the third way out. For in almost all contemporary theories of reference, like those upheld by Frege, Russell, Quine, Kripke and others, it has been admitted that an object of reference must be provided with an absolute criterion of identity and an adequate apparatus for individuating the object. According to Quine, the latter task is performed by the apparatus of quantification. Even then, that object alone can be properly individuated which is capable of being a *definite* value of a bindable variable of which names, descriptions and indexicals are substituends. So the criterion of identity that can be associated with any object of reference must be absolute and the object, in its turn, must be discrete and complete. The idea of indeterminateness in identity is so abominable that some philosophers will concede 'a *small* and manageable amount of fuzzy boundedness'[52] (which can be rationalized or explained away)[53] rather than tolerating indefinite identity.

The question of the fate of vague objects is put in the shade by fascinating debates over problems of reference if the existence of vague objects is to be solved within the framework of reference. So it is better to delink the issue of *de re* vagueness from the issues concerning reference. Sainsbury, therefore, demands:

> There ought to be a way of saying what it is for an object to be vague which talks simply of objects, and not of sentences, and is thus neutral about theories of reference.[54]

The delinking can be easily done if we talk in terms of identity relation associated with a vague object and not about identity statements containing precise names.

In the second section of this chapter we have differentiated amongst three types of vague objects: those which are (i) compositionally vague, (ii) temporally vague and (iii) Individuatively vague following Sainsbury. He thinks that vague objects of the third type are *prima facie* good candidates for possessing vague identity relation. For convenience of discussion let me repeat the definition of an individuatively vague object.

> x is individuatively vague = (defined) x is such that, for some y, it is vague whether y is identical with x.

A vague identity relation in this context will mean that the pair x and y are neither definitely related by it nor definitely not related by it. We might conveniently redefine it in terms of property: the property of 'being identical with' is such that it neither definitely applies nor definitely fails to apply to the pair x, y. But this definition of identity relation gets vitiated by a counter-example. The counter-example is a variant of our example of 'the sun'. Supposing that the mountain Snowdon is compositionally vague, it can be shown that the precise property of having a surface area of just 1500 acres neither definitely applies to Snowdon nor definitely fails to apply to it. Hence one can argue that whenever a property is such that it neither definitely applies to a vague object, nor definitely fails to apply to it, it is not always the case that the property is vague. So the 'property of being identical with' or the relation of identity applicable to a vague object need not necessarily be vague.

But it may be objected that we have shifted our ground. We were discussing vague identity relation in respect of an individuatively vague object and not in respect of a compositionally vague one.

Let us, therefore, consider the example of Theseus' ship. It is vague whether Theseus' ship after replacement of its fiftieth plank (henceforth $TS_{50}$) is identical with the original ship of Theseus' (TS) though $TS_{50}$ continues to sail on the same route. Yet one can conceive that there is a TS-like-precise-object and a $TS_{50}$-like-precise object which are distinct and that there is a TS-like-precise object and $TS_{50}$-like-precise-object which are identical. Hence one may conclude with Sainsbury,

> If you blame the objects for the vagueness, you need not blame the relation. . . . The slogan is: vague object without vague identity.[55]

Though Sainsbury has attempted to delink the theory of vague objects from the theory of reference yet by his supervaluationist stance of precisification he has reinstated the classical notion of absolute identity. A serious supporter of vague objects will have reservations against the notion of precisification as well as any absolute criterion of identity. It is justified on his part to question the ideas of precise designator, definite quantification, definite identity and discreet existence.

Since with Sainsbury we have already entered into the metaphysical arena leaving behind the logico-linguistic arguments, it is high time that we review the problem of vague objects in the backdrop of the realist-conceptualist debate. By this exercise I do not want to press the point that the metaphysical realm can be kept separate from the logico-linguistic realm; my intention is to alter the thrust of the arguments.

The Fregean version of realism, we have seen, cannot give any quarters to any vague object. For Frege would not budge an inch from the following commitments. (1) There is nothing in the world which is inherently incompletely specified and (2) we need not and should not go beyond the bounds of classical logic. But for these beliefs, Frege could have formulated his criteria of identity for objects and concepts differently.

Moreover, Frege used 'objects' in a highly technical sense meaning referents of singular terms. In subsequent literature, this usage has come to stay. We are not therefore surprised when we find Quine insisting both in *Word and Object* [56] and in *Ontological Relativity*[57] that objects must have in-built individuating features in them. We have also seen that Quine is a staunch supporter of absolute identity. That is why, when Quine is confronted with an example like Theseus' ship, he construes this problem not as a problem of the 'same' but of 'ship'. To Quine it is not so much a problem whether $TS_{50}$ is the same as TS but whether $TS_{50}$ is the same *ship* as TS. To accommodate an entity like $TS_{50}$ in his framework, he is ready to go to the length of redefining the notion of 'Ship'.[58] He may precisify 'ship' as 'strict ship' the planks of which cannot be replaced and as 'laxship' the planks of which can be replaced. Then there will be no vague object; $TS_{50}$ being a laxship and TS a strict ship. This theory, however, will have the absurd consequence that there will be no ship in the world. Ordinary ships will thus go out of existence along with vague objects. So it is clear that Quine will not admit vague objects though he has dealt at length with the nature and use of vague expressions in a language.

A conceptualist like Wiggins upholds that there are no lines in reality, we slice out objects by imposing our own conceptual framework. In keeping with this view he very consistently upholds that identity is sortal-dependent. So if we are conceptualists we shall have to maintain that whenever we want to individuate an object we individuate it depending on some sortal or other. Some sortals like 'mountain', 'cloud', etc. are fuzzy. So whenever we individuate something as a mountain, the singled out object appears to be vague even though there is no vagueness in reality. In *Sameness and Substance* Wiggins upholds, granting that the sortals like 'mountain' are vague, there is no necessity of describing some item of reality as 'mountain' or 'plain'. That is, reality need not be sliced in this manner. If we have a different scientific theory we shall slice reality in a different way making necessary adjustments in our descriptions of reality. At this point Quine and a conceptualist come very close to each other.

Besides, Wiggins points out, words like 'heap' do not necessarily lead us to admit vague objects because each collection can be said to be constituted of a definite number of constituents. Hence vagueness of *sortals* or that of *terms* need not entail corresponding vagueness in reality.

Still there remains an important issue to be settled. Let us grant that reality can be described without using the terms like 'mountain'. Even then we shall have to use some other sortal, some other word in lieu of it to pick out and to describe reality. But can we be ever sure that there is a range of ultimate states of affairs that can be described without using any vague expression at all? Or, can there be, in the ultimate analysis, such terms which are free from all vagueness and can depict reality as it is?

The question is a very involved one; 'yes' or 'no' or 'meaningless' whatever may be our answer, we shall have to go beyond conceptualism. Indeed, the question is a tangle of many issues of which two, at least, must be kept distinct:

(1) Whether there exists a range of precise facts/states of affairs or not,

(2) Whether the human conceptuo-linguistic framework is adequate to those facts/states of affairs.

We are more interested in settling the first issue here. But the second one is not insignificant either. If the human conceptual framework is inherently imprecise then vagueness becomes an essential feature of our thought and talk and no representation of reality can ever be precise. If, on the other hand, our conceptual framework mirrors reality then at least some elements of vagueness in our thought and talk are due to *de re* vagueness. This is, no doubt, a simplistic picture. Actual state of affairs may be much more complex.

The other half of the question is equally tricky. A direct realist claiming direct confrontation with reality will be able to give a straightforward 'yes/no' answer to the questions: whether reality contains anything which is inherently indeterminate or whether reality is precise; whether there are clear-cut demarcations in reality or whether reality is demarcationless. To an internal realist the questions will appear meaningless.

Of course there is a sure way of repudiating the vagueness-in-reality thesis. That is by way of upholding that reality is what it is, vagueness creeps in at the level of representation. Sure, reality is what it is, but *what* is it really? Philosophy will end if we stop raising this question. Sure, what reality is, is known through our conceptual framework, is justified through our web of belief, but it is not sure that whatever we know or believe about reality cannot be a feature of reality. Just because there is vagueness in our representation, it does not follow that there is no vagueness in reality. If it is objected, *de re* vagueness is still a bias, it has not yet been established, I would humbly point out that it does not stand condemned either. Hence by following the legal principle 'not guilty, until proved guilty' I am inclined to take a charitable attitude towards fuzzy objects.

## NOTES AND REFERENCES

1. Bertrand Russell (1923), p. 85.
2. Ibid.
3. Michael Dummett (1970).
4. Bertil Rolf (1980).
5. David Wiggins (1979).
6. D. Wiggins (1986), p. 173.
7. Michael Tye (1990).
8. R.M. Sainsbury (1989).
   Compositional vagueness is different from the vagueness arising out of having fuzzy boundaries. For an object can be compositionally vague even with precise spatial boundaries.
9. B. Rolf (1980).
10. Ibid., pp. 317–8.
11. Sainsbury (1989).
12. Gottlob Frege (1979), p. 155.
13. M. Dummett (1973b), p. 647.
14. Frege (1979), p. 120.
15. Ibid.
16. Ibid., p. 155.
17. Ibid., p. 155.
18. Ibid., p. 122.
19. Garrett Evans (1978), p. 208.
20. Nathan Salmon (1982).
21. Wiggins (1986).
22. Comments within parentheses are mine.
23. Brian Garrett (1991).
24. J. Broom (1984).
25. B. Johnsen (1989).
26. Ibid., p. 109.
27. David Lewis (1988).
28. D.E. Over (1989).
29. F. J. Pelletier (1989).
30. R. Thomason (1984).
31. Ibid., p. 331.
32. Lewis (1988), p. 128.
33. Wiggins (1986), p. 174.
34. J. A. Burgess (1989).
35. G. Evans (1976).
36. J.A. Burgess (1989), p. 118.
37. D.E. Over (1989), p. 99.
38. Wiggins (1986), p. 173.
39. B. J. Garrett (1988).
40. Wiggins (1986), p. 175.
41. Ibid., p. 174.
42. Wiggins (1980).
43. Salmon (1982), p. 243.

44. B. Johnsen (1989), p. 111.
45. N. Salmon (1982).
46. L. Pena (1984).
47. F.B. Fitch (1976).
48. S. Kripke (1972).
49. E. Trilas and A. Valverde (1984).
50. D. Lewis (1988).
51. Kit Fine (1975), p. 299.
52. J.A. Burges (1989), p. 118.
53. M. Tye (1990) speaks of manageable fuzzy boundedness. Let x be an object and there are some space-time points which do not definitely belong to it. But the object x is such that its parts, non-parts and borderline parts can be clearly distinguished from one another. x is not in fact vague in the true sense for its borderline cases form a well defined grey area distinct from the 'inside' and the 'outside' of x. Now, if such a grey area can be eliminated by some device, x becomes precise.
54. R.M. Sainsbury (1989), p. 99.
55. Ibid., p. 103.
56. W.V.O. Quine (1960).
57. W.V.O. Quine (1969).
58. W.V.O. Quine (1981).

CHAPTER 4

# Logics of Vague Sentences

After having discussed some philosophical issues about vagueness in the previous chapters, it is time now to investigate whether vague expressions are formalizable, whether any of the formal apparatus so far used is adequate, if not, then what sort of alternative logic should we develop, and what are the benefits consequent upon an alternative logic.

## 4.1 THE CLASSICAL APPROACH

Vague sentences do not follow the laws of classical bivalent logic. We have seen that a particular shade of colour in the red-orange continuum may be neither red nor orange. In that case the sentence 'This shade is red' is not true, for the shade in question cannot be called definitely red nor is the sentence false, for there is no fact of the matter to determine that the given shade is not red. So under the circumstances the said sentence turns out to be neither true nor false. But, if every sentence must be either true or false, i.e. if the law of excluded middle (LEM, henceforth) holds without exception as the classical 2-valued logicians claim, then how can we account for the recalcitrant sentence? Classical logic either has to ignore vague sentences or has to thrive with inconsistencies. Neither alternative appears to be acceptable. Hence in this chapter we are going to enquire: What is the logic of vague sentences?

We may begin our enquiry with a very innocuous question: Why should one at all try to develop a logic for vague sentences? What we have said so far commits us to the view that vague sentences are ineliminable from ordinary language. Must this commitment be reflected in our logic? History of logic provides us with a negative answer. Logic in the Frege-Russell tradition would have no truck with vague sentences. Frege and Russell have set aside these peccant sentences to keep their logic impeccable. Following in their footsteps will surely render our logic inadequate. For, logic as a theory of inference must be capable of handling any valid argument. Vague sentences very often occur essentially in valid arguments. No adequate logic should, therefore, set aside vague sentences. Yet Russell did ignore vague sentences. His strong commitment to bivalence supported by an assumption of *discrete predication*[1] set him against vague sentences. This is in consonance with Russellian Calculus of Classes adopted in the *Principia Mathematica* where Russell upholds the equivalence thesis:

$$\vdash x \in {\sim}\alpha \equiv x \sim\in \alpha$$ [2]

So when one is unable to assert definitely that x is P, one is justified in asserting 'it is not the case that x is P' and then by virtue of the above equivalence, 'x is non-P'. Thus even if we are doubtful about P being a predicate of x we can easily uphold 'x is non-P'. Borderline cases thus explained Russell did not feel any urge to make any provision for vague sentences within his logic.

It is obvious that Russell did not take vague expressions seriously in *Principia Mathematica.* So PM cannot be our model for logic. Our logic should be able to tackle sentences like 'x is bald', 'y is tall', 'z is red', etc., when such sentences are neither true nor false.

In logical literature usually the 'neither true nor false' status of a vague sentence has been equated with 'truth value gap'. But any sentence involving a truth value gap is not a vague sentence since truth value gap may be due to failure of reference or failure of presupposition and not necessarily due to vagueness.

Of the various logical approaches to the 'truth value gap' thesis we shall discuss only two: (a) the three-valued logic and (b) the supervaluational logic.

## 4.2 THREE-VALUED LOGIC AND VAGUE SENTENCES

All systems of 3-valued logic posit a third truth value, viz. *I* (*Indefinite* or *Indeterminate*) over and above the two classical values *Truth* and *Falsity* (*T, F*). *Indefinite* has been given various different interpretations in different many-valued systems. Sometimes *I* is taken to be a third objective truth value, sometimes just a truth value gap. Again, *I* signifies 'meaninglessness' in some systems while in some others it has an epistemological undertone, e.g. *I* may mean neither known to be true nor known to be false. Sometimes *I* has been treated as a halfway house between truth and falsity and is placed in between *T* and *F*, and sometimes it is considered simply a different value other than *T* and *F* without any algebraic, geometric or topological specifications.

Not only *I* has been differently interpreted, the calculi involving *I* have also been variously defined. All standard 3-valued calculi may be brought under two different approaches; the approaches being (a) the I-dominant approach where any compound sentence involving an indefinite component yields I and (b) the I-recessive approach where a compound sentence having an indefinite subsentence may get a definite classical value. The 3-valued system of Bochvar ($B_3$) and Kleene's weak system ($K_3^W$) may be taken as representatives of the former approach whereas Lukasiewicz's 3-valued system ($L_3$) and Kleene's strong system ($K_3^S$) are good examples of the latter approach.

The I-dominant approach is not suitable for our purpose because it has no explanatory value. In such systems an indefinite input always yields an indefinite output. But it is not always the case that one vague component renders the whole sentence vague. The I-dominant approach is suitable for formalizing meaningless sentences as meaningless components are really capable of affecting meaningful sentences. Historically speaking both Bochvar and Kleene developed their systems $B_3$ and $K_3^W$ respectively with this motivation.

But the case is different with $L_3$ and $K_3^S$, their approach being I-recessive. Of these two systems, $K_3^S$ is better suited to represent truth value gap. *I* in $L_3$ is an *objective* intermediate truth value between *T* and *F*. But $K_3^S$ does not force on us any such notion. Originally $K_3^S$ was developed with the aim of accommodating those mathematical formuli which are neither proved nor disproved; it should therefore be appropriate for dealing with the 'truth value gap' situation. Besides, in $L_3$, $p \rightarrow p$ is a tautology. It does not, however, appear quite correct to uphold that $p \rightarrow p$ is always true, even when p is indeterminate. In $K_3^S$ this point also can be taken care of. Hence, it appears, if any 3-valued system can at all tackle vague sentences, it should be $K_3^S$.

Interestingly enough, we are not alone in our faith in the logical power of $K_3^S$. Michael Tye[3] in one of his very recent papers has also taken $K_3^S$ as the base logic for handling sentences possessing 'truth value gap'.

Let us recapitulate the truth-table definitions of '¬', '∧', '∨' and '→' following Kleene.

| p | ¬p |
|---|---|
| T | F |
| I | I |
| F | T |

| | p∧q | p∨q | p→q | p↔q |
|---|---|---|---|---|
| p\q | T I F | T I F | T I F | T I F |
| T | T I F | T T T | T I F | T I F |
| I | I I F | T I I | T I I | I I I |
| F | F F F | T I F | T T T | F I T |

It is obvious from the above table that neither LEM nor the law of non-contradiction (LNC in future) can be tautologies of $K_3^S$ as they will have the truth value I when p is I. But we can treat them as quasi-tautologies since they can never be false. Similarly $p \wedge \neg p$ will be a quasi-contradiction since it will never be true. The quasi-tautological nature of LEM and LNC instead of being a defect of $K_3^S$ turns out to be a merit in the present context. It serves as an additional justification for adopting $K_3^S$ as the base logic. Under the circumstances $p \vee \neg p$ should not always be true, not when p is indefinite or a borderline case of a vague predicate is involved.

Tye has sketched a formal semantics of vague sentences that goes well with $K_3^S$ . A brief resumé of it follows immediately.

Given a non-empty domain D, an extensionally vague monadic predicate F is assigned an extension S and a counter extension S'. S is the set of objects of which F is true; S' is the set of objects of which F is false. Since F is vague, both S and S' are vague sets. A set is vague iff

(i) It has borderline members and
(ii) There is no determinate fact of the matter about whether there are objects that are neither members, borderline members nor non-members.

In the context of vague sets the Axiom of Extensionality becomes indefinite. This axiom states: two sets S and S' will be identical iff, for any x, x belongs to S, iff, x belongs to S'. In symbolic notation

$$S = S' \leftrightarrow (x)\,(x \in S \leftrightarrow x \in S').$$

But this principle does not hold where S and S' are vague sets for there is no fact of the matter to determine whether x belongs to S or not. So both $x \in S$ and $x \in S'$ are indefinite. Since '$\leftrightarrow$' in $K_3^S$ has been defined as $(p \rightarrow q) \wedge (q \rightarrow p)$, it gets the value I when both p and q are *indefinite.* So the Axiom of Extensionality becomes *indefinite.*

For any individual constant c, let $i_c$ be the object in D assigned to c. Then $F_c$ is true if $i_c$ belongs to S; $F_c$ is false if $i_c$ belongs to S'; and $F_c$ is indefinite if there is no determinate fact of the matter about whether $i_c$ belongs to S (or to S').

$(\exists x)$ Fx is true if Fx is true for some assignment of an object of D to x; false if Fx is false for all assignments; and indefinite otherwise.

$(\forall x)$ Fx is true if Fx is true for all assignments of objects of D to x; false if Fx is false for some assignments; and indefinite otherwise.

Kleene's 3-valued system sketched above, though simple and elegant, fails to retain the spirit of vagueness. For $K_3^S$ also subscribes to the theory of discrete predication. The trichotomy of values will ultimately lead us to some sharp borderline. It is well-known that all substitutions of a vague sentence do not receive the value I; some specifications of a vague sentence are true and some others are false and some are indefinite. So we have to know which instances are borderline instances and have got to differentiate them from definite instances. But in order to succeed in such differentiation we have to maintain that the grey zone extends thus far and no further. In terms of the formal semantics the situation becomes something like this. We know for certain which elements definitely belong to S and which elements belong to S' and the rest are vague. That means we need sharply demarcate an area about which there is no fact of the matter to determine whether the individual in question belongs to the positive or the negative extension or not. Thus contrary to our intuitive understanding, a standard 3-valued logical system will compel us to draw some arbitrary borderline between true cases and indefinite cases on the one hand and indefinite cases and false cases on the other.

To improve on this situation Tye has introduced the notion of a vague set—a set which has no distinct boundary. While spelling out the notion of 'indefinite' in terms of a vague set Tye has anticipated the charge of circularity. He responds to the charge by pointing out that the definition of 'indefinite' in terms of 'there is no determinate fact of the matter whether. . .' does not involve any circularity, for a given sentence is indefinite since there is no determinate fact of the matter whether an individual belongs to an appropriate set or not and not the other way round.

But if that is the case, Tye must explain how he interprets the notion of 'belonging to' in his system. In naive set theory '$\in$' or *belonging to* is a primitive notion the intuitive rendering of which admits of dichotomous possibilities; either some element belongs to a set or it does not. But when there is no fact of the matter to determine whether some element belongs to a set or not, 'belonging to' must mean something other than what it means in classical set theory. So, the semantics of Tye suffers from inadequacy unless he clearly explains the notion of belonging to in the context of a vague set.

Tye has also foreseen that the charge of circularity may be raised in another level. Tye's semantics of vague sets is essentially dependent on his logic. His logic, on the other hand, refers to vague sets. Hence a vague set cannot be made intelligible at all. Against this objection Tye maintains that it is not the case that the concept of a vague set cannot be understood without prior understanding of the base logic. He elucidates this point by citing an analogous case. The concept of disjunction essentially depends on the logic of disjunction. But the logic of disjunction uses the notion of disjunction, e.g. $p \vee q$ is true when p is true or q is true. But understanding the logic, says Tye, cannot be a precondition for understanding the concept. It is not the case that the truth conditions for a disjunctive sentence analyze the meaning of 'or'. The truth condition obtains because 'or' means what it does. 'One who understands the concept will use it in accordance with the logic but a full grasp of the metalinguistic sentences which utilize the concept in the logic is no part of that understanding.'[4]

Tye admits of higher order vagueness and $K_3^s$ can be extended to n-valued, even to infinite valued systems. But unless and until Tye gives up the idea of discrete predication, neither his logic nor his semantics will be adequate for vague sentences. He will be committed to some sharp division, however thin the wedge may be.

### 4.3 THE SUPERVALUATIONAL APPROACH

The term 'supervaluation' is a coinage of B. van Frassen. He called his theory of empty terms a supervaluational theory. But he was in no way concerned with sentences having truth value gap due to vagueness. The pioneering work in this area was done by Kit Fine.[5] So it is mainly Fine's theory that we are going to survey critically under the head 'the supervaluational approach'. The most important feature of this approach is that it reinstates the truths of classical logic even in the contexts of 'empty terms' and 'vague sentences'.

Fine's paper 'Vagueness, Truth and Logic' has two distinct parts—polemical and positive. Fine's polemics is directed against the three valued systems of logic and in the positive part he offers an alternative framework for logic of vague sentences.

Vagueness to Fine is a semantic notion and is an outcome of deficiency in meaning. This deficiency can be overcome, thinks Fine, by linguistic adjustment, i.e. by 'appropriate linguistic decision'. This linguistic decision, we shall see in a shortwhile, is regarding the question, how to extend the meaning of a given expression.

Fine proposes to tackle both extensional and intensional vagueness in his theory. 'A predicate F is extensionally vague if it has borderline cases'. Intensional vagueness is nothing but the possibility of something being extensionally vague. This notion comes very close to Waismann's idea of an expression having an open-texture.

Before giving an exposition of his positive theory Fine builds his case against three valued systems laboriously. He starts by showing how we can and do assign T, F and I to sentences of a language L. Let assignment of T, F and I to atomic sentences of L be a partial specification. A specification is appropriate if it conforms to the intuitive understanding of the given sentence. For example, if we assign T to 'Satyajit Ray is tall', F to 'Lalbahadur Shastri is tall' and I to 'Jawaharlal Nehru is tall' where Nehru is a borderline instance of tallness then our specification will be appropriate. Once assignments have been made for the atomic sentences of the language, we should be able to determine the truth value of the compound sentences uniquely from the truth value of its components. So such a system of logic is truth functional.

Fine thinks that any specification must obey a couple of constraints, but actually both of them relate to *definite* atomic sentences.

(a) The classical truth conditions should be retained as far as possible.

This shows that the 3-valued systems that Fine wants us to consider are standard systems. Next he introduces the notion of a complete specification. A complete specification yields only T or F. So the first constraint christened fidelity condition (F) states that a sentence is true (or false) for a complete specification iff it is classically true or false.

The second constraint is formulated as the stability condition(S) which in its simplest form reads:

(b) If a sentence has a definite truth value under a specification t, it enjoys the same definite truth value under any specification u that extends t.

A detailed analysis of the notion of extending will be taken up later. Here I would mention this much only that u extends t if u assigns to an atomic sentence a truth value not less than the one assigned by t.

The conditions of Fidelity and Stability deal with definite or classical values of a sentence. If any of the subsentential components were I, then either the I-dominant (minimal in Fine's terminology) or the I-recessive (maximal, according to Fine) approach has to be adopted. The minimal approach, upholds Fine, has no explanatory value and in the maximal approach truth functionality fails to hold. How? We know that in all standard I-recessive 3-valued systems conjunction gives us the minimum value. That means I and I should yield I. Let 'This shade is pink' (P) be indefinite, then P and P should give the result I. But supposing 'This shade is pink' (P) and 'This shade is red' (R) are both vague sentences, then P and R, says Fine, will yield F and not I. For P and R are contraries and cannot be true together. So conjunction ceases to be truth functional as I and I sometimes yield I, sometimes F.

A 3-valued logician may counter the objection by showing that Fine is adopting a double standard here. In case of P and P, he is simply following the truth table definition of conjunction of an I-recessive system. But while evaluating P and R he is not simply following the calculus. If he had done that, both P and R being indefinite sentences, he would have assigned the value I to both of them and then I and I would have yielded I and not F. Consequently conjunction would have retained its truth functionality. But Fine has brought in a different consideration; the contrariety of P and R is indeed an extra stipulation. Nor is it obvious that even when P and R are vague sentences they clearly exclude one another. The additional premise that Fine is using is: if some shade is pink, then it cannot be red. When the sentence in question is vague, because the shade talked about is in the borderline of pink and red, the relation of contrariety becomes suspect.

If we could have known that the shade cannot be red since it *is* pink, P would not have an indefinite status.

The second charge that Fine presses against the systems of 3-valued logic is that they fail to account for truths of logic in the penumbral region. He maintains that we very naturally uphold the truth of $(p \vee \sim p)$ and the falsity of $(p \& \sim p)$ even in the grey area of vague sentences. A particular shade about which we are unsure whether it is pink or red still cannot be both pink and red at the same time. At best it can be either of them. Again, suppose that 'This shade is pink' is indefinite and 'This shade is non-pink' is also indefinite. But as 'pink' and 'non-pink' exhaust the whole universe of discourse, $p \vee \sim p$ holds. This is once again a highly debatable point.

Fine's intuition concerning penumbral truths differs from that of a 3-valued logician simply because while making appropriate specifications for vague atomic sentences Fine is taking into consideration not only the actual meaning of a sentence but also its possible meaning that may be brought out by complete extension. But a 3-valued logician makes assignment only at a particular point depending on the intuitive meaning of a sentence at that particular point. So it appears natural to them that the laws like LEM fail in the penumbral region. The issue between a supervaluationist and a many-valued logician is too deep—it is really a matter of perspectives hence cannot be settled superficially.

Even then we may try to find out Fine's reason for upholding penumbral connections. According to Fine, upholding penumbral connections is a demand forced on us by ordinary language; it is not a whim on the part of a supervaluationist. Our ordinary understanding of the natural language predicates 'red', 'pink' and 'small' is such that we cannot maintain at the same time 'This dot is red' and 'This dot is pink', not even in the penumbral region but we can easily conjoin 'this dot is red' with 'this dot is small' without involving any inconsistency. Fine claims that his supervaluational logic can capture this understanding. So he should be given a serious hearing.

The pivot around which the supervaluational theory turns is the notions of precisification and extension relation taken together. Fine has explained the semantical notion of precisification with the help of the geometrical notion of a space and points contained in that space. The space referred to is the specification space. We have already seen that by precisification is meant assignment of truth values to atomic sentences. In the supervaluational theory such truth assignments are made with respect to a particular space.

A specification space is a non-empty set of elements called specification points with a partial ordering ≥ (read: extends) on it. A partial ordering relation is always reflexive, transitive and anti-symmetric. A space is appropriate if each point of the space corresponds to a particular precisification. It is required that there should be a one-one correspondence between a specification and a precisification. Fine describes the nature of correspondence as follows: each point in the space assigned a particular truth value that is appropriate to the corresponding precisification. One specification point extends another if there is a natural extension relation among the corresponding precisifications. The truth valuation is to be made uniform by using those specification points only where the atomic sentences are true or false.

It should be noted that the intensional notion of 'appropriateness' as used by Fine is dependent on the intensional notion of precisification. The way in which a particular expression is precisified depends on the intuitive understanding of the expression by a particular person at a particular moment of time. Fine also speaks of an admissible specification which makes the space that contain them appropriate. The notion of admissibility is primitive to Fine. But we can relate it with our sociohistorical background.

Fine has imposed some restrictions on extension of a specification point. Let us enumerate them one by one.

Every specification chain has a base point or an appropriate specification point. The precisification corresponding to the base point is that of which every other precisification is an extension. Not only that, any point in a specification space can be extended to a complete point within the same space. So the first condition is the condition C or completability. C states

$$(\forall t) \quad (\exists u \geq t) \quad (u \text{ complete})$$

i.e. for every specification point t there exists a u such that u extends t and u is complete. Let us consider the example 'A man whose height is 5' 5" is tall'. At the base point this sentence will receive the value I. But with further precisifications its truth status may change. Let us suppose that we are precisifying the sentence by adding 1 inch to the given height at each step. Then the four subsequent precisifications may correspond to the assignment I. But when we precisify the sentence by saying that 'the person whose height is 5' 5" would have been tall if his height were 5' 10" ', then the specification point corresponding to this precisification would have been complete. Just as in classical valuation van Frassen[6] assigns truth (T) and falsity (F) to sentences disregarding the possibility that a sentence might suffer from a failure of reference, at complete points Fine assigns truth (T) and falsity (F) to sentences disregarding the possibility that the sentence might be vague.

Next Fine reformulates the conditions of *Fidelity* and *Stability* with respect to the complete point.

F: $t \models A \leftrightarrow t \models A$ (classically) for t complete. In other words, the complete points always receive classical or definite truth values.

S : $t \models A$ and $t \leq U \rightarrow U \models A$.
$t =\!| A$ and $t \leq U \rightarrow U =\!| A$.

That is, truth values are preserved under extensions of a point within a given space. The significance of this condition is that a sentence that was true (false) before extension cannot become less true (less false) after extension. This follows from the meaning of 'precisification' itself.

Besides the conditions of F and S, three other conditions have been laid down by Fine for adequate understanding of vague sentences under varied circumstances.

Principle of Uniformity (U) : The extension of a compound $\phi$ $(A_1, \ldots, A_k)$ is a function $F\phi$ of the extension of its parts.

Principle of Monotonicity (M) : If extensions $x'_1, \ldots, x'_k$ extended extensions $x_1. \ldots, x_k$ respectively, then $f\phi$ applied to $x_1', \ldots, x_k'$ extends $f\phi$ applied to $x_1. \ldots, x_k$.

Uniformity and Monotonicity hold with respect to intensions too. This point is important for precisification is an intensional notion. Though Fine does not want to enter into the debate on the nature of intension yet he generally believes in the Fregean slogan: intension determines extension. This belief together with the principles of intensional uniformity and monotonicity lead to the following result:

X extends Y (where X and Y are intensions) iff x extends y.

These conditions as a whole are responsible for coveted stability of recorded truth values in the ever changing scenario of meaning.

The last condition, but by no means the least, is the Resolution condition.

R: an indefinite atomic sentence can be resolved in either of the classical ways upon improvement in precision.

From R follows the most important feature of the supervaluational theory: 'Indefinite sentences are born, as it were, to be true or false.'[7] Fine justifies this tenet with the help of the following observation: 'There is no point in withholding truth from a sentence that can be made true by improvement in precision.'[8]

Since the truth conditions of a vague sentence can be specified only in relation to a particular precisification and precisification is a linguistic concept, Fine finds it necessary to give an account of the development of language. According to him, it is from the seeds of penumbral connections that the whole language-tree grows. The penumbral region is to be treated as the initial repository of truths of logic and language. These penumbral truths are $C_2$–tautologies. Some of these connections, he points out, are internal, some are external. 'If Herbert is to be bald, then so is the man with fewer hairs on his head' is Fine's example of an internal connection, for the connection is between the different borderline cases of a single predicate. But the connection underlying 'If the blob is to be red, it is not to be pink' is external since it is related to the common borderline cases of different predicates.

On the basis of the notion of extension Fine next formulates his notion of *super-truth.* He, of course, follows a special type of maximization technique in the context of indefinite sentence. In his own words:

> A sentence is true (or false) at a partial specification point iff it is true (or false) at all complete extensions. A sentence is *true simpliciter* iff it is true at the appropriate specification point . . . . Truth is super truth, truth from above.[9]

A comparison with van Frassen's[10] account of supervaluation over empty terms at this stage will enable us to understand Fine's theory of super truth better. We have already mentioned that van Frassen while developing his supervaluational logic was actually responding to the challenge of determining the truth value of a sentence containing a non-denoting singular term. Let us consider the following sentences:

(1) Lightning has a white forelock and

(2) Pegasus has a white forelock.

Supposing Lightning is a horse taking part in the coming Ascot Race and Pegasus is the mythical horse of Bellerophone, the problem is to determine the truth value of (2). Usually a simple sentence (an n-adic predicate followed by n proper names) has a truth value if and only if all the names it contains have referents. Pegasus being an empty name, (2), according to van Frassen, is neither true nor false. But what happens when such a non-denoting singular term occurs in a classical logical truth and a classically valid inference? van Frassen answers that they remain valid. So the problem to van Frassen was much deeper since he thought that logic should in no way be affected by contingencies. The problem of van Frassen, therefore, can be reformulated as: how can one retain $C_2$–tautologies and $C_2$–valid arguments even when they involve some sentential component which is neither true nor false? van Frassen's supervaluational logic and semantics provide an answer to this question.

Ermano Bencivenga has captured this spirit of supervaluation perfectly.

> The set of logical truths should be absolutely independent of the philosophy of language we decide to adopt. There will be conventions assigning True to (2), again conventions assigning False to it. . . . Logic can be at best committed to the logical product of all possible conventions, to what is going to be true (or false) no matter what convention you adopt.[11]

To present the supervaluational semantics *a la* van Frassen we need a specific language L having a domain of discourse D and extensions for the predicates. The language L consists of variables, predicates, quantifiers, usual propositional connectives and a set of names. Let D be the domain set, a non-empty set of things and f be an assignment function such that if F is a predicate of L then f(F) is the extension of F in D. Then ⟨f; D⟩ is a model of L.

We shall now present a few important definitions.

*Definition 1*
*True in a model.* A sentence will be *true in a model* if f(F) of F is in the domain D. Then (∀x) Fx will be true in this model exactly if the extension f(F) of F is the whole of the domain D.

*Definition 2*
*Logically true.* A sentence is *logically true* iff it is true in any model ⟨f; D⟩, no matter how D and f are chosen.

*Definition 3*
*Defined names.* A name e will be defined in D if its referent f(e) is a member of the extension f(F) of the predicate F.

*Explanation 1*
If e is defined in the above manner then Fe will be true in this particular model. If, on the other hand, the name e does not have a referent in D then Fe is neither true nor false in that model.

*Definition 4*
*Classical valuation.* A classical valuation over a model is a function V that assigns T or F to each statement subject to :

(a) If A is an atomic statement containing no non-referring names, then V(A) is determined by the model in the indicated manner.
(b) If A is a complex statement, then V(A) is determined by what V assigns to the simpler statements in the usual manner.

*Explanation 2*
A classical valuation is a method of eliminating the truth value gap by assigning truth values to indefinite sentences in an arbitrary manner. Now if there is any name e that has no reference in the domain of a given model and A is an atomic sentence containing e, then there is at least two classical valuations over this model; one which assigns T to A and one which assigns F to A.

van Frassen says that the classical valuations go beyond the model to which they belong in all possible ways. Since a classical valuation 'is an assignment of truth (T) and falsity (F) to sentences, which disregards the possibility that a sentence might suffer from a failure of reference'.

*Definition 5*
*Admissible valuation.* An admissible valuation is to correspond to a possible situation such that it assigns T to the sentences true in that situation, F to the sentences false in that situation and does not assign a truth value to those sentences which are neither true nor false in that situation.

*Definition 6*
*Supervaluation.* A supervaluation over a model is a function that assigns T(F) by all the classical valuations over that model.

*Explanation 3*
Let us suppose that L contains exactly one monadic predicate F and exactly two names, a and b, such that f(a) is defined and f(b) is not defined. There are here exactly two classical valuations $V_1$ and $V_2$; F(a) $\in$ f(F) and all of D is included in f(F). Then the supervaluation assigned to sentences is shown in the following table.

| | $V_1$ | $V_2$ | S |
|---|---|---|---|
| Fa | T | T | T |
| ~ Fa | F | F | F |
| Fb | T | F | – |
| ~ Fb | F | T | – |
| Fb ∨ ~ Fb | T | T | T |

The dashes in the last column show truth value gaps.

*Definition 7*
*Supervaluationally true.* A sentence is Supervaluationally true if and only if it is assigned T by all supervaluations.

An atomic sentence containing an undefined name will never be Supervaluationally true yet a sentence like

Fb V ~ Fb is always true in supervaluational semantics even when its only atomic component is truth valueless. The supervaluationist considers Fb V ~ Fb to be true even when b is an empty name because if b were denoting then it would have been true.

Similar is Fine's notion of super truth. A true sentence is true for all ways of making it precise. A vague sentence might be true at some complete specification point and false at others. Then its truth value remains indefinite. But a vague sentence is considered true if it is true for all admissible and complete specifications. Thus though 'This blob is pink' may be indefinite 'Either this blob is pink or non-pink' is true. Even when at the base point 'This blob is pink' is assigned I, by conditions C and R, it will get either the value T or the value F at complete points.[12] So it will be true or false in that particular specification space just as a sentence containing an empty name can be true in a model without being supervaluationally true; but as it will not get any uniform valuation, the truth value gap will remain in supervaluation. But as in the complete points 'This blob is pink' will be assigned either T or F so 'Either this blob is pink or non-pink' will be true at all complete specification points. Thus LEM and other penumbral truths will be retained. Super truth theory thus vindicates the classical position. 'For the truth conditions are, if not classical, then classical at a remove.'[13]

Fine realizes that the condition C or the completeability condition is the most troublesome of all the conditions specified by him. C can be easily understood where the specification space concerned possesses finite extension points. C is then guaranteed by F, S and R. It cannot be determined *a priori* how many steps one is to take before reaching the complete point. There is no upper limit to the number of extension points that connect the base point to the complete point, nevertheless it is not infinite. If one maintains that C holds in a specification space with infinite points, then one's move becomes unintelligible. That is why Fine says that the super truth theory can be shown to hold even if we do away with the condition of completeability. In that case the truth of a sentence will be an anticipatory truth, i.e. an indefinite sentence would have been true if it had been extended in such and such manner.

In fact Pinkal[14] is right in upholding that to suppose that completeability holds within a specification space having infinite extension points is impracticable as well as unnecessary. It is impracticable because human communication process is always of finite length; it is unnecessary for in any discourse situation only a limited range of topics is at issue.

What Fine actually wanted to convey through spatial metaphors can be narrated in a different language following Sainsbury.[15] In Sainsbury's language (also in that of Kamp[16]) 'precisification' is replaced by 'refinement' or 'sharpening'. A vague predicate can be sharpened if we can replace it by a sharp predicate. Take, for instance, 'tall'. Suppose a height of 5' 6" lies at the penumbral region and it is vague whether somebody of this height can be called tall or not. We may 'precisify' or 'sharpen' it by replacing it with a sharp predicate, say, 'P-tall' such that heights equal to or above 5' 6" will fall in its positive extension and all heights below 5' 6" will fall in its negative extension. Replacing 'tall' by 'P–tall' is just one way of sharpening; we could have sharpened it by various different ways by shifting the borderline this way or that and by redistributing the instances of the penumbral region to the positive and to the negative extension of the new sharp predicates. These sharpenings cannot have less intensional content than the original predicate and if they are also in accordance with our established linguistic usage they will be 'admissible' or 'eligible'. A vague sentence will be true or false at each sharpening but it will be true *simpliciter* if and only if it remains true in all admissible sharpenings.

But there is a problem. A supervaluationist seriously claims to admit vagueness in language while at the same time he wants to precisify it. The question is: is vagueness compatible with precisification? The supervaluationist will undoubtedly answer in the affirmative. In his support he will draw our attention to the fact that he is nowhere making the cut-off points absolute except at the complete points. The complete points, however, represent the extremes where the classical logic holds its sway. Besides, the notion of 'precisification' itself is vague to a supervaluationist and so he does not hesitate to admit higher-order vagueness.

Yet we cannot accede to the supervaluational thesis. The reason is, we cannot give up tolerance of vague predicates in the penumbral region. It defeats our original intention. We wanted to explain vague sentences which are neither true nor false. We do not want to explain them away. Besides, removal of penumbra leads to some practical difficulties too. This point has been brought out by Sainsbury with a very apt example. He denies that the sentence 'either he is an adult or he is not' is a tautology. For the following argument is not acceptable.

> Either he is an adult or he is not. If he is an adult, then watching the hard-porn movie will do him no harm. If he is not an adult, then he will not understand it . . . either way, it will do him no harm to watch it.[17]

But, observes Sainsbury, watching a hard-porn movie might harm an adolescent for he is in a stage between adulthood and childhood. Making LEM artificially true forces us to keep such instances out of our consideration. The theory is, therefore, not strong enough to be acceptable.

## 4.4 SUPERVALUATIONAL FORMAL SEMANTICS

Joachim Ballweg[18] has worked out a formal semantics for vague sentences from the supervaluational point of view following van Frassen, Fine and Kamp. Ballweg's system, in his own words, is a 3-valued first order logic with supervaluation. His model can be treated as the standard semantic model of the supervaluational logic. Special features of different supervaluational systems can be taken care of by a little addition to or alteration of this semantics. We shall discuss Ballweg's semantics just to give the reader an idea of how a supervaluational formal semantics may be developed.

### Syntax of a first order language L

*Symbols*

| | | |
|---|---|---|
| Individual Constants | : | {Fine, Kamp, Parikh} = IC |
| Individual Variables | : | $\{x_1, x_2, \ldots, x_n \ldots\}$ = IV |
| Individual Expressions | : | IV U IC = IE |
| Predicate Constants | : | {IT RAINS} = $O^{pc}$ |
| | | {WRITE, SLEEP, JUMP} = $1^{pc}$ |
| | | {SEE, LOVE} = $2^{pc}$ |
| Quantifiers: | : | $\forall$ |
| One-place connective | : | $\neg$ |
| Two-place connective | : | $\wedge$ |
| Auxiliary Symbols | : | [ ], ( ) |
| Well formed Formulae | : | WFF, the set of well-formed formulae of L, is the smallest set such that for any string of symbols $\alpha$, — if $\alpha \in O^{pc}$, then $\alpha \in$ WFF |
| | | – If $\alpha = \beta\ (\gamma_1, \ldots, \gamma_n)$, and $\beta \in n^{pc}$, and $\gamma_1 \in$ IE, . . . $\gamma_n \in$ IE, $\alpha \in$ WFF |
| | | – If $\alpha \in$ WFF, and $\gamma \in$ IV, then, $\forall\gamma\ [\alpha] \in$ WFF |
| | | – If $\alpha \in$ WFF, $\neg\alpha \in$ WFF |
| | | – If $\alpha \in$ WFF, and $\beta \in$ WFF, $[\alpha \wedge \beta] \in$ WFF |

Let us now sketch the classical semantics for L.

A classical model for L is a structure

M = $\langle$D, {f, k, p}, $\vartheta$, $\langle$Ext $\alpha\rangle$ $\alpha \in n^{pc}$, V$\rangle$, where
D = is the individual domain, a non-empty set, the set of truth values, {0, 1} is in D.

{f, k, p}$\subset$D—is a set of designated elements of D.
$\vartheta$ is a function from IV into D.

$\langle$Ext $\alpha\rangle$ $\alpha \in n^{pc}$ is a family of sets, indexed by the set of n-place predicates, the extensions of predicates, for any $\alpha \in n^{pc}$, Ext $\alpha \subset D^n$.

V is the valuation function for any expressions $\alpha$, $\beta$, $\gamma$:

(1) If $\alpha$ = Fine, $V(\alpha) = f$
(2) If $\alpha$ = Kamp, $V(\alpha) = r$
(3) If $\alpha$ = Parikh, $V(\alpha) = p$
(4) If $\alpha \in$ IV, $V(\alpha) = \vartheta(\alpha)$
(5) If $\alpha \in n^{pc}$, $V(\alpha) = \text{Ext}\ \alpha$
(6) If $\alpha \in$ WFF, $V(\alpha) \in \{0, 1\}$
(7) If $\alpha = \neg B$, $V(\alpha) = 1$ iff $V(\beta) = 0$
(8) If $\alpha = [B \wedge \gamma]$, $V(\alpha) = 1$ iff $V(\beta) = V(\gamma) = 1$

The other connectives are defined in terms of $\neg$, $\wedge$

$[B \vee \gamma]$ = df. $\neg(\neg\beta \wedge \neg\gamma)$
$[B \rightarrow \gamma]$ = df. $\neg(\beta \wedge \neg\gamma)$
$[B \leftrightarrow \gamma]$ = df. $[\beta \rightarrow \gamma] \wedge [\gamma \rightarrow \beta]$

(9) If $\alpha = \forall\gamma\,[B]$, $V(\alpha) = 1$ iff all $d \in D$, $V^+(\beta) = 1$, and $V^+$ is like V, with the possible difference that $V^+(\gamma) = d$.

$\exists\gamma\,[B]$ = df. $\neg\forall\gamma\,[\neg B]$

(10) If $\alpha = \beta(\gamma_1, \ldots, \gamma_n)$, where $B \in n^{pc}$, $\gamma \in$ IE, . . ., $\gamma_n \in$ IE, $V(\alpha) = 1$ iff $\langle V(r_n), \ldots, V(\gamma_n)\rangle \in V\beta$.

A WFF $\alpha$ is said to be true relative to a model M iff $V(\alpha) = 1$ in M, and a WFF $\alpha$ is said to be true in L iff $V(\alpha) = 1$, for all models M', which differ from M at most having V' instead of V.

To accommodate predicates of comparison, vagueness, etc., we need to introduce a scale with a threshold. So we shall have to add the following semantic elements to our language L.

$\Sigma\alpha$ is a set (of values, heuristic) and $|\Sigma\alpha| \geq 2$. $<_\alpha$ is a transitive, irreflexive and connected ordering on $\Sigma\alpha$, so $\langle\Sigma\alpha, <_\alpha$ is a scale for $\alpha$ (if $|\Sigma\alpha| = 2$, it is a nominal scale, if $|\Sigma\alpha| > 2$, it is at least an ordinal scale.)

*Observation:* The scale could be antisymmetric as well, i.e.

there is no formal reason behind not taking $\leq \alpha$ as the ordering relation. Formally, a precisification can be that precisification itself but informally sharpening or precisification means some improvement on the original predicate.

$\mu\alpha$ is a function from $D^n$ into $\Sigma\alpha$, so $\langle \Sigma\alpha, <\alpha, \mu\alpha \rangle$ is a scalar measurement for $\alpha$. $\tau\alpha$ is a designated element of $\Sigma\alpha$, the threshold value $\langle \Sigma\alpha, <\alpha, \mu\alpha, \tau\alpha \rangle \; \alpha \in n^{pc}$ can be used to determine extensions of predicates.

Here the valuation function V has to be changed suitably. We shall call the amended valuation function V'. Now if $\alpha \in n^{pc}$, then $V'(\alpha) = \{d: \mu(d) \geq \tau\alpha\}$

But to explain a vague predicate we need two thresholds to capture the notion of the positive and the negative extension of the vague predicate. So $\tau\alpha$ for a predicate $\alpha$ will be replaced by $\tau\alpha^+$ and $\tau\alpha^-$. Then the positive extension of one-place predicate $\alpha$ will be the set of all $d_1$ such that $\tau\alpha^+ \leq \mu(d_1)$; the negative extension will be the set of all $d_2$ such that $\mu(d_2) \leq \tau\alpha^-$ and the indeterminate cases lying in the penumbral region will be the set of $d_3$ such that $\tau\alpha^- < (d_3) < \tau\alpha^+$.

So in this model the scale with two thresholds finally takes the following form:

$$\langle \Sigma\alpha, <\alpha, \mu\alpha, \langle \tau\alpha^+, \tau\alpha^- \rangle \rangle \; \alpha \in n^{pc}.$$

It also needs a set of completions, viz. C and an additional one-place connective ~ standing for weak negation.

But it follows from the supervaluational thesis that any element c of C will always be associated with a classical scale with one single threshold so that extensions are plotted unidirectionally.

In view of the above additions there will be the following changes in the valuation.

(1) If $\alpha \in n^{pc}$, $V(\alpha) \in \{0, *, 1\} D^n$, such that for all $\langle d_1, \ldots, dn \rangle \in D^n$,

$$V(\alpha)(\langle d_1, \ldots, dn \rangle) = \begin{cases} 1 \text{ iff } \tau\alpha^+ \leq \mu\alpha(\langle d_1, \ldots, dn \rangle) \\ 0 \text{ iff } \widehat{\mu\alpha}(\langle \hat{d_1}, \ldots, \hat{dn} \rangle) \leq \tau^-\alpha \\ * \text{ otherwise} \end{cases}$$

(2) If $\alpha \in$ WFF, $V(\alpha) \in \{0, *, 1\}$ — this set being the set of characteristic functions of predicates.

(3) If $\alpha = \neg \beta$, $V(\alpha) = \begin{cases} 1 \text{ iff } V(\beta) = 0 \\ 0 \text{ iff } V(\beta) = 1 \\ * \text{ iff } V(\beta) = * \end{cases}$

(4) If $\alpha = \sim \beta$, $V(\alpha) = \begin{cases} 1 \text{ if } V(\beta) = 0 \text{ or } * \\ 0 \text{ if } V(\beta) = 1 \end{cases}$

(5) If $\alpha = [\beta \wedge \gamma]$, $V(\alpha) = \begin{cases} 1 \text{ if } V(\beta) = V(\gamma) = 1 \text{ or} \\ \text{if } V'(\alpha) = 1 \\ 0 \text{ if at least one of} \\ V(\beta), \text{ for all } c \in C, \\ V(\gamma) = 0 \text{ or if } V'(\alpha) = 0 \\ \text{for all } c \in C \\ * \text{ otherwise} \end{cases}$

(5) states that a conjunction is true in a vague model if it is classically true in that model, and if it is classically true in all completions; that it is false if it is classically false in the original model as well as in all completions and undecided otherwise. If a sentence is true in the original model, so is it in all its completions, but not vice versa.

(6) If $\alpha = \forall \gamma [\beta]$, $V(\alpha) = \begin{cases} 1 \text{ if for all } c \in C, \text{ for all } d \in D, \\ V'^{+}(\beta) = 1 \text{ and } V'^{+} \text{ is like } V' \text{ with} \\ \text{the possible difference that} \\ V'^{+}(\gamma) = d \\ 0 \text{ if for all } c \in C, \text{ for at least one} \\ d \in D\ V'^{+}(\beta) = 0 \\ * \text{ otherwise} \end{cases}$

(7) If $\alpha = \beta(\gamma_1, \ldots, \gamma_n)$, where $\beta \in n^{pc}$, $\gamma_1, \ldots \gamma_n \in$ IE,
$V(\alpha) = V(\beta)\ (\langle V(\gamma_1), \ldots, V(\gamma_n)\rangle)$

The scales that have been constructed is adequate for predicates like ‘tall’, ‘red’, ‘long’, etc., but not for evaluative predicates like ‘nice’ or ‘clever’. For representation of multi-dimensional vague predicates we need a family of scales and measurements.

The thresholds that the supervaluationists have fixed are not absolute; they vary from speaker to speaker from context to context. So Ballweg adds to this supervaluational semantics the notion of context dependence. Though a context may have various parameters, Ballweg only includes speaker and time within context.

Such a context dependent supervaluational scalar semantics will have the following model.

$\langle D, \{f, k, p\}, V, S, \langle T, \prec\rangle, \langle \Sigma\alpha, s, t, <\alpha, s, t, \mu\alpha, s, t, \langle \tau\alpha^{+}, s, t, \tau\alpha^{-}, s, t\rangle\rangle\, \alpha \in n^{pc}, s \in S, t \in T, C, VT\rangle$.

S is a subset of D, the set of (possible) speakers.

T is a set (of points in time)

α is an ordering on T which is irreflexive, transitive, dense and connected in T.

The whole scale has been indexed by speaker and time since the construction of the scale depends on the set of speakers and on time. VT is the evaluation function, and it is such that for all s ∈ S, for all t ∈T,

If α = Fine, VT (α, s, t) = f for all t ∈ T, for all s ∈ S

If $\alpha = n^{pc}$, $VT(\alpha, s, t) \in \{0, *, 1\}^{D^n \times T \times S}$

such that for all $\langle d_1, \ldots, d_n\rangle \in D^n$

$$
\begin{aligned}
VT(\alpha, s, t)(\langle d_1, \ldots, d\hat{n}\rangle) &= 1 \text{ iff } \tau^{+}_{\alpha, s, t} \leq \mu d, s, t\,(\langle d_1, \ldots, d_n\rangle) \\
&= 0 \text{ iff } \mu_{\alpha, s, t}(\langle d_1, \ldots, d_n\rangle) \leq \tau^{-}_{\alpha, s, t} \\
&= * \text{ otherwise.}
\end{aligned}
$$

In this way all other semantic elements are to be indexed by speaker and time.

This semantics still has a serious drawback. It is effective when one and the same speaker uses a predicate in different ways at different times or when different speakers at different times have different ways of using a predicate. But it cannot do justice to cases when one speaker at a particular moment of time is unable to put certain objects clearly into the positive or the negative extension of a predicate. This is really the problem of vagueness and this problem remains unsolved even in a context dependent supervaluational scaler semantics. Nor can this semantics represent multi-dimensional vagueness.

The above analysis of the supervaluational logic together with its proposed formal semantics highlights one point. The supervaluational technique fails in the context of vagueness for like the classical 2-valued logic and the 3-valued logics, this theory also subscribes to the thesis of discrete predication. It is true that to account for the notion of extension they have introduced a scale but the associated truth value set has only three elements, viz. 1, 0,*. To explain vagueness adequately we need to give up the notion of discrete predication and require a graded truth set to associate with a continuous predicate. This is precisely the stance taken by the fuzzy logicians. Hence we shall be engaged in a thorough critical survey of the field of fuzzy logic as a prospective model for vague sentences in 4.6.

## 4.5 A TOPOLOGICAL REPRESENTATION

Rohit Parikh[19] represents vagueness with the help of a metric space. Parikh's representation makes it absolutely clear why it is necessary for any sound logic of vagueness to discard discrete predication. Parikh establishes this point by introducing four definitions mentioned below.

*Definition A*

A metric space is a non-empty set together with a metric or a distance function d defined for all points and which satisfies for all points x, y, z

(1) $d(x, y) = 0$ iff $x = y$

(2) $d(x, y) = d(y, x)$

(3) $d(x, z) \leq d(x, y) + d(y, z)$

The values of d are non-negative real numbers.

*Definition B*

A metric space is $\alpha$– connected if for all partition A, B, $A \neq \phi \subset X$, $B \neq \phi \subset X$, $A \cup B = X$, there exist x and y such that $x \in A$, $y \in B$ and $d(x, y) < \alpha$ where $\alpha > 0$. $\alpha$ may be arbitrarily small.

*Definition C*
A non-trivial predicate P will be defined on an α–connected metric space only if there are two points x, y such that d(x, y) < α and the predicate P applies to x but not to y.

*Definition D*
A space is observationally connected if it is α–connected for some α which is smaller than the limits of observation.

Therefore, no non-trivial observational predicate can be defined on an observationally α–connected metric space. Hence if something looks like a predicate, but is observational and non-trivial at the same time, it can at best be a vague predicate. This is the correct representation of vague observational predicate as envisaged by Dummett and Crispin Wright. Not only predicates like 'tall' and 'red' but also those like 'bald' and 'heap' can be explained with the help of an observationally connected space. Though in the latter case we deal with integral numbers of hairs or grains yet spaces corresponding to them may be observationally connected. For difference of one hair or one grain does not make significant observable difference.

It is evident from the metric representation of vagueness that we should give up the distinction between 'discrete' and 'continuous'. Another important point that we should keep in mind is that a set may have more than one relevant metric on it. So the same set may give rise to several observationally relevant metric spaces and on no such metric space a non-trivial observational predicate can be defined.[20]

## 4.6 THE FUZZY APPROACH

The characteristic feature of the fuzzy approach is that a vague expression is represented as a fuzzy set and the sorites paradox is solved in terms of approximate reasoning. Since fuzzy logic has for its base fuzzy set theory we shall have to be involved with the nuances of fuzzy set theory.

Roughly speaking, a fuzzy set is a class which lacks sharp boundary, i.e. it is a class in which the transition from membership to non-membership is gradual and never abrupt. The classes of tall men, small cars, young boys, red flowers are all examples of fuzzy sets. Fuzzy set theory is a brain-child of L.A. Zadeh[21] who introduced this theory with a view to minimizing the gap between human reasoning and machine reasoning. Human brain has the power to think and reason in terms of imprecise, non-quantitative fuzzy concepts which a computer lacks. Mainly to make such fuzzy terms intelligible to machines Zadeh devised fuzzy set theory when he realized that classical logic and classical mathematics together with classical set theory are ill-suited for the purpose.

Before Zadeh propounded his theory there were two prevalent approaches to deal with inexact concepts. One was to artificially precisify an inexact concept in the manner of Carnap;[22] the other was to recognize the penumbral region but leave it out of the consideration of logic. According to this theory, an *ostrich* which is a borderline member of the class *bird* will not be considered one of the falsifying instances of the proposition: 'All birds can fly'. Zadeh has shunned both these extremes of 'having no borderline' and 'possessing a definite borderline' and proposes instead a continuously graded degree of membership to a set. This is Zadeh's point of departure from the classical set theory where membership has always been an all-or-none-affair, i.e. either an element belongs to a set or it does not, there is no third possibility.

It is time now that we present the features of fuzzy set theory formally. In the last two decades there have been so much development in this area that it will not be possible for us to cover all its aspects. I shall highlight only those features without which a proper representation of vagueness cannot be accomplished.

A fuzzy subset A of a universe of discourse U is characterized by a membership function $\mu_A$ (x) which associates with each point x in U its 'grade of membership' in A. When U is a classical set of objects whose generic elements are denoted by x, membership in a classical subset

A of U is usually defined by a characteristic function $\mu_A$ from U to {0, 1} such that

$$\mu_A(x) = \begin{cases} 1 \text{ iff } x \in A \\ 0 \text{ iff } x \notin A \end{cases}$$

{0, 1} is called a *valuation set.* If the valuation set is allowed to be the real interval [0, 1], A is called a fuzzy set and $\mu_A(x)$ is the grade of membership of x in A. So in a fuzzy set, the grade of membership is always a number between 0 and 1, with 0 and 1 signifying non-membership and full-membership respectively. For example, if U is the set of integers from 0 to 100, then the grade of membership of a man who is, say, 23 years old in the class of young men might be 0.9. Zadeh thus avoids ascribing discrete predication.

So a fuzzy set A can be completely characterized by the following set of pairs.

$$A = \{(x, \mu_A(x)), x \in U\}$$

A more convenient notation was proposed by Zadeh in 1972.[23] When U is a finite set $\{x_1, \ldots, x_n\}$, a fuzzy set on U is expressed as

$$A = \mu_A(x_1)/x_1 + \ldots + \mu_A(x_n)/x_n$$
$$= \sum_{i=1}^{n} \mu_A(x_i)/x_i$$

When U is *not finite* we write

$$A = \int_U \mu_A(x)/x$$

Two fuzzy sets A and B are said to be equal (denoted A = B) iff

$$\forall x \in U, \mu_A(x) = \mu_B(x)$$

The elements of U such that $\mu_A(x) = 0.5$ are said to be the cross-over points of A. This notion of cross-over point may present some difficulty. Zadeh's theory is not affected in any way if we never use this idea.

The empty set $\phi$ is defined as

$$\forall x \in U, \mu\phi\ (x) = 0$$

and $A \subseteq B$ iff

$$\mu_A (x) \leq \mu_B (x), \forall x \in U$$

We are going to list below a few important observations on fuzzy set.

1. A fuzzy subset is actually a generalized subset of a classical set.

2. What we call a universe of a fuzzy subset is never fuzzy. This lends support to our thesis that not all expressions, not even all predicates of our language are fuzzy.

3. In general, the grades of membership are a matter of definition rather than experimentation or analysis.

4. The theory of fuzzy subsets is not a variant of probability theory. A basic property of the latter is *additivity* but the former exhibits a weaker property of *monotonicity* with respect to inclusion.

5. Fuzziness can be introduced in a more general way if the characteristic function of a set can be allowed to take values in a finite or infinite distributive lattice.

6. Zadeh's theory of fuzzy subsets may be viewed as a very significant generalization of the many-valued systems of Lukasiewicz.

Now we shall define some useful operations on fuzzy sets following Zadeh.

(a) *Complementation*

It is a unary operation. The complement of a fuzzy set A is denoted by $\neg$ A and is defined by the relation:

$$\mu_{\neg A} (x) = 1 - \mu_A (x), x \in U$$

If a is a term whose meaning is given by M(a), then the meaning of M (not a) is given by M(not a) = $\neg$ M(a).

(b) *Intersection*

This is a binary operation. The intersection of two fuzzy sets A and B is a fuzzy set denoted by $A \cap B$ and defined by $\mu_{A \cap B}(x) = \mu A(x) \wedge \mu B(x)$, $x \in U$, where for any real a and b, $a \wedge b$ denotes Min (a, b), i.e.

$$
\begin{aligned}
a \wedge b &= a \text{ if } a \leq b \\
&= b \text{ if } a > b
\end{aligned}
$$

*Prima facie*, the conjunctive connective *and* may be identified with the intersection of fuzzy sets. So if u and v are terms, then the meaning of a composite term x = (u and v) is given by M (u and v) = M (u) $\wedge$ M (v).

If $u = \int_U \mu A(x)/x$ and $v = \int_U \mu B(x)/x$,

then $(u \text{ and } v) = \int_U (\mu A(x) \wedge \mu B(x))/x$.

*Example:* Let U = 1+ 2+ 3+ 4+ 5+ 6
u = 0.8/3 + 1/5 + 0.6/6
and v = 0.7/3 + 1/4 + 0.5/6
Then (u and v) = 0.7/3 + 0.5/6

(c) *Union*

It is also a *binary* operation. The union of two fuzzy sets A and B is a fuzzy set denoted by $A \cup B$ or A+B and is defined by $\mu_{A+B}(x) = \mu_A(x) \vee \mu_B(x)$, $x \in U$ where $a \vee b$ denotes Max (a, b), that is,

$$
a \vee b = \begin{aligned} & a \text{ if } a \geq b \\ & b \text{ if } a < b. \end{aligned}
$$

More generally $(u \text{ or } v) = \int_U (\mu A(x) \vee \mu B(x))/x$

If we reconsider the previous example

(u or v) = 0.8/3 + 1/4 + 1/5 + 0.6/6

The union and intersection of fuzzy sets are associative and distributive operators. They also satisfy the De Morgan identities.

The membership of x in $A \cup B$ or $A \cap B$ cannot decrease when the membership of x in A or in B increases. Besides, a small increase in $\mu_A$ (x) or $\mu_B$ (x) cannot induce a strong increase in $\mu_{A \cup B}$ (x) or $\mu_{A \cap B}$(x).

(d) *Product*

The product of two fuzzy sets A and B is denoted by AB and is defined by

$$\mu_{AB}(x) = \mu_A(x)\,\mu_B(x),\ x \in U$$

More generally, using the integral representation of A and B, we can write

$$AB = \int_U \mu_A(x)\,\mu_B(x)/x$$

*Example*: Let A $= 0.7/2 + 0.8/4$ and
B $= 0.5/2 + 0.6/4 + 0.5/5$
then AB $= 0.35/2 + 0.48/4$

The product operation distributes over the union and the intersection, so,

$$A(B + C) = AB + AC$$
$$A(B \cap C) = AB \cap AC.$$

The product of A and B as defined above differs from the Cartesian Product of A and B.

If A is a fuzzy subset of U and B is a fuzzy subset of V, then

$$A \times B = \int_{U \times V} \mu_A(u) \wedge \mu_B(v)/(U,V)$$

where U × V denotes the Cartesian product of the non-fuzzy sets U and V and $u \in U$, $v \in V$.

When A and B are non-fuzzy the above equation reduces to the conventional definition of the Cartesian product of non-fuzzy sets. The need for differentiation between *product* and *Cartesian product* becomes particularly important when A = B. Since $A^2$ is commonly used to denote A × A (When A is non-fuzzy) whereas in fuzzy set theory $A^2$ = AA. We shall choose between the product operators depending on the context.

Here we need to introduce two lattice-theoretic concepts, (*a*) infimimum and (*b*) supremum.

*Infimimum:* Let B be a subset of a partially ordered set A. An element m in A is called a lower bound of B if for every $x \in B$, $m \leq x$. If a lower bound of B dominates every other lower bound of B, then it is called the g.l.b. (greatest lower bound) or infimimum of B and is denoted by inf (B).

*Supremum:* Let B be a subset of A as before. An element M in A is called an upper bound of B if for every $x \in B$, $x \leq M$. If an upper bound precedes every other upper bound of B, then it is called the l.u.b. (lowest upper bound) or supremum of B and is denoted by sup (B).

We may now go back to our list of fuzzy operations.

(*e*) *Normalization*

Let $\bar{\mu}_A$ denote the supremum of a membership function over the universe of discourse, i.e.

$$\bar{\mu}_A = \sup_{U} \mu_A(x)$$

A fuzzy set A is said to be *normal* if $\bar{\mu}_A = 1$, otherwise A is *subnormal.* A subnormal fuzzy set can be normalized by dividing $\mu_A$ by $\bar{\mu}_A$. So

$$\text{NORM}(A) = (\bar{\mu}_A)^{-1} A, \mu_A \neq 0$$

*Example:* Let A = 1/John + 0.8/Jim + 0.6/Tom
hence normal, while
A' = 0.6/John + 0.8/Jim + 0.6/Tom
is subnormal.
Norm (A') = 0.75/John + 1/Jim + 0.75/Tom

(*f*) *Concentration*

It is a unary operation. Application of this operation on a fuzzy set A yields a fuzzy subset of A in which the grades of membership are reduced. But reduction is small for those x's which have a high grade of membership in A and comparatively large for the x's having low membership grade.

Zadeh usually assumes that the operation of concentration has the same effect of squaring the membership function of A. So

$\mu_{CON(A)}(x) = \mu_{(A^2)}(x), x \in U.$
or CON (A) = $A^2$

Concentration distributes over the union, intersection and product. Therefore,

$$\text{CON }(A + B) = \text{CON }(A) + \text{CON }(B)$$
$$\text{CON }(A \cap B) = \text{CON }(A) \cap \text{CON }(B)$$
$$\text{CON } AB = \text{CON }(A) \text{ CON }(B)$$

*Example:* Let few = def. 1/1 + 1/2 + 0.8/3 + 0.6/4
Then CON (few) = 1/1 + 1/2 + .64/3 + .36/4

(g) *Dilation*

Dilation is another unary operation and its effect is just the opposite of that of concentration. DIL (A) is defined by

$$\text{DIL }(A) = A^{0.5}$$

which implies that

$$\mu_{DIL(A)}(x) = \sqrt{\mu_{(A)}}(x), x \in U$$

*Example:* If 'few' is defined as before, then
DIL (few) = 1/1 + 1/2 + 0.9/3 + 0.78/4.

(h) *Contrast Intensification*

The operation of contrast intensification, denoted by INT, increases the value of $\mu_A(x)$ which are above 0.5 and diminishes those which are below 0.5. Thus

$$\mu_{INT(A)}(x) \geq \mu_{(A)}(x) \text{ for } \mu_{(A)}(x) \geq 0.5$$
$$\mu_{INT(A)}(x) \leq \mu_{(A)}(x) \text{ for } \mu_{(A)}(x) \leq 0.5$$

INT also distributes over the union, intersection and product.

(i) *Convex Combination*

The convex combination is an n-ary operation which combines a set of n fuzzy sets $A_1, \ldots, A_n$ into a single fuzzy set A.

The fuzzy set A is a weighted combination of $A_1, \ldots, A_n$ in the sense that the membership function of A is related to those of $A_1, \ldots, A_n$ by the expression

$$\mu_A(x) = w_1(x)\,\mu_{A1}(x) + \ldots + w_n(x)\,\mu_{An}(x)$$

where the weights $w_1(x), \ldots, w_n(x)$, $0 \leq w_i(x) \leq 1$ $i = 1, \ldots, n$

such that $w_1(x) + \ldots + w_n(x) = 1$ for all x in U.

*Example:* Let $U = 1 + 2 + 3 + 4 + 5 + 6$

$$u = 0.8/3 + 1/5 + 0.6/6$$
$$v = 0.7/3 + 1/4 + 0.5/6$$

The convex combination of u and v with constant $w_1 = 0.8$ and $w_2 = 0.2$ is given by

$$\begin{aligned} A = {} & (0.8 \times 0.8 + 0.2 \times 0.7)/3 + 0.8/5 + 0.2/4 + \\ & (0.8 \times 0.6 + 0.2 \times 0.5)/6 \\ = {} & 0.78/3 + 0.2/4 + 0.8/5 + 0.58/6. \end{aligned}$$

(j) *Fuzzification*

The operation fuzzification transforms a fuzzy or (non-fuzzy) set A into an approximating set $\underset{\sim}{A}$ which is more fuzzy than A. The fuzzifier is denoted by the wavy bar, e.g. if '=' denotes the relation of equality then '$\underset{\sim}{=}$' represents approximate equality.

There are various ways of fuzzification but at the basis of all lies a process called *point fuzzification.* This last named operation transforms a singleton set $1/u$ in U into a fuzzy set which is concentrated around u; $\underset{\sim}{u}$ is written as $\underset{\sim}{u}$ = K (u), i.e. the kernel of fuzzification. Generally, the grade of membership of u in K(u) is assumed to be 1. K(u) is a fuzzy set whose membership function $\mu_{k(u)}(x)$ is a non-increasing function of the distance between u and x.

Consider a fuzzy set represented by

$$A = \underset{\sim}{\mu_i}/x_i + \ldots \underset{\sim}{\mu_n}/x_n$$

where $\mu_i$ is the grade of membership of $x_i$ in A. When fuzzified the above equation turns out to be $\underset{\sim}{A} = \mu i/\underset{\sim}{xi} + \ldots + \mu_n/x_n$. There may be two special cases of fuzzification.

I: Support fuzzification: where we hold $\mu_i$ constant and fuzzify each point in the set so that $\mu_i/x_i = u_i/\underset{\sim}{x_i}$, $i = 1, \ldots, n$.

II: Grade fuzzification: where we hold $x_i$ constant and fuzzify the membership grade such that $\mu_i/x_i = \underset{\sim}{\mu}/x_i$.

> Case I: If $K(x_i)$ is the kernel then the support fuzzifier SF (A; K) is defined by $\underset{\sim}{A}$ = SF (A; K) = $\mu_1 K(x_1) + \ldots \mu_n K(x_n)$ where K $(x_i)$ is the fuzzy set which is the product of a scalar constant $\mu_i$ and a fuzzy set K $(x_i)$ and + stands for the union of fuzzy sets.
>
> Case II: Supposing that the point fuzzification which transform $\mu_i$ into $\underset{\sim}{\mu i}$ is defined by the kernel K (i),
>
> $$GF(A; K) = \underset{\sim}{A} = K(\mu_1)/x_1 + \ldots + K(\mu_n)/x_n.$$

All these operations are required for representing different vague expressions and fuzzy modifiers which are usually called the linguistic hedges.[24] We may cite a few examples from Zadeh that involve various different operations.

Suppose young is defined as follows:

$$\text{Young} = \int_0^{100} (1 + (U/30)^2)^{-1}/U$$

$$\text{Then very young} = \text{CON } (|\text{ young }|)$$

$$= \int_0^{100} (1 + (U/30)^2)^{-2}/U$$

$$\text{More or less young} = \text{DIL } (|\text{ young }|)$$

$$= \int_0^{100} (1 + (U/30)^2)^{-0.5}/U$$

Let F be any vague predicate. Then

| sort of (F) | = INT (DIL (| F |) $\cap$ INT (DIL (NEG (| F|) )))
| Pretty (F) | = INT (| F |) $\cap$NEG (INT (CON (| F |)))
| Rather (F) | = INT (CON (| F |))

'More or less recent' may be expressed in terms of support fuzzifier.

More or less recent = SF (recent; K)
Let recent = 1/1991 +0.8/1989 +0.7/1988
and K (1991) = 1/1991 +0.9/1990
K (1989) = 1/1989 +0.9/1988
K (1988) = 1/1988 +0.8/1987
Then|more or less recent| = 1/1991 +0.9/1990 +0.8/1989 +0.7/1988 +0.56/1987.

Zadeh uses the operation of convex combination to represent expressions like 'essentially', 'Technically', etc.

To determine the degree of membership Zadeh has introduced two membership functions.

(*i*) S–function has been defined from the real line to [0, 1] by the equations

$$S(\mu) \triangleq 0 \quad \text{for } \mu < 0$$
$$\triangleq 2\mu^2 \quad \text{for } 0 \leq \mu \leq 0.5$$
$$\triangleq 1 - 2(1-\mu)^2 \quad \text{for } 0.5 < \mu \leq 1$$
$$\triangleq 1 \quad \text{for } \mu > 1$$

(*ii*) Putting two S–functions back to back we get a π–function. The definition equations for π (μ) are

$$\pi(\mu) \triangleq 0 \quad \text{for } \mu < -1$$
$$\triangleq 2(\mu+1)^2 \quad \text{for } -1 \leq \mu < -0.5$$
$$\triangleq 1-2\mu^2 \quad \text{for } -0.5 \leq \mu \leq 0.5$$
$$\triangleq 2(\mu-1)^2 \quad \text{for } 0.5 < \mu \leq 1$$
$$\triangleq 0 \quad \text{for } \mu > 1$$

Let us suppose that we would like to assign grade of membership to the class of young people. Supposing further that a young person of 25 years is assigned the grade 1, we may arrive at the following generalized equation by computing the S–function.

$$\text{Young} = \int_{0}^{25} 1/y + \int_{25}^{100} \left[1+\left(\frac{y-25}{5}\right)^{2}\right] - 1/y$$

A 30 year old man will get the membership grade .96 if we put y = 30.

On the basis of Fuzzy Set Theory the classical propositional and predicate logic can be extended to the corresponding *fuzzy logics.*

Let us take the syntax of the classical propositional logic with '¬' , '∧', '∨', '→' as connectives and 'P', 'Q', . . . as propositional variables. Let us allow 'P', 'Q', . . ., to have values in [0, 1]. Let p, q . . . signify the values of the propositional variables so that valuations of the connective are defined as follows:

$$|\neg p| = 1 - |p|$$
$$|p \wedge q| = \text{Min}\ (|p|, |q|)$$
$$|p \vee q| = \text{Max}\ (|p|, |q|)$$
$$|p \rightarrow q| = \text{Min}\ (1, (1-|p|) + |q|)$$

The valuation is similar to $L_n$, the n-valued system of Lukasiewicz.

It is apparent from the above valuation set that p ∨ ¬ p will not be a tautology (uniformly 1-assuming) nor p ∧ ¬ p is a contradiction (uniformly 0-assuming) in a fuzzy logical system. An example will make the point clear.

Let p = 'The colour of my dress is orange' receive the truth value 0.7. Then

$$|p \vee \neg p| = 0.7 \vee 0.3 = 0.7$$

and $|p \wedge \neg p| = 0.7 \wedge 0.3 = 0.3$

Such outcomes are quite in accordance with our intuition. We cannot assume p ∨ ¬ p to be true and p ∧ ¬ p to be false when p is not definitely true.

We shall now see which of the $C_2$–tautologics are valid in fuzzy propositional logic and which are not.

*Valid in FPL*

1. $P \rightarrow P$
2. $(P \rightarrow (Q \rightarrow R)) \rightarrow ((P \rightarrow Q) \rightarrow (P \rightarrow R))$
3. $(\neg P \rightarrow \neg Q) \rightarrow (Q \rightarrow P)$
4. $\neg\neg P \leftrightarrow P$
5. $(P \wedge \neg P)\ \neg P$
6. $((P \rightarrow Q) \wedge \neg Q) \rightarrow \neg P$
7. $(P \rightarrow Q) \rightarrow ((Q \rightarrow R) \rightarrow (P \rightarrow R))$
8. De Morgan's Laws
9. Associative Laws
10. Distributive Laws
11. Commutative Laws.

*Not valid in FPL*

1. $P \vee \neg P$
2. $P \rightarrow (Q \rightarrow P)$
3. $\neg P \rightarrow (P \rightarrow Q)$
4. $((P \wedge Q) \rightarrow R) \leftrightarrow (P \rightarrow (Q \rightarrow R))$
5. $(P \rightarrow (Q \wedge \neg Q) \rightarrow \neg P$
6. $(P \wedge \neg P) \rightarrow Q$
7. $Q \rightarrow (P \vee \neg P)$

In fuzzy logic *semantic entailment* is defined as:

$p \Vdash q$ iff $|p| \leq |q|$ in all models.

It is obvious that

$p \Vdash q$ iff $\Vdash p \rightarrow q$

Modus ponens is a valid form of inference and can be generalized so that it preserves degrees of truth.

$$\vdash_{\overline{\alpha}}\ p$$
$$\vdash p \rightarrow q \mid \therefore \vdash_{\overline{\alpha}}\ q$$

That means if p is true at least to degree $\alpha$ and $p \rightarrow q$ is true, q is true at least to degree $\alpha$.

To extend Fuzzy Propositional Logic to Fuzzy Predicate Logic we need to define valuations for predicates and quantifiers. Let F be an n–place predicate. The value of $Fx_1, \ldots, x_n$ is defined as the degree of membership of the ordered n–truple $(x_1, \ldots, x_n)$ in the Fuzzy set F, where $\tilde{x}_i$ is the denotation of $x_i$ on a given valuation. That is,

$|Fx_1, \ldots, x_n| = \mu_F\ (\tilde{x}_1, \ldots, \tilde{x}_n)$, then

$|\forall x\ Fx|$ = def. Min $\{\,|Fx|\,\}$ for all assignments to x of elements of the universe of discourse.

In other words, $| \forall x\, Fx | = \inf_x | Fx |$

$| \exists x\, Fx | =$ def, Max { | Fx | } for all assignments to x of elements of the universe of discourse.

or. $| \exists x\, Fx | = \sup_x | Fx |$.

The link between fuzzy set theory and fuzzy logic can be easily established by introducing Zadeh's notion of fuzzy restriction.[25] A fuzzy restriction denoted by R(v) is a fuzzy relation R that acts as an elastic constraint on the values, elements of X, that may be assigned to a variable v. Any variable, therefore, will be viewed as a triple (v, X, R(v)), v being the name of the variable. The meaning of a proposition of the form x is p (where x is the name of an object and P is a fuzzy predicate) may be expressed in terms of fuzzy restriction as a relational assignment equation of the form R (A (x)) = p. Here A(x) is an implied attribute of x, R is a fuzzy restriction on x and p is the unary fuzzy relation assigned to R. An informal account of fuzzy restriction follows immediately.

Let us consider the following sentences:

(1) Arna is *young.*
(2) Rohit has *red hair.*
(3) Shefali and Malini are *approximately equal in height.*

Starting with the first example, let age (Arna) denote a numerically valued variable which ranges over the interval [0, 100]. With this interval regarded as our universe of discourse U, *young* may be interpreted as a label of a fuzzy subset of U which is characterized by a compatibility function (degree of membership). Our calculus will tell us that the degree to which a numerical age, say, u = 28 is compatible with the concept of young is 0.7 whereas the degree of membership of 30 and 35 year-old men to the fuzzy set young is 0.5 and 0.2 respectively.

As 'young' is a vague predicate lacking a sharp boundary, the usual interpretation of 'Arna is young' in terms of the classical set theory will not qualify as adequate. Rather it should be explained in terms of an assertion of a restriction on the possible values of Arna's age not in terms of membership of Arna in a class of young individuals. Thus while denoting the restriction on the age of Arna by R (Age (Arna) ), the above function may be expressed as an assignment equation

R (Age (Arna) ) = young,

the unary fuzzy relation young is assigned to the restriction on the variable Age (Arna). The restriction in this context is undoubtedly a fuzzy restriction.

Following the same analysis the second sentence may be read as

R(colour (Hair (Rohit) ) ) = red.

Here the fuzzy set *red* is assigned as a value to the fuzzy restriction on the variable colour (Hair (Rohit) ) and colour (Hair) is the implied attribute. An implied attribute may have a nested structure like

$A_k$ ($A_{k-1}$ (. . . .$A_2$ ($A_1$ (x) . . . .) ) ).

Though uptill now we have always been talking about numerical values, it is not necessary to have a numerically valued base variable, i.e. the variable ranging over the universe of discourse U. We may proceed by exemplification and the variable we use may be a linguistic base variable.

So far we have been dealing with examples of fuzzy restrictions which are unary. But in our third example there are two variables to consider, viz. Height (Shefali) and Height (Malini). The corresponding assignment equation will have the form R (Height (Shefali), Height (Malini)) = approximately equal. Here *approximately equal* is a binary fuzzy relation characterized by a compatibility matrix. The matrix of approximately equal (u, v) is shown in the following table.

| u \ v | 5'6 | 5'8 | 5'10 | 6' | 6'2 | 6'4 |
|---|---|---|---|---|---|---|
| 5'6 | 1. | 0.8 | 0.6 | 0.2 | 0 | 0 |
| 5'8 | 0.8 | 1 | 0.9 | 0.7 | 0.3 | 0 |
| 5'10 | 0.6 | 0.9 | 1 | 0.9 | 0.7 | 0 |
| 6' | 0.2 | 0.7 | 0.9 | 1 | 0.9 | 0.8 |
| 6'2 | 0 | 0.3 | 0.7 | 0.9 | 1 | 0.9 |
| 6'4 | 0 | 0 | 0 | 0.8 | 0.9 | 1 |

Thus if Shefali's height is 5'8 and Malini's is 5'6, then the degree to which these are approximately equal is 0.8.

Let us suppose we are given two interrelated sentences.

(1) u is tall.

(2) u and v are approximately equal

(1) and (2) translated in terms of fuzzy restriction will be

(1') R(u) = tall

(2') R(u, v) = approximately equal.

Depending on the knowledge of a fuzzy restriction on u and a fuzzy restriction on (u, v) we can derive a fuzzy restriction on v, e.g., R(v) = R(u) o R(u, v) where o stands for the composition of fuzzy restrictions. Now,

$$\mu_{AOB}(v) = \text{def. } V\,(\mu_A(u) \wedge B(u, v))$$

Where A is a unary fuzzy restriction in U and B is a binary fuzzy restriction in U X V and V signifies the supremum over $u \in U$.

So (1') and (2') will yield (3'), i.e. R(v) which in our example is the composition of *tall* and *approximately equal.* Then by applying the technique of *linguistic approximation* we shall derive: v is more or less tall. This type of inference is known as approximate reasoning. It is a very handy tool in a fuzzy situation and is being widely used by the computer scientists especially in the field of Artificial Intelligence and Expert Systems. We shall discuss the process of approximate reasoning in detail in the next chapter.

Fuzzy logic compels us to admit degrees of truth. The sentence 'my dress is red' is true to the degree 0.7 if my dress is red to the degree 0.7. But our familiarity with the classical set theory and bivalent logic has conditioned our thought to such a great extent that degree of truth theory appears unacceptable to us at first glance. Truly speaking, the notion of degree of truth is not stranger than that of the degree of correspondence. Those who admit the latter notion formally represent propositions as functions from possible worlds to a new truth set containing as many values as is required to deal with the logical phenomena in question. Similarly in fuzzy logic the grade of membership is assigned to each element belonging to a fuzzy set by associating it with the valuation set [0, 1].

Degree of truth is a notion which does not appear counter-intuitive to common man though philosophers have various reservations against it. In ordinary language we very often use expressions implying degrees of truth. But our ordinary understanding of degree of truth is much wider than our technical understanding. Ordinarily speaking, we assert P to be truer than Q when P is epistemically more certain than Q. Sometimes we say that P is truer than Q. When P and Q are both false but P is somewhat more accurate than Q. In fuzzy logic by degree of truth we mean a number of the truth set with which a given element is associated. That is, some sentences may not be completely true yet true to some degree. Here we know truth and falsehood (in the classical sense) to be the limiting values of an ordered truth set. Since there is no sharp demarcation within a fuzzy set and since the truth set taken is continuous what is true to some degree may also be said to be false to some degree when we proceed from the side of the complement. Therefore, if 'my dress is red' is true to the degree 0.7 then it is false to the degree 0.3. Such a view helps us to understand easily how we can meaningfully assert in our ordinary conversation, 'It is raining and it isn't' without giving rise to any contradiction.

We have already seen that fuzzy sets are extensional. It follows from the extensionality of fuzzy sets that '$A \leftrightarrow B$'

is true iff A and B are true to the same degree. Depending on this Peacocke[26] has attempted to give a Tarski-type truth definition: true ('red(Uranus) ') $\leftrightarrow$ red (Uranus). That is to say that the degree to which the predicate 'is true' applies to the sentence 'Uranus is red' matches exactly the degree to which Uranus is red. But such simple truth definition fails in case $\leftrightarrow$ is graded. So we require a more sophisticated truth definition and a matching notion of validity.

In classical logic, we know, the notion of validity is intimately connected with the notion of a tautology or a uniformly T-assuming formula. In many systems of many-valued logic the notion of tautology has been extended to the notion of quasi-tautology by designating certain truth values. Thus by designating I as truth like, the tautology can be redefined as a formula which never takes the truth value F. Similarly, some fuzzy logicians have suggested that a formula which always takes a value $\geq 0.5$ should be considered a tautology.

The validity of an inference in classical logic is usually related with the notion of implication. The inference from p to q is said to be valid in classical logic if the corresponding implication $p \rightarrow q$ gets the value 1 in all models. In a valid inference the conclusion always preserves the truth of the premisses. So an argument in fuzzy logic is said to be valid when its conclusion is at least as true as the falsest premiss. The way in which we have defined the validity of *modus ponens* is in accordance with the above principle. It has been said when p is true to the degree x and $p \rightarrow q$ is true, then q is true at least to the degree x. This definition of validity is consistent with our notion of semantic entailment too.

One may ask: What happens when p is true to the degree $\alpha$ but $p \rightarrow q$ is not definitely true? Fuzzy logicians differ on this issue. Some hold that q should at least get the value equal to the Min of $|p|$ and $|p \rightarrow q|$ while some others maintain that q should be $\geq$ the product of $|p|$ and $|p \rightarrow q|$. Moreover, the entailment also admits of degree; it is not always cent per cent truth-preserving. Consequently the notion of validity also becomes graded. To accommodate such cases we shall put forward a generalized formula of graded consequence relation.[27]

Tarski[28] has taught us that any consequence relation, '$\vdash$' should possess three properties:

I. $\alpha$–overlap
II. Dilution
III. Cut.

A fuzzy consequence relation should also possess these three properties. A relation from the power set of V (the non-empty universe) to V is called a conclusion relation on V. A conclusion relation is denoted by '$|\!\sim$' and the grade in which a subset X of V is related to an element B of V is denoted by $gr(X |\!\sim B)$.

A conclusion relation $|\!\sim$ is said to be an $\alpha$–consequence relation iff it satisfies the conditions:

(1) $\alpha$–overlap : If $B \in X$ then $gr(X |\!\sim B) \geq \alpha, \alpha > 0$
(2) Dilution: If $X' \subseteq X$ then $gr(X' |\!\sim B) \leq gr(X |\!\sim B)$
(3) Cut: $gr(X |\!\sim B) \geq gr(X \cup Z |\!\sim B) \wedge \inf.\ gr(X |\!\sim A)$, $A \in Z$.

for any subsets X, Z of V and any element B.

In 2–valued logic, B is a consequence of X iff for all T, $X \subseteq T$ implies $B \in T$, where T is the ordinary subset of the universe of discourse of true propositions determined by a particular state of affair.

In multiple-valued fuzzy logic each element of V is assigned values ranging from 0 to 1 by any state of affairs. Under the circumstances, the graded subset is defined as

$$gr(A \subseteq B) = \inf_{x \in V} \left(\mu_A(x) \rightarrow \mu_B(x)\right)$$

where V is the universe, A and B two fuzzy subsets of V, $\mu_A$ and $\mu_B$ are respectively membership grades and $\rightarrow$ is any fuzzy implication operator.

Now we are in a position to define a graded consequence relation as follows:

$$gr\,(X \mid\!\sim B) = \inf_{T_i} \left( \bigwedge_{x \in X} (\mu_A(x) \rightarrow Ti\,(x) \Rightarrow (1 \rightarrow Ti\,(B)\,)\,\right)$$

Here Ti is any particular state of affair which is a fuzzy subset of V, $\rightarrow$ is an implication operator for which $0 \rightarrow a = 1$, and $\Rightarrow$ is a fuzzy implication operator satisfying the conditions:

(i) $a \Rightarrow a = 1$
(ii) $a \leq b$ implies $a \Rightarrow c \geq b \Rightarrow c$
(iii) $a \Rightarrow c \geq a \Rightarrow b \wedge b \Rightarrow c$

Once we admit such a graded consequence relation, it becomes very much plausible that in a long chain of arguments validity gradually passes onto invalidity, just as truth gradually merges into falsity.

Granting that the notion of degree of truth and that of graded consequence are admissible, one may question the correctness of and justification for assigning a particular degree of truth to a particular proposition or a particular grade of membership to a particular element of a fuzzy set. Previously we mentioned that a grade of membership is a matter of definition. It is subjective in the sense that it may vary depending on the user and the context. So raising the question of whether the degree assigned is correct or not will be meaningful only relative to a context.

But whether a particular assignment is justified in a particular context can be answered only if we look at the actual process of assigning grades of membership. There are several alternative methods of degree-assignment prevalent in fuzzy logic. We shall, however, discuss only Zadeh's method.[29]

Zadeh takes U to be the universe of discourse and A, a fuzzy subset of U. He then estimates $\mu_A$ of finite number of samples depending on the partial information that he has of A. Suppose we are trying to determine whether a man with n number of hairs is bald or not. Zadeh will allow us to use some linguistic truth values. Say, true, more or less true, borderline, more or less false, false. We shall then assign one of these values to the case at hand and associate these linguistic truth values with their numerical counterparts, say 1, 0.75, 0.5, 0.25 and 0 respectively. Once we fix these positions on the scale we can make still further calibrations on our scale in the intermediate positions measuring the approximate distance between the point fixed and the given instance. By repeating this process for a number of cases we can construct the membership function of A = bald.

A question may be raised, and indeed a legitimate one, why shouldn't we regard assignation of membership grade as an act of precisification. Surely it is one thing to say that somebody is more or less bald and quite another to say that he is bald to the extent 0.8. The latter way of putting things is really a step towards precisification. And have we not said time and again that vagueness and precisification are totally incompatible? When precisified, vagueness loses its essence. So any theory that wants to take vagueness seriously should not attempt to precisify it.

Zadeh might not find anything wrong with assignment of membership grade. For his aim is to make vague statements intelligible to machines. Without this sort of precisification vague expressions will not be amenable to formalization or generalization. Consequently vague sentences will lie outside the ambit of our logic. So what Zadeh has actually been doing may be reconstructed and summarized in the following steps.

(*a*) Zadeh has observed that human beings reason with inexact concepts of different kinds including vague expressions with ease and there is some parity amongst the conclusions reached by different persons from inexact premisses.

(*b*) Machines cannot handle inexact concepts unless some algorithm can be devised for them.

(*c*) To devise such algorithms we require some well-defined method of assigning degree of membership and some calculus to deal with fuzzy predicates, relations, etc.

(*d*) The results obtained by following the calculus are then checked against the results arrived at through intuitive human reasoning. If the two sets of results are found to tally significantly then it is assumed that the calculus and the rules adopted underlie the intuitive reasoning process.

(*e*) Machines are fed with these devices and if these are found to be *effective* we accept them as the correct rules for handling fuzzy expressions.

Obviously there are alternative methods to arrive at the same conclusions and to choose amongst them we shall be guided by the usual criteria of theory choice like generality, simplicity, etc.

So the method that we are following in the area of fuzzy reasoning is quite different. We are not starting with the calculus and then interpreting it, we are starting with established usages and then are trying to formulate a suitable calculus for them.

In the light of the above comments we might reformulate the charge brought against the fuzzy approach; whether the rules and calculus devised so far can adequately handle vague sentences.

Fuzzy logicians can defend their position against the charge of precisification by offering several different arguments.

Assignment of degree of membership to different elements of a fuzzy set does not amount to precisification from the common sense point of view. Our ordinary understanding of precisification is: to make something completely precise but in fuzzy logic vague expressions are being precisified only to a certain extent. Moreover, fuzzy logicians have given up the notion of discrete predication. So by saying that some shade of red is red to the degree 0.7, they are not actually drawing any sharp line between red shades that are red to the degree 0.7 and shades which are not red to that particular degree. What they want to emphasize is that the given shade of red is sort of red, though not completely red, and it is more red than non-red. Besides the degree of membership assigned is not an absolute one, Fuzzy logicians have pointed out repeatedly; nor have they ever ruled out the possibility of there being higher order vagueness. It is also to be kept in mind that the points on the real line are continuous so even if for a particular purpose we draw some divide, the points on the real line on both sides of the cut are really continuous and there is a smooth passage between one point and another. Hence by assigning some numerical values to the membership grades Zadeh and his followers are not precisifying vague expressions in such a manner so as to lose the flavour of vagueness.

## 4.7 A MODIFIED APPROACH

We have some reservations against Zadeh's representation of vague sentences. Zadeh, we have seen, has admitted the possibility of higher order vagueness but has always given a first-order analysis of vague sentences. We think that this horizontal first order analysis needs to be supplemented. A general account of representation of vagueness cannot disregard the fact that a vague sentence involving a vague predicate when satisfied by objects in the penumbral region is vaguely vague. I would like to quote from Russell once again,

> All the vagueness which apply to the primary use of words apply also when we try to fix a limit to their indubitable applicability.[30]

This point can be established with a very simple experiment. A person who knows the meaning of 'red' is shown a red strip the shade of which is a bit lighter than the shade taken as the paradigmatic red. He is then requested to assign a membership grade to the presented shade of red. He is always found to hesitate, to vacillate. He hesitates because he feels that he cannot be sure that the grade assigned by him is absolutely correct. Suppose he assigns the grade 0.7 to the red presented to him. Then the sentence 'This shade is red' will be true to the degree 0.7. But if challenged, the person is found to revise his opinion very often since the sentence x is red to the degree 0.7 is itself vague. So assignment of membership grade as well as degree of truth to a first order vague sentence must take into consideration some vertically higher orders.

Let us spell out the rationale of our representation in greater detail. To represent any vague sentence like 'a is red' we are to proceed as follows:

(a is red) is vague . . . . (1)

Supposing a is sort of red, say, to the extent 0.7, it may be said that:

(a is red) is true to the extent 0.7 . . . . (2)

Suppose, I ask myself (or even a third person who shares our linguistic background and understands 'red' in our sense) whether I am sure about the assignment of degree, I usually answer in the negative. So the original vague sentence ((a is red) is vague) becomes neither true nor false. . . . (3)

Now, at the second level too, I may raise the same question after assigning grade, say, 0.8 to 3. Then we have:

( (a is red) is vague) is vague is neither true nor false. . . . (4)

This vacillation is not due to my psychological debility or epistemological laziness. It follows from the nature of vagueness itself. But human reasoning process cannot go on like this *ad infinitum.* I shall have to stop vacillating at some point and assert that I am certain about my assertion. And once we reach certainty we do not once again lapse into uncertainty. Such being the case, an adequate logic/semantics of vagueness should take into account successive higher-order truth grades assigned to a vague sentence till certainty is reached.

This situation can be very elegantly represented in terms of a Heyting algebra.

Let x be an object of the domain U and P be a vague predicate the extension of which is the fuzzy set P'. Let $\alpha_0$ be the degree of membership of x in P'. Then the vague sentence x is P is true to the extent $\alpha_0$. So the representation of 'x is P' will have the following steps.

a. ( x is P ) . . . . . $\alpha_0$
b. ( (x is P) is $\alpha_0$) . . . $\alpha_1$
c. ( ( (x is P) is $\alpha_0$ ) is $\alpha_1$) . . . , $\alpha_2$ . . . ., where $\alpha_1, \alpha_2, \ldots$ are the degree of truth of the nested sentence.

The generalized form of representation will be:

(x is P) . . . . . $\langle(\alpha_0, (\alpha_1, \alpha_2 \ldots) ), \leq\rangle$

where (i) $\alpha_0 \in [0, 1]$
(ii) $\alpha_1 \geq 0.5$
(iii) $\alpha_{i+1} \geq \alpha_i$ where i = 1, 2, 3 . . .
(iv) $\alpha_i = 1$

Next follows the justification for (i) – (iv).

$\alpha_0$ is the degree of truth of the original vague sentence which can be obtained by fuzzy restriction on the value of P and so may take any value within the interval [0, 1]. $\alpha_1$ is the degree of truth of *x is p* being vague, or, to say the same thing, being true to some extent. If $\alpha_1$ gets a grade $< 0.5$, then we have to admit that there was something grossly wrong with the original degree assignment. Hence the subject should be asked to revise the original membership grade. We are here subscribing to the view that any assertion possessing lesser degree of certainty than 0.5 is no assertion at all. That is why $\alpha_1, \alpha_2 \ldots$ cannot get a value less than 0.5.

Number (iii) above states that the successive degrees of truth assigned to the higher levels cannot decrease from the immediately preceding one. So if the degree of truth of the sentence *x is p* to the extent 0.8 is 0.7, then the next level cannot get a value less than 0.7. It must be either greater than or equal to 0.7. This is a stipulation insisted and required for developing a workable calculus. So we have to admit that $\alpha_{i+1} \geq \alpha_i$ where i = 1, 2, 3 . . .

Number (iv) above is difficult to justify. For theoretically it is possible that i may take any value up to $\alpha$. But actually uncertainty in the human reasoning process comes to a halt at some point. Normal human reasoning cannot ultimately rest on any uncertain stance. That is why, we have taken $\alpha_i = 1$. When we are certain about some point (may be with respect to a particular context) we remain certain about it provided all other things remain the same. Actually at which level we are to reach the value 1 can be determined by statistical generalization of the relevant empirical data.

We should note that if $\alpha_0 = 0$, then $\alpha_1 = \alpha_2 \ldots . = 1$. For 0 is a classical value and when a sentence is assigned 0, we are absolutely certain about the falsehood of the sentence. So if (x is P) is false, the corresponding set of degrees of truth will be $(0, 1, 1, \ldots)$. Similar is the case of a sentence which is definitely true. In that case the accompanying set of grades will be $(1, 1, 1, \ldots)$

$\leq$ : it is the coordinatewise ordering of all points excepting where $\alpha_0 = 0$.

That is, $\alpha_i \leq \beta_i$, i = 0, 1, 2.

Now $(0, 1, 1, \ldots) \leq \alpha$ for all $\alpha \in$ (the truth set).

So, $(0, 1, 1 \ldots .)$ may be taken as the least element. It is obvious that $(1, 1, 1, \ldots)$ is the greatest element.

In our logic *and* is defined as the co-ordinatewise Min or $\wedge$ of all points except $(0, 1, 1 \ldots)$ as $(0, 1, 1 \ldots)$ is the least element.

*Example:* $R = (\alpha_0, \alpha_1, \alpha_2 \ldots \ldots)$
$S = (\beta_0, \beta_1, \beta_2 \ldots \ldots)$
Then $(R \text{ and } S) = (\alpha_0 \wedge \beta_0, \alpha_1 \wedge \beta_1, \alpha_2 \wedge \beta_2, \ldots)$
But if $S' = (0, 1, 1 \ldots .)$
then, $(R \text{ and } S') = (0, 1, 1, \ldots)$ whatever may be the evaluation set of R.

Disjunction ($\vee$) is defined as

$$\alpha \vee \beta = (\alpha_0 \vee \beta_0, \alpha_1 \vee \beta_1, \alpha_2 \vee \beta_2 \ldots .)$$

Implication ($\rightarrow$) is defined as

$$\alpha \rightarrow \beta = \operatorname*{Sup}_{x} (x \mid \alpha \wedge x \leq \beta)$$

It can be easily proved that modus ponens, i.e. $\alpha \wedge (\alpha \rightarrow \beta) \leq \beta$ from the definition of $\rightarrow$.

$$\neg \alpha = \alpha \rightarrow 0$$
$$= (\alpha_0, \alpha_1, \alpha_2 \ldots) \rightarrow (0, 1, 1, \ldots)$$
$$= \{(x_0, x_1, \ldots) / (\alpha_0, \alpha_1, \alpha_2 \ldots) \wedge (x_0, x_1, \ldots) \leq (0, 1, 1, \ldots)$$

This negation, it is obvious is the intuitionistic negation. The reason behind opting for it is that a Heyting algebra with intuitionistic negation is decidable. If necessary, a stonger negation can also be defined by taking an additional assumption, viz. $x = \neg\neg x$.

Now ≤, the ordering relation, can easily capture '|—' or entailment. Of course, as we have already discussed '|—' will be a graded entailment relation. The grade of entailment will depend upon the grade of premisses and the connectives involved.

*Example 1*: x is very young ∴ x is young.
Let us suppose x is young has the grade
(0.7, 0.7, 0.9, 1.1)
Then the grade of very young will be calculated by
CON | young |, i.e. (.49, .49, .81, 1, 1)
Now (.49, .49, .81, 1, 1) < (0.7, 0.7, 0.9, 1, 1)
Hence, x is very young |~ x is young.

*Example 2:* P ∧ Q / ∴ P
Let P = (0.7, 0.6, 0.9, 1, 1)
Q = (0.9, 0.9, 1, 1, 1)
Then P ∧ Q = (0.7, 0.6, 0.9, 1, 1)
So P ∧ Q / ∴ P and also P ∧ Q / ∴ Q
Other valid forms of arguments can also be checked in this way.

We have seen that a fuzzy set *per excellence* should have graded consequence relation. Identity in the context of a fuzzy set is also indeterminate or graded. The law of identity of indiscernibles takes the following form in the presence of vague predicate.

> If x falls under the concept X to the extent α and relative to the concept, if y is identical with x to the extent β, then y falls under the concept X to the extent not less than α * β.

Here * is the object-level 'anding' operation. The indeterminate identity is an equivalence relation that satisfies the conditions of reflexivity, symmetry but weak transitivity.

A semi-formal description of genesis of indeterminate identity compatible with our mode of representing vagueness is given below.[31]

To start with, we have a universe of discourse U with objects x, y, z, . . . . . . . . . A concept is defined as a fuzzy subset of $U^k$, k = 1, 2, . . . identified with a function called the membership function of the fuzzy subset and is denoted by X, Y, Z . . . . . We also have a set L with an ordering relation $\propto$ which generates quite naturally other operators, viz. $\wedge$, $\vee$, etc. Next we introduce a binary operator* with the properties of associativity, symmetry, identity, isotonicity, etc. This new operator with the basic structures in L will give rise to other operators like $\rightarrow$, $\neg$, etc., in L. All these equip L with a structure adequate for truth value computations. We then define basic unary concepts as fuzzy sets of some universe having membership grades in L such that:

x belongs to the concept X to the grade 'a'
iff the truth value of 'x is X' is 'a'.

Now an indeterminate identity can be induced in the universe of object via each unary concept. Let $\upsilon^*$ denote the indeterminate identity operator and we define it as follows.

$\upsilon^* (x, y) = \text{def. } (x \rightarrow y) * (y \rightarrow x).$

$\upsilon^*$ satisfies the following condition

(1) $\upsilon^* (x, x) = 1$ (reflexivity)

(2) $\upsilon^* (x, y) = \upsilon^* (y, x)$ (symmetry)

(3) $\upsilon^* (x, y) * \upsilon^* (y, z) \propto \upsilon^* (x, z)$ (weak transitivity)

The operator $\upsilon^*$ induces a function $\upsilon_X : U^2 \rightarrow L$ via a unary concept X such that

$\upsilon_X (x, y) = \text{def. } \upsilon^* (X (x), X (y))$[32]

and $\upsilon_X$ is the indeterminate identity induced in the universe via the concept X. $\upsilon_X$ also satisfies the properties of reflexivity, symmetry and weak transitivity.

An indeterminate identity amongst concepts can also be defined in terms of graded inclusion.[33] The identity among concepts is also an equivalence relation defined as

$\tilde{\upsilon}$ (X, y) = gr(X ⊂ Y)* gr(Y ⊂ X) satisfying reflexivity, symmetry and weak transitivity.

This notion of indeterminate identity required for representing nearness relation amongst instances of vague predicates however does not supplant classical identity but only supplements it. The indeterminate identity reduces to the classical identity relation in a crisp context.

## NOTES AND REFERENCES

1. T.K. Sarkar (1990).
2. Russell (1927), p. 27.
3. Michael Tye (1990).
4. Ibid., p. 547.
5. Kit Fine (1975).
6. B. van Frassen (1966).
7. Kit Fine (1975), p. 279.
8. Ibid.
9. Ibid., p. 278.
10. B. van Frassen (1966).
11. E. Bencivenga (1986), p. 401.
12. That is why, Fine writes, indefinite sentences 'are born, as it were, to be true or false.'
13. Ibid., p. 278.
14. Manfred Pinkal (1983), p. 29.
15. R.M. Sainsbury (1988).
16. H. Kamp (1981).
17. R.M. Sainsbury (1988), p. 40.
18. Joachim Ballweg (1983), pp. 59–78.
19. Parikh (1988), pp. 245–46.
20. A topological reading of vague predicates has also been presented by Walther Kindt (1983).
21. L.A. Zadeh (1965a, 1965b).
22. Rudolf Carnap (1950).
23. L.A. Zadeh (1972).
24. G. Lakoff (1973).
25. L.A. Zadeh (1975a).
26. Cristopher Peacocke (1981).
27. M.K. Chakraborti (1988).
28. Tarski (1956).
29. Following D. Dubois and H. Prade (1980), pp. 256–60.
30. See note 7, Chapter 1.
31. For a formal account see M.K. Chakraborti and A. Chatterjee (forthcoming).

32. X(x) signifies x falls under the concept X. Any object will fall under a certain concept to a certain degree, say, α. Hence identity of objects is bound to be graded in a vague context and is relative to a particular concept.
33. For a definition of graded inclusion see 4.6 above.

CHAPTER 5

# Sorites Paradox

IT IS A PARADOX, whose importance familiarity fails to diminish. *Max Black*

## 5.1 NATURE OF A PARADOX

The sorites paradox or *the paradox of the heap* is an age-old paradox usually attributed to the megarian Eubulides. Like any other paradox, it is also an outcome of our conflict between reason and common sense. Let me be a little more explicit on this point. In a paradoxical argument the conclusion which is derived 'by apparently unexceptionable means from apparently unexceptionable first principles'[1] appears to be exceptionable and contrary to common sense. Thus in a paradox though we start with acceptable premises and our process of reasoning is valid, yet we arrive at an absurd conclusion.

In philosophical literature we have come across paradoxes and paradoxes. Some of them are veridical or *truth-telling*[2] where the conclusion of the argument is only apparently absurd but can be explained with the help of some rules. Take, for example, the case of a man whose age is twenty-five only after his sixth birthday. The puzzle is resolved the moment we realize that the man must have been born on the 29th of February and, therefore, can celebrate his birthday only once in four years.

Some other paradoxes may be grouped under the head 'falsidical' where the absurdity of the conclusion is due to the adopted reasoning procedure which is really unsound though does not appear to be so. One instance of such a paradox is the famous De Morgan's paradox the conclusion of which asserts that 2 = 1; but the proof of it can be shown to be unsound on closer scrutiny.

There is another group of paradoxes quite unlike the above two types which may be called the genuine paradoxes. Here the conclusion is really absurd but is justified by the sound process of reasoning. That the sorites paradox belongs to the third group will be evident if we state the different versions of the paradox.

(*a*) *Eubulides's Version*
Let us suppose there is a heap of sand in front of us. If we take away one grain of sand from the heap, it remains a heap. If we take away another grain, it remains a heap. If we take away still another grain, it remains a heap. If this process continues, a time will come when all the grains are removed but our logic will prompt us to say that still there is a heap.[3]

(*b*) *Wang's Version*

O is small.
If n is small, (n+1) is small
Every number is small.[4]

(*c*) *Russell's Version*
A man with no hair is bald. If a man with no hair is bald so is the man with one hair. If a man with one hair is bald so also is the man with two hairs. Hence, in the long run, a man with 10,000 strands of hair on his head will also be bald.[5]

(*d*) *Parikh's Version*
Take a can of red paint, a can of yellow paint, a brush, an ink dropper and a stack of cards. You dip the paint brush in the can of red paint and colour one card, the card will be red. Now add a few drops of yellow paint to the red can, mix thoroughly and dab one of the remaining cards with the brush, the colour of the cards will still be red. You repeat this procedure and you will find that the cards painted are no longer red but orange.[6]

(*e*) *Goldstein's Version*

*The Mona Lisa sorites:* Imagine an experiment where I am presented with a perfect reproduction of the Mona Lisa and asked to assess it beautiful or ugly. I assert that '$ML_1$ is beautiful'. The next reproduction I am asked to consider is just like $ML_1$, except that an imperceptibly tiny quantity of the original colour had been replaced by a shade of puce. I call this second reproduction $ML_2$ and judge it beautiful. But the subsequent Mona Lisa reproductions become pucer and pucer though two successive reproductions are indistinguishable from one another. Somewhere in the line my ratings start to change and I find the last few reproductions definitely ugly.[7]

The general form of the sorites paradox gleaned from the above examples may be stated as follows:

$x_i$ is P.
For any i, if $x_i$ is P, then $x_{(i+1)}$ is P.
$\therefore x_{(i+1)}$ is P.
........................
........................
........................
$\therefore x_n$ is P.

At first glance (a) might not appear to be conforming straightforwardly to the general form. So let us reformulate it.

(a) One grain of sand cannot make a heap. For any number of n, if n grains of sand cannot make a heap, n+1 grains cannot, either. Thus arbitrarily many grains of sand cannot make a heap.[8]

It does not require great logical acumen to realize that there is nothing wrong with the general form. The argument form involves one categorical premiss and one hypothetical premiss. Then by application of two simple rules of logic, viz. modus ponens (M.P.) and universal instantiation (U.I.) we derive the conclusion. In the next argument in the chain, the conclusion of the previous argument is taken as the first premiss, the hypothetical premiss is suitably altered, once again M.P. is employed and we get the second intermediate conclusion and so on. Thus the general form of sorites argument comprises a long chain of valid modus ponens argument forms.[9] The absurdity becomes patent only when we replace the variables by constants, especially, the predicate letter P by vague expressions like 'heap', 'small', 'bald', 'red', 'beautiful', etc. Hence the general consensus is: 'the paradox is evidently due to the vagueness of the predicate(s)'.[10]

The above observation helps us to establish two points about sorites paradox: (i) it is a genuine paradox and (ii) it is a semantic paradox.

The sorites paradox is genuine simply because here the patently absurd (for no one will ever uphold that a man with 10,000 hairs on his head is bald or 1,23,45,678 is a small number) conclusion is backed by a valid rule of inference.

The necessary involvement of vague expressions in the sorites paradox leads us to distinguish it from logical paradoxes like the paradox of material implication, the paradox of types, etc. The paradoxes of the latter group can be expressed by employing only logical terms and hence are aptly characterized as logical.[11]

Granting that the use of vague predicates lies at the root of the paradox, let us now see how the paradox is actually generated. The following are the conditions which make a sorites argument paradoxical.

(1) In the categorical premisses of the argument some vague predicate is asserted about the subject terms. It is necessary that the objects referred to by those terms can be arranged in a series.
(2) The series must have a first member which is to be taken as the paradigm instance of the concept represented by the vague predicate in question and be incorporated in the first premiss.
(3) The series in question may be infinite but for the purpose of highlighting the paradox, a finite subsection of the infinite series suffices. The series may be taken to terminate at the point where the element

*surely* does not fall under the concept under which the first element falls.

(4) Each element of the series must be discrete.

(5) No two successive elements of the series, though discrete, should be distinguishable with respect to a particular property, i.e. they must be *non-discriminably different.*

(6) This relation of being non-discriminably different with respect to a property[12] in question has got to be non-transitive. That means, somewhere in the middle of the ordered series $x_i$ ceases to be indistinguishable from $x_{i+2}$ though $x_i$ is indistinguishable from $x_{i+1}$ and $x_{i+1}$ is indistinguishable from $x_{i+2}$.

(7) But it must be indeterminate with respect to which $x_i$ the relation ceases to be transitive.

(8) The series should be ordered in such a manner that elements lower down the series fall under a concept diametrically opposed to the concept instantiated by the first element.

We shall now check these conditions against Parikh's version of the paradox. Let us arrange a stack of painted cards in the following manner. The first card is painted by the paint from the red can before any yellow drop is added to it. The next card is painted by the red paint having one drop of yellow in it. The third card is painted by the red paint with two drops of yellow in it and so on. Let us name the cards $C_1$, $C_2$, $C_3$, . . . We shall terminate the series with the card, say, $C_{115}$ the colour of which is undoubtedly orange. We may go on diluting the colour further by reducing the portion of red more and more but that is not necessary to show the paradox.

Now each card in the series is indistinguishable in colour from its immediate predecessor and its immediate successor. Let us assume that we are never shown more than two cards of the ordered series at a time. When we are shown the first card, $C_1$, in the series we naturally find it red. Then $C_2$ is shown and as $C_2$ is non-discriminable from $C_1$, $C_2$ is also red. $C_3$ is indistinguishable from $C_2$ in colour, to $C_3$ is red too. In this manner, if we proceed along the series, $C_{115}$ should also be red. But our observation tells us that $C_{115}$ is surely not red but orange. However, the situation is such that we shall never be able to tell exactly at which point the card has first stopped to be red, or when the relation of non-discriminability with respect to colour has lost its transitivity. Even if one hundred and fifteen cards are displayed all at a time, the paradox will not be solved. For uncertainty over identification of the last red card and the first orange card will continue to persist.[13]

Of all the conditions mentioned above, no. 6 is the most crucial one. For if the relation among the non-discriminably different members of a series with respect to a particular property were transitive, the paradox would never have arisen. This trait of the sorites argument follows directly from the tolerant character of vague predicates.[14] But before that, two successive elements may be non-discriminably different with respect to an observational property.[15] For, negligible differences[16] among objects below a certain threshold cannot be detected by human observation. That is why two objects $x_1$ and $x_2$ may appear to match exactly without being actually identical with respect to a property. When such negligible differences in a chain add up to a significant difference we decide by *backward reasoning* that there must have been some difference, however insignificant that might be, between $x_1$ and $x_2$ otherwise $x_1$ could not have been so different from, say, $x_6$.

Can't aided observation be of some help? I don't think so. It is true that differences not detectable by an unaided sense organ can be detected when aided by suitable instruments. Thus $x_1$ and $x_2$ may become discriminable when instrument detection facility is available. But even the most sensitive instruments operate within some limits and it is always possible for two things to have a difference smaller than the smallest difference notable by a powerful instrument. That means, in between $x_1$ and $x_2$ we can find inserted two objects, say $x_1'$ and $x_1''$ such that the difference between $x_1$ and $x_1'$ remains undetected by the most effective of instruments. So, aided observation can at best shift the problem to a subtler level, but does not solve it.

Another characteristic of the series, we have seen, is that its first element and its (so-called) last element fall under two different concepts. Take, for instance, the red-yellow colour series. Since red merges into orange, orange may be taken as a shade of red. But the paradox arises only when red and orange are considered opposed to one another.

Some are, therefore, inclined to uphold that there is a series the special trait of which is, in the terminology of Michael Dummett,[17] being both 'weakly finite' and 'weakly infinite'. A series is 'weakly infinite' if there exists a well-ordering[18] of it with no last member; a series, on the other hand, is 'weakly finite' if for some finite ordinal n, there exists a well-ordering of it with no nth member. Now the red subseries is weakly infinite for every shade of the series is still considered red when the next shade is presented. On the other hand, such a series is weakly finite for it is possible to point out a shade of the series which is definitely not red, i.e. the red series does not contain the nth shade.[19] So the series in question is such that though it is not possible to say which is the last red shade yet we may discern some upper bounds of the series beyond which the shades appear to be distinctly orange. A weakly finite series which is also weakly infinite, says Dummett, following a strict finitist, constitutes the extension of a vague predicate.

We are now in a position to sum up the above discussion. The sorites paradox by which it can be established that a red shade is orange or a eighty year old man is young or some such proposition, arises because of the essential occurrence of some vague predicate in the body of the argument. A vague predicate always refers to a well ordered series in which no two contiguous members are discernible with respect to the property in question. This sort of indiscernibility results, we have seen, from the tolerant nature of vague predicates. By appealing to this feature of tolerance we can explain the curious phenomenon of non-transitivity of non-discernibly differents which is directly responsible for the paradoxical outcome.

### 5.2 SOLUTIONS

We can no longer avoid raising the million-dollar question: how to solve the paradox? Before we come up with our own answer we are going to make a historical survey of the field. The logical solutions so far offered may be classified into two broad categories: (a) solutions that question one or more of the premisses and (b) solutions that doubt the soundness/validity of the reasoning procedure. The tri-valent, the supervaluational, the intuitionistic and the context-theoretic accounts belong to the first category. But the solutions provided by the strict finitists, the fuzzy logicians and by Parikh can be included in the second group.

While analyzing different solutions we shall be using the baldman version of the paradox as the typical example[20] which says

(1) A man with no hair on his head is bald.
(2) For any number, n, if a man with n hairs on his head is bald, then a man with n + 1 hairs on his head is bald.

Therefore,

(3) A man with ten thousand hairs on his head is bald.

It becomes clear in no time that no solution of the paradox can be provided remaining within the framework of the bivalent classical logic. For, here, the first premiss is undoubtedly true, the conclusion is undoubtedly false (if we stick to the standard English usage of 'bald'), and the rules of inference applied, viz. universal instantiation and modus ponens are valid and truth-preserving. So the only plausible way in which the falsity of the conclusion can be explained is by declaring the second premiss false. The falsity of the second premiss (since it is a conditional sentence) will imply that there is some n (number of hairs) the possession of which is sufficient to brand a man 'bald' but if the same man gains one single hair (n + 1), he will not be bald. That is, there is some assignment of n under which the antecedent of the conditional premiss is true but the consequent is false. Such a supposition, however, will make 'bald' precise; for only a precise expression can have a sharp cut-off point. But surely there is nothing precise in the natural import of 'bald'. We shall, therefore, find that all who seek to solve the paradox try to come up with a solution that does not undermine the vague character of the predicate involved.

## 5.3 THE TRIVALENT SOLUTION

One such solution has been offered by Michael Tye[21] following the 3-valued logic of S.C. Kleene.[22] The strategy adopted by Tye in dealing with the paradox is: to attack the second premiss but to hold it indefinite. Thus he gains on two counts: (*i*) he need not declare 'bald' to be precise and (*ii*) the sorites is checked. Tye maintains that the statement schema:

(2') If a man with n hairs on his head is bald, then a man with n + 1 hairs on his head is bald

is indefinite and not false. For, under some assignment of n, it can be shown that both the antecedent and the consequent of the above statement schema are indefinite. So by Kleene's table (2') will be indefinite. Such assignment suits our intuitive understanding of 'bald' too. The borderline member of the set of bald men does not become a non-member simply by gaining one single hair. This shows that on Tye's view the principle of tolerance holds in the penumbral region too. Hence by the rule of quantification, the universally quantified sentence (2) also become indefinite. Now if we grant that $(\forall x)\ Fx$ is equivalent with $\neg \exists x \neg Fx$, then

(2'') It is not the case that there is a number n such that a man with n hairs is bald and a man with n + 1 hairs is not must also be considered indefinite. Again, since in Tye's system the negation of an indefinite statement is also indefinite,

(2''') There is a number n such that a man with n hairs is bald and a man with n + 1 hairs is not

is indefinite. So the argument does not warrant our drawing a sharp line between 'bald' and 'not-bald' thus 'bald' remains vague.

Tye has not shown explicitly how the sorites argument fails. We can reconstruct his reasoning in the following manner. Since (1) is true and (2) is indefinite, the premiss set is indefinite (since $T \wedge I$ yields I in $K_3$ ). (3), Tye upholds, is unquestionably false. Hence the conditional underlying the argument is false ($I \rightarrow F$ gives F). So the argument cannot be valid. Then the sorites paradox cannot be treated as a genuine paradox as neither the premiss set nor the reasoning process is unexceptionable.

At this point Tye rejects the possibility of a sorites paradox at the metalinguistic level. The sorites paradox, as we have stated it, condenses ten thousand application of U.I. and M.P. Naturally in (2), n ranges from 0 to 9999. Let us name these instantiations $M_0$, $M_1$, . . ., $M_{9999}$. Since $M_{9999}$ is indisputably false, there must be some statement $M_k$ which is true but $M_{k+1}$ is not true. So we must admit that there is a sharp transition from the true statement in the chain to the non-true statements.

Tye proposes to solve the meta-level sorites in the same way as the object level one. He rightly points out that as we cannot know exactly at which stage the embedded statements become indefinite, it is not possible for us to locate the exact M which first ceases to be true though we cannot but admit that $M_0$ is true, so is $M_1$, $M_{7500}$ may not be true and $M_{9999}$ is definitely false. So the statement

(4) It is not the case that, for some k, there is a statement $M_k$ such that $M_k$ is true but $M_{k+1}$ is not true

may be indefinite. Consequently

(5) For some k, there is a statement $M_k$ such that $M_k$ is true and $M_{k+1}$ is not true

will also be indefinite. Hence the meta-level sorites will fail. But at the same time this solution will commit us to the view that 'is true' is a vague predicate like 'is bald' and we cannot drive a clean wedge between true and not true. Tye is willing to admit not only second order vagueness but also still higher order vagueness. He realizes that to accommodate higher order vagueness he will have to extend his 3-valued logic to more than 3-valued logic. For, the moment he allows us to say

It is indefinite that $M_k$ is neither true nor false (i.e. indefinite)

he gets committed to a fourth truth value indefinitely indefinite. Tye does not envisage any logical difficulty here for both Kleene's strong 3-valued system as well as his adaptation of Kleene permit n-valued extensions where $n > 3$.

Tye's solution has some merits. It is comparatively simple and gives due attention to the vagueness of the central notion involved in the sorites. Yet a few worries continue to nag me. Tye admits that the conclusion of the sorites is derived by ten thousand applications of U.I. and M.P. The first few applications of U.I. do not make (2) indefinite. So M.P. smoothly goes through since the premiss set remains true. But at a later stage we realize that we have arrived at a borderline case of bald, i.e. the number assigned to n at that stage will make (2) indefinite though we do not know for certain which step first leads to indefiniteness. Now, in a sorites argument, we know, the first premiss of every successive argument is the same as the conclusion of the immediately preceding argument in the chain derived by M.P. If M.P. is truth-preserving then how can we at all arrive at an indefinite premiss given that at the starting point both (1) and (2) are true?

One possible way out may be not merely to follow the argument chain but check at each assignment whether the number assigned to n still makes the man undoubtedly bald or makes him a doubtful instance of baldness. Then in spite of our not being able to identify the first doubtful case we may declare (2) to be indefinite under some assignment of n. But now we start facing too many problems like, can we still apply M.P.? Perhaps we might apply a weaker form of M.P. When the premiss set is indefinite, M.P. may turn out to be just a *quasi-tautology*. Here we may raise similar questions once again. If M.P. is truth-preserving then how can we at all arrive at a false conclusion? Modus ponens as a quasi-valid argument form can at best yield an indefinite conclusion, not a false one.

Besides, people might have reservations against acknowledging 'true' as vague. Even if we concede this point and consider true to be vaguely vague, then we have no reason not to admit predications that are vaguely vaguely vague and so on. But need we proceed *ad infinitum*? What will constitute the legitimate stopping place? If Tye says that there are fringes within fringes and all instances of a vague predicate are affected by vagueness of different order excepting the limiting cases, then that will amount to giving up the notion of discrete predication. Actually Tye by his semantics, his theory of vague objects and admitted hierarchies of vagueness are hinting towards continuous predication but he has never made this tacit bias explicit. Nor is his logic commensurate with this position.

Tye's solution, therefore, fails to satisfy us and we are left with the task of exploring alternative avenues. The supervaluational approach is one such alternative.

## 5.4 THE SUPERVALUATIONAL SOLUTION

We have already discussed in some details the supervaluational semantics in the previous chapter. So here we shall recapitulate only the characteristic features of supervaluation. A supervaluationist like Kit Fine thinks that his approach is superior to other alternative approaches for supervaluation alone can formulate 'the correct logic of vagueness'. This superiority claim has been justified on the ground that supervaluation can account for vagueness retaining at the same time truths of classical logic.

The central notion on which Fine founded his supervaluational edifice was that of 'precisification' or 'refinement' or 'sharpening'. Fine explains precisification with the help of specification space. But we can try to understand it more informally. One predicate may be called a precisification of another if the former is at least as precise as the latter. The relation of 'being as precise as' is definitely reflexive, transitive and anti-symmetric. We can easily define the relation of 'being more precise than' in terms of 'being as precise as'. A precisification is appropriate in a given situation if it does not violate standard linguistic usage. If, for instance, someone precisifies 'tall' by meaning 'tiny' then in accordance with the standard English usage it will be improper. But if someone precisifies 'tall' by meaning 'taller than six feet' then the precisification is appropriate. Fine upholds some precisifications to be admissible but considers the notion of admissibility to be primitive. But Pinkal maintains that admissibility and appropriateness are matters of 'historical and social contingencies'[23] and depend to a large extent on speakers and times.

Fine has imposed five restrictions on precisification and its corresponding specification. These are the conditions of fidelity (F), stability (S), completeability (c), monotonicity (M) and resolution (R).[24] F states that all complete specifications must be classical. S requires that *definite* truth value assignments remain unchanged even after precisification. C states that any point can be extended to a complete point. M is the correlate of S and may be viewed as the counterpart of the Fregean principle of functionality. R enjoins that an indefinite atomic sentence can be made precise in either classical way.

On the basis of these conditions Fine defines his notion of truth. A vague sentence is true (or false) if and only if it is true (or false) at all complete extensions. A sentence is true *simpliciter* if and only if it is true at the appropriate specification point as well as at the complete point.

Let us now see how a solution to the sorites paradox is conceived by a supervaluationist. Like Tye, Fine also attempts to resolve the paradox by rejecting the second premiss. The second premiss can be shown to be false by showing that under a particular precisification/sharpening the antecedent of the premiss is true but the consequent is false. That is, 'bald' can be precisified in a way such that n number of hairs will make a man bald but (n+1) number of hairs will not. In Fine's own language, '. . . the second premiss is false. This is because a hair-splitting n exists for any complete and admissible specification of "is bald".'[25]

The conditional premiss of the paradox is not true, says a supervaluationist. To understand their position we have to recall to our minds their idea of extension. We already know what is meant by an extension of a predicate. A vague predicate, say, 'bald' can be precisified by redistributing its penumbral objects between its positive and negative extensions. Such redistribution may be effected in various different ways and each such redistribution will be considered a precisification of 'bald'.

Now let us suppose that a man with 2000 hairs on his head is a borderline bald. Then some precisification of 'bald' will make the proposition 'a man with 2000 hairs on his head is bald' true. Let us assume that by virtue of a particular precisification men with 2000 or lesser number of hairs on their heads fall in the positive extension and men with more than 2000 hairs on their heads fall in the negative extension of 'bald'. But there would be various other precisifications and the proposition may not be true under all precisifications and, therefore, according to the supervaluationist semantics the said proposition is not true in general. Now under this particular sharpening possession of 2000 hairs on the head will make a man bald but 2001 hairs will not. So at least under this precisification or extension of 'bald' the conditional sentence:

> If a man with n hairs on his head is bald, then a man with (n+1) hairs on his head is bald

turns out to be false. Since the conditional proposition is not true for this precisification, it is not true for all precisifications, hence it is not true. But wherever we draw the imaginary line persons with n number of hairs will fall in the positive extension of 'bald' after sharpening and those with n+1 number of hairs will fall in its negative extension. So the conditional, being false at all complete ways of making it precise, is indeed supervaluationally false.[26] Thus, claims the supervaluationist, the sorites chain can be blocked without harming the essence of vagueness.

But can the supervaluationist really justify this claim? Isn't he actually drawing a sharp borderline between 'bald' and 'non-bald' at some arbitrary specification point and thus going against our intuitive notion of vagueness? Isn't he giving up the principle of tolerance in the borderline area? The supervaluationist's attempt to justify his position by appealing to the concept of higher order vagueness will not hold water either. It is true, he admits borderline cases of a borderline bald and in the process makes precisification or sharpening itself a vague concept. But he has to admit at the same time that his solution to the paradox presupposes a shifting but sharp borderline for vague predicates. Besides, as Wright (1987) rightly points out, the notion of a sharpening inherits sorites susceptibility. The supervaluationist has set before him an impossible end to attain and that is to retain vagueness in the language and at the same time to precisify it. There is no doubt that their approach towards vagueness is rather simplistic. This should not come as a surprise at all. For the supervaluationists, after all, consider vagueness as a shortcoming of language. I, therefore, wholeheartedly agree with Putnam's observation.

> It seems to me that the whole 'speak as if every sentence had determinate truth value' approach to logic cannot be the right one when we wish to honestly face the fact that there are sentences which have no determinate truth value.[27]

### 5.5 THE INTUITIONISTIC SOLUTION

Hilary Putnam has offered a very simple solution to the sorites paradox relying on the intuitionistic logic. He has taken the same *bald man* version of the paradox, but has stated the premisses in the reverse order. For convenience of discussion we shall stick to our ordering. Putnam thinks that the vague predicates should receive the same treatment as that meted out to the undecidable predicates by the intuitionists. To an intuitionist, there may be two types of undecidable statements. A statement p is *simply* undecidable if there is a proof to show that there can be no mathematical construction in support of p.[28] A statement p is weakly undecidable in case there is no proof (as far as our knowledge goes) for p or against p. That is, p has not yet been proved or disproved.[29] The former statements, it goes without saying, are false but the latter are neither true nor false and, therefore, may be treated as analogues of vague predicates of natural language.

Putnam contends that the falsity of the conditional premiss is responsible for the falsity of the conclusion. But unlike the classical two-valued solution, here the denial of the conditional premiss will not amount to giving up the essential vague character of the predicate involved.

In intuitionistic logic ~ (n) Fn does not imply (∃n) ~ (Fn). Hence Putnam's acceptance of the proposition

(4) ~ (n) (If a man with n hairs is bald, then a man with (n+1) hairs is bald)

does not imply

(5) (∃n) ~ (If a man with n hairs is bald then a man with (n+1) hairs is bald)

In classical logic, (5) would have implied (5') : (∃n) (A man with n hairs is bald. A man with (n+1) hairs is not bald) [since ~ (p ⊃ q) ⊃ p & ~ q]

In intuitionist logic ~ (p ⊃ q) implies (~ ~p &~q). So following the intuitionist route from (5) we can at best reach to (5") that reads

(5") (∃n) (A man with n hairs is not not-bald. A man with (n+1) hairs is not bald).

And by virtue of the intuitionist rule of negation [ $p \supset \sim \sim p$ but $\sim \sim p \supset p$ ] we can deny that Putnam is not bald without admitting thereby that Putnam is bald.

Therefore, it does not follow that there is at least one number n such that a man with n number of hairs is bald but a man with (n + 1) number of hairs is not bald. Hence, there is no sharp cut-off point between bald and not-bald; consequently the predicate bald is not crisp.

Putnam's solution to the sorites paradox is undoubtedly simple, clever and elegant. We should have been satisfied with it but for a very *slight* semantic hitch.

The intuitionists are out and out constructionists. So they assert ~ p if and only if they have a construction such that if the construction p were carried out, it leads to a contradiction. Such an interpretation is easily intelligible when p is a mathematical proposition. But the intuitionist logicians intend to extend this interpretation to the negation of other propositions too. In that case, the natural language rendering of (4) says:

> It is absurd that for each and every number n, if a man with n hairs is bald then a man with (n + 1) hairs is bald.

Then acceptance of (4) is tantamount to discarding the principle of tolerance which is a necessary feature of sentences involving vague expressions.

## 5.6 PARIKH'S SOLUTION

We propose to discuss Parikh's solution at this juncture because it serves as a bridge between the first group of solutions (that doubt one or more of the premisses of the sorites argument) and the second group of solutions (that doubt the reasoning process involved in the sorites chain).

It is a peculiarity of Parikh's position that he has envisaged the possibility of the sorites type paradox not only at the phenomenal level but also at the level of predicates that correspond to physical properties. He realizes that a general solution will not be available for paradoxes occurring at different levels. He has, therefore, offered an intuitionistic solution (having some flavour of supervaluation) for the paradox occurring at the physical level but holds a long chain of reasoning responsible for the sorites paradox breaking out at the phenomenal level. To quote Parikh,

> The way of looking at vague predicates that I shall propose has elements of both the last mentioned proposals.[30]

The last mentioned proposal are those of Kit Fine and Lotfi Zadeh. In the same paper he also says quite emphatically,

> The proper logic for vague predicates is intuitionistic logic or something very like it. . . . However this approach doesn't work with vague predicates like 'phenomenal red' which are presumably defined in terms of direct observation.[31]

The paradox at the level of physical colour predicates arises due to inaccuracy of measurements. We have already stated this version of the paradox in Chapter 2. So here we shall present it in bare outlines and then pass on to Parikh's solution.

Though pure spectrum colours are available only under controlled conditions, Parikh states the paradox in terms of one-dimensional pure spectrum colours to avoid unnecessary complications. In a hypothetical situation, a physicist, having fixed the range of wavelengths in micromillimetres for a particular colour, say, red, is measuring the wavelength corresponding to the observed shades of red with a sensitive instrument and recording the measures. Theoretically it is possible to measure the wavelength almost accurately yet in actual circumstances some amount of deviation does take place and that is why every theory of measurement always keeps room for a little deviation. Suppose that the deviation allowed in this case is up to ± 0.4. So whenever the physicist is recording the measurement, he is recording a range of numbers and not only one single number. But in all these cases there is a belief that each measurement can be improved. And we can conceive a sorites paradox breaking out in this situation. Let us suppose that the physicist has taken two readings. Since the deviation allowed in this context is ± 0.4, if the second reading is found to be discrepant within the specified limit, then we take both the readings to be correct. Now suppose that the third reading once again slightly deviates from the second one but still remains within the limit of deviation and we must take this reading to be correct too. If however, the experiment is repeated a number of times, a sorites paradox can be plausibly construed.

To solve such paradoxes Parikh formulates his Theory of Vague Real Numbers (TVR in future). It might appear puzzling that Parikh is proposing TVR in the context of measurement. For, actual measurements are done in terms of rational numbers. Parikh's reason for taking up real numbers are two-fold: (*i*) Parikh, we have seen, has given a representation of vague predicates in terms of topologically connected spaces and the real numbers are uniquely ordered Archimidean fields which are topologically connected. (*ii*) Ideal measurements can be expressed in terms of real numbers without any hassle.

Parikh has worked out TVR in considerable detail. We shall give a partial exposition of his position—only those definitions, proofs and lemmas which are absolutely necessary for understanding Parikh's solution to this particular version of the paradox.

Let us begin by considering three measurements of a physical property corresponding to the predicate of physical red. The first measurement gives us the open interval (5.9, 6.3), the second one gives (6.4, 6.6) and the third gives (6.1 and 6.3). The first two intervals are disjoint, therefore, incompatible and unequal. But the first and the third are overlapping and so are not unequal. But we cannot uphold for that reason, says Parikh, that the first and the third measurements are equal. So here we have to deal with unequal relations. This relation is a much weaker relation than equality as the former is reflexive, symmetric but not transitive. In TVR Parikh incorporates a weaker relation of transitivity and hopes to solve the problems of measurement with the help of it.

Let us now take a conducted tour of the land of vague reals.[32]

*Definition 4.1*

A vague real number ($V_r$) is a pair (a, b) where a, b are rationals and a < b.

*Definition 4.2*

(a, b) < (c, d) iff, b < c

(a, b) ≠ (c, d) iff, (a, b) < (c, d) or

(c, d) < (a, b)

(a, b) ≈ (c, d) iff, it is not the case that

(a, b) ≠ (c, d). So ≈ means not unequal. But ≈ is not identical with equality for, it is reflexive and symmetric but not transitive. This definition of ≈ reminds us of the intuitionistic negation where ~ ~ p ≠ p.

*Definition 4.3*

(*i*) (a, b) + (c, d) = (a + c, b + d)
(a, b) – (c, d) = (a – d, b –.c)

(*ii*) $(a, b)^{-1} = (b^{-1}, a^{-1})$ if (a, b) have the same sign . = is undefined otherwise.

(*iii*) (a, b) . (c, d) = (ac, bd) if a, b, c, d are all positive.
If a, b, c, d are not all positive then (a, b), (c, d) = (e, f) where e = min (ac, ad, bc, bd) and f = max (ac, ad, bc, bd)

(*iv*) (a, b) ≤ (c, d) iff c ≤ a ≤ b ≤ d and (a, b) will be called *a refinement of* (c, d). If c < a < b < d then (a, b) will be a *proper refinement of* (c, d) and it may be designated as (a, b) ∝ (c, d).

Now we shall define two languages L and L' a la Parikh.

*The language L*

| | | |
|---|---|---|
| Constants | : | for the vague reals – (a, b), (c, d) etc. |
| Functions | : | +, ., –, $^{-1}$. |
| Predicate | : | < (to be interpreted as in definition 4.2) |

No equality symbol has been taken. So $\alpha \neq \beta$ will mean $(\alpha < \beta) \vee (\beta < \alpha)$, i.e. [ (a, b) < (c, d) ∨ (c, d) < (a, b) ]

Logical symbols : $\rightarrow, \vee, \sim \wedge, (\exists x)$.

In the language L' we have an additional negation symbol '$\neg$' which means 'not as far as we know'. Then $\sim (\exists x) \sim$ will be represented by $(\forall x)$ and $\neg (\exists x) \neg$ will be represented by (x).

*Definition4.4*
This definition gives us the meanings of the symbols. *Atomic wffs* are of the form $\alpha < \beta$; $\alpha, \beta$, being terms (closed).

(i) $\models \alpha < \beta$ iff (a, b) < (c, d), i.e. b < c where (a, b) and (c, d) are denotations of $\alpha, \beta$ respectively.

Non-atomic *wffs* are

(ii) $\models A \vee B$ iff $|= A$ or $|= B$

(iii) $A \wedge B$ iff $|= A$ and $|= B$.

(iv) $\models \neg A$ iff $\not\models A$, i.e. it is not the case that $\models A$ as far as we know.

(v) $(\exists x)$ A (x) iff there exists $\alpha$ such that $|= A (\alpha)$, i.e. loosely speaking, for some (a, b), A ( (a, b) ) holds. This is also the usual meaning of $\exists x$.

(vi) $\models \sim A$ iff there is no refinement A' of A such that A'.

*Explanation*: $|= A$ does not hold and for any refinements $\beta_1, \ldots, \beta_n$ of the terms $\alpha_1 \ldots\ldots, \alpha_n$ in A, $|= A \ (\beta_1, \ldots, \beta_n)$ does not hold.

*Example:* $\models \sim (\alpha_1 < \alpha_2)$ iff
(a, b) < (c, d) does not hold for any refinement (a', b') of (a, b) and (c', d') of (c, d), (a' b') < (c', d') does not hold.
This is possible only if (c, d) $\leq$ a

(vii) $\models B \rightarrow C$ iff there is no refinement $B' \rightarrow C'$ of $B \rightarrow C$ such that $|=$ B' and $\models \sim C'$, i.e. $|=$ B and $|= \sim$ C do not hold together and also for any refinement B' of B, C' of C, $\models$ B' and $|= \sim$ C' do not hold together, i.e. $|\neq B'$ and $|\neq C'$ and $|\neq (C')'$

(viii) $= (x)\ A(x)$, i.e. $|= \neg (\exists x) \neg A (x)$ iff
$\not\models \exists x \neg A(x)$ iff
there is no $\alpha$ such that $|= \neg A (\alpha)$ iff

there is no $\alpha$ such that $\not\models A(\alpha)$ iff
for all $\alpha$, $\models A(\alpha)$

(ix) $\models (\forall x) A(x)$ iff
$\models \sim (\exists x) \sim A(x)$ iff for all refinements A' of A $\not\models (\exists x) \sim A'(x)$ iff for all refinements A' of A, it is not the case that [there exists $\alpha$ such that $\models \sim A'(\alpha)$ ] iff for all refinements A' of A, it is not that [there exists $\alpha$ such that { there is no refinements $A''(\alpha)$ of $A'(\alpha)$ such that $\models A''(\alpha)$ } ] iff
[for all $\alpha$, there is some refinement $A''(\alpha)$ of $A'(\alpha)$ such that $\models A''(\alpha)$ ] iff
for all refinements A' of A for all $\alpha$ there exists a refinement A'' of A such that $\models A''(\alpha)$.

*Lemma 4.5:* If A is an L – formula and $\models$ A then $\models$ A' of A.

*Proof:* Suppose A be atomic, say $\alpha < \beta$ and let $\models \alpha < \beta$. Then by definition (a, b) < (c, d) or b < c holds, where (a, b) corresponds to $\alpha$ and (c, d) corresponds to $\beta$. Obviously for any refinement $\alpha' < \beta'$ of A, $\models \alpha' < \beta'$.

Now, apply induction on the complexity of A.

A is $B \wedge C$.

and refinement A' is $B' \wedge C'$

$\models B \wedge C$ implies $\models$ B and $\models$ C, and hence

$\models$ B' and $\models$ C' so $\models B' \wedge C'$.

A is $B \vee C$—exactly similar

A is $(\exists x)B$.

$\models$ A implies there is $\alpha$ such that $\models B(\alpha)$.

This implies $\models B'(\alpha)$

Now A' is $(\exists x)$ B' since $\models$ A' holds.

A is $\sim$ B

$\models$ A implies $\not\models$ B and $\not\models$ B'

Now, any refinement A' of A is $\sim$ B'. To prove $\models$ B' we have to show that $\not\models$ B'' for any refinement B'' of B'. A refinement B'' of B' being a refinement of B, the result holds, i.e. $\models$ A'.

The case for $\rightarrow$ is similar.

This proves the lemma.

An L–formula is called a permanent formula.

The binary relations $\propto$, $\underline{\propto}$ are not permanent and cannot be defined in L though they can be defined in L'.

*Lemma 4.6:* If $\not\models \sim$ A, then there is a refinement of A' of A such that $\models$ A'. $\not\models\sim$ A means that $\models$ A may not hold but for some refinement A', $\models$ A' should.

If $\models$ ~~A then $\models$ A' for some refinement of A

$\models$ ~~ A implies $\not\models\sim$ A

implies $\not\models$A"

i.e. $\models$ A' for some refinement of A and not for A.

This, according to Parikh, is the closest thing to the Law of Excluded Middle.

In TVR two distinct trends are easily noticeable. The logic of vague reals, especially, in its interpretation of negation is intuitionistic whereas in its notion of refinement it is distinctly reminiscent of Fine's supervaluational theory. The only difference between them is that as a result of precisification of Fine's system indeterminate values converge towards the limiting values, i.e. either towards 1 or towards 0 while refinement in Parikh's system leads to the closing of the gap between the end points of the value range so that we get a specific real number as the value of a given physical property corresponding to a vague physical predicate instead of a value range or a real interval.

Since in TVR no predicate has a classical negation, the sorites-type paradox does not arise here. Through TVR Parikh wants to establish that though no physical property is exactly measurable yet the difference between slightly varying measurements is not transitive; 'being not equal' being reflexive and symmetric but non-transitive. But TVR together with its logic is appropriate for situations where accurate measurement is at least theoretically possible. Parikh rules out the possibility of applying this technique to phenomenal predicates the quantities corresponding to which is never accurately measurable. The reason why vague predicates considered at the phenomenal level cannot be accommodated in a theory of the intuitionist type has been explained by Termini very lucidly.

Let us suppose that some questions can be answered at a certain level of accuracy at a certain time; if the accuracy can be in principle, improved, then it makes sense to leave questions unsettled. An answer which is neither clearly positive nor clearly negative at a certain level of accuracy can be, in fact, definitely answered. When, however, vague predicates are considered at a phenomenal level there is no future improvement to which one can refer and then it makes no sense to reserve judgement.[33]

It is clear, therefore, that Parikh readily admits to redistribution of the grey zone into positive and negative extensions of a predicate where refinement is at least theoretically possible and does not subscribe to 'as if every sentence has a classical truth value' stance of Kit Fine. But the question that remains unanswered is how to solve the paradox at the phenomenal level.

At the level of observational predicates Parikh is a Dummettean. He maintains with Dummett that the use of colour predicates in our language is sure to lead us to inconsistency. In practical life we can avoid inconsistencies since we do not want to discriminate between colours directly but do so usually with reference to objects possessing colours and colours could then easily be identified and differentiated with the help of the criterion of identification of objects. But when colour names are ascribed directly to colour patches and colour patches are qualitatively similar in all respects, then the sorites paradox creates problems.

We know that any solution to the sorites paradox must be able to explain the non-transitivity of non-discriminably differents. Parikh is well aware of that and he introduces the notion of chain-transitivity for that purpose.

A relation R is chain transitive if given $x_1 \ldots, x_n$ such that R holds between $x_i, x_{i+1}$ for $i = 1, 2, \ldots, n-1$, then R hold between $x_1$ and $x_n$. A transitive exact relation is chain-transitive. It cannot be transitive if it is not chain-transitive. But in the context of vague predicates the case is different; the relation involved may be (apparently) transitive and yet be clearly not chain-transitive.

The situation of colour discrimination then can be described in the following way. The more the distance between two colour patches is in a series, the more is the probability of distinguishing between them. On the basis of several trials a discrimination threshold could be defined. It would be the point where at least in fifty percent of trials a difference has been noticed and the point where difference has been noticed in most of the trials is called a jpd point (jpd stands for just perceptible difference).

Let us take three colours $c_1$, $c_2$, $c_3$ such that the possibility of distinguishing $c_1$ from $c_3$ is greater than that of $c_1$ from $c_2$ or $c_2$ from $c_3$. But the distinguishability relation even in the pair ($c_1$, $c_3$) is not strongly intransitive in the sense that $P(c_1, c_3) \geq 0.9$ whereas $P(c_1, c_2)$ and $P(c_2, c_3)$ is nearly 0. But this weak transitivity relation can be made strongly intransitive only in chains. One can have chain $c_1$, . . . $c_n$ such that $P(c_i , c_{i+1})$ is really small, say, 0.1 but $P(c_1, c_n)$ is 0.9.

It is this notion of chain-intransitivity that Parikh uses to solve the paradox at the phenomenal level. He reconstructs the paradox once again. Let $P_1 . . . . P_{1000}$ are colour patches arranged in a series. $P_1$ is red, $P_{1000}$ is not red. $P_i$ and $P_{i+1}$ cannot be distinguished. Let $\mathcal{S}$ be a formal system in the lower predicate calculus where there is only one unary predicate R and thousand constants, viz. $P_1, . . . .,$ $P_{1000}$. Let the system have the following axioms:

(*a*) $R(P_1)$
(*b*) $\neg R(P_{1000})$
(*c*) $R(P_i) \leftrightarrow R(P_{i+1})$ for $i = 1, . . . ., 999.$

In this system an explicit contradiction can be reached at 1001st step.

In our everyday life arguments are never that long. That is why vague predicates do not create practical problems. Due to chain intransitivity of vague relations, arguments involving vague predicates, if too long, lead to inconsistencies. But if an argument is 'reasonably short' then the paradox does not arise.

This solution, however, leaves one important question unanswered: how short is reasonably short?

Parikh in his treatment of vague predicates has combined elements of intuitionistic logic, supervaluational logic and fuzzy logic. His constructivist, finitist attitude is reflected in keeping the arguments involving vague predicates reasonably short. His interpretation of negation is intuitionistic. From the supervaluational approach of Kit Fine Parikh has derived his notion of refinement. He has also admitted a weak version of excluded middle with respect to a particular refinement. But as intuitionists do not accept the principle of excluded middle, he will not admit the tautologousness of $A \vee \sim A$ where A is a permanent well-formed formula. Consequently he cannot uphold that penumbral connections always hold.

In case of phenomenal properties Parikh has borrowed the concept of approximate reasoning and adopted an amended version of it. His notion of inference involving any vague predicate is approximate in the sense that depending on the accuracy of observation behind his axioms, he will consider his chain of reasoning intransitive. At the beginning of the chain it may be only weakly intransitive but as the chain proceeds it is sure to become strongly intransitive and that generates the paradox.

Like Zadeh he also wants to assign truth values to sentences between [0, 1]. But Zadeh's system is normal and truthfunctional. Parikh, on the other hand, disputes that the truthvalues of compound sentences can be recursively determined. He proposes to assign truth values to all sentences of the system simultaneously and in terms of certain inequalities. But the proposal does not appear satisfactory for then his system has got to be narrowly finite and closed. The law of excluded middle will be a casualty of this system too. Not only that, here penumbral connections will always fail to hold.

Before pointing out the drawbacks of Parikh's theory let me first offer the plaudits we owe to him. He is the only person to realize that the sorites paradox that may arise at the phenomenal level is different from the paradox arising at the level of physical predicates and therefore cannot be solved in the usual manner. Besides, his topological representation of vague predicates is also very effective in bringing the actual problem to focus. But Parikh has not developed fully the logic of vague sentences involving references to phenomenal properties. His treatment deviates from that of Zadeh in some respects but he has not given any justification for such deviations. For example, he has never explicitly stated what benefits will be gained if he makes his fuzzy logic non-truth-functional. We shall see before long that approximate reasoning procedure may have different forms. He has not given us any clue regarding what form his version of approximate reasoning takes. Moreover, we are at a loss when we try to guess what Parikh's overall logical framework will be. For intuitionistic supervaluational systems and intuitionistic fuzzy systems are plausible. But supervaluational and fuzzy approaches are not compatible and they cannot be combined without both the systems losing their identity.

We cannot wholeheartedly agree with Parikh for we have already seen in the previous section that intuitionistic approach is inadequate and fails to provide a satisfactory solution.

### 5.7 STRICT FINITISM, WANG'S PARADOX AND MICHAEL DUMMETT

Another school of thought that has taken vague expressions seriously and finds fault with the reasoning process involved in the sorites paradox is known as strict finitism. Strict finitism is basically a philosophy of mathematics which joins issue with both platonism and traditional constructivism. This position *vis-à-vis* sorites paradox has been discussed by Michael Dummett in connection with *Wang's Paradox*. So to understand and evaluate the strict finitist solution we should concentrate on Dummett's treatment of Wang's Paradox.

Wang's paradox, it has been mentioned, takes the following form:

(i) O is small
(ii) If n is small, n + 1 is small
(iii) Therefore, every number is small.

The paradoxical character of the above argument might not become apparent at once. If by 'small' we mean 'smaller than most natural numbers', then 'small' is applicable to every natural number since any natural number is smaller than infinitely many natural numbers.

But surely there will be no dearth of interpretation of 'small' which will make the premisses true and the conclusion false. For example, 'small' may be taken to mean 'n grains of sand is too few to make a heap' or 'It is possible in practice to represent any n in Arabic notation', etc. And wherever the paradox arises, the interpretation is found to be vague. But how does vagueness exactly contribute to the generation of the paradox? Dummett offers, at the outset, two usual alternative answers: (*a*) either the second premiss is false or (*b*) the process of reasoning is invalid in the presence of vague predicates.

The above argument form has been taken by Dummett as a mathematical induction where (*i*) constitutes the basis step, (*ii*) is the induction step and the process of inference involved is mathematical induction.

The induction step appears to be innocent for its rejection will imply that a number is small but its successor is not. This is not acceptable to our intuition. But the apparently absurd sentence which is said to follow from the rejection of induction step, viz. 'For some n, n is small but n + 1 is not' can be deduced only if we stick to the following rules of inference.

(a) The principle of bivalence which says that every sentence must be either true or false. This principle is responsible for our assertion to the effect that if the induction step is not true, then it is false,

(b) The principle of quantifier negation which says that the negation of 'For every n, A(n)' yields 'For some n, not A(n)',

(c) The rule that from the negation of, 'If A then B' one can infer the truth of A.

None of these principles is universally accepted. Dummett, for example, rejects the principle of bivalence though he accepts the principle of *tertium non datur*, i.e. no statement is neither true nor false. In presence of vagueness Dummett is willing to admit the principle of excluded middle only by introducing a new logical operator, 'It is definite that'. This operator is actually a modal operator the addition of which Dummett thinks will generate a modal logic weaker than $S_4$. But this is beside the point.

Let me be a little more explicit about Dummett's version of LEM. Consider, for example, the sentence 'This is orange'. If the corresponding shade is definitely orange then the given sentence is definitely true; if the corresponding shade is definitely not-orange then the given sentence is definitely false. But if the shade is a penumbral one then the sentence is neither definitely true nor definitely false. Even if the given shade is a borderline shade, it must be between orange and, say, yellow. With reference to this particular shade the sentence 'This shade is yellow' will be neither definitely true nor definitely false. But since the shade lies in the borderline of orange and yellow, the sentence 'This shade is either orange or yellow' will be definitely true though neither of its disjuncts is so. Moreover our understanding of colour concepts is such that no shade can be both orange and yellow, that is, orange and yellow are understood to be mutually exclusive. So yellow will imply 'not orange'. Therefore by substituting 'not orange' in the previous sentence we shall get 'This is either orange or not orange' and this disjunctive statement is definitely true. That is why Dummett writes, 'when vague sentences are involved, then we may legitimately assert a disjunctive statement without allowing that there is any determinate answer to the question which of the disjuncts is true.'[34]

But from this analysis it does not follow that every sentence is either simply true or simply false in presence of vague predicates.

The second and the third rules mentioned above will not be accepted by the intuitionists either. For the validity of the rules depend on the principle of double negation, or more specifically, on the validity of the formula $\sim\sim p = p$.

Granting the validity of the rules of classical logic, one cannot doubt the soundness of the induction step. So the burden of explaining the paradox lies on the process of induction or the underlying process of universal generalization. One may very plausibly conjecture that the process of universal generalization is not valid in the context of a vague predicate. So the passage from (*ii*) to (*iii*) is not warranted.

But the above conjecture is easily refutable and has, in fact, been refuted by Dummett. It is true that if induction or universal generalization fails in the presence of vague predicates, we cannot draw the conclusion, 'for every n, n is small', but we can easily establish any specification of the above general proposition given the premisses by the application of *modus ponens* in a chain. So universal instantiation and *modus ponens* will justify the deduction of the conclusion. Dummett is not ready to give up U.I. and M.P. as invalid since these rules of inference are constitutive of the meanings of 'every' and 'if'.

Now it appears that the only way to explain away the paradox is to uphold that though modus ponens in itself is a valid rule of inference yet when applied in chain it might yield an invalid conclusion. That amounts to calling in question the established notion of proof which is equally unacceptable to Dummett. But the strict finitist upholds this alternative by redefining the notion of proof. 'A proof', according to a strict finitist, 'is valid just in case it can in practice be recognized by us as valid; and, when it exceeds a certain length and complexity, that capacity fails.'[35] So the solution, if stated in a simplistic fashion, is this: the chain of modus ponens arguments involved in a sorites paradox is *too long* to be recognized as valid by us and hence to yield a valid conclusion.

It might be objected that this solution is too general, for any long chain of proof will be suspect to a strict finitist even if it has no connection with vagueness. Moreover, 'small' can always be given such interpretations that even following the strict finitist notion of proof will not enable one to avoid Wang's paradox. One such interpretation has been suggested by Dummett. The strict finitist understanding of any totality of natural numbers imposes at least three conditions on the totality: (1) it is closed under the successor operation; (2) for any number n belonging to the totality, there are n numbers smaller than it in the totality; and (3) it has an upper bound, i.e. a number, say, M can be cited which is large enough not to be a member of the totality. Let us now define a natural number n to be apodictic if it is possible for a proof (which we can recognize as such) to contain n number of steps. Now, suppose, 'n is small' means '(n+100) is apodictic.' If (M–100) which is also apodictic is considered to be the upper bound for the totality of apodictic numbers, then by application of a chain of modus ponens containing M–100 steps we shall arrive at the conclusion: 'M–100 is small' which is definitely false.

Against strict finitism Dummett has other reservations too. He finds strict finitism as a theory quite unsatisfactory since the strict finitist explanation of vague predicates in terms of queer totalities leads to incoherence.

Arithmetic acknowledges four distinct kinds of well-ordered totalities. A *strongly finite* totality has a last number, a *strongly infinite* totality is not finitely bounded. A *weakly* infinite totality has a well-ordering with no last member and a totality of some finite ordinal n is *weakly finite* when there is no nth member. Usually the possibility of there being a totality which is both strongly finite and strongly infinite or which is both weakly finite and weakly infinite has been ruled out. But to explain vagueness, we have to take into consideration a series which is both weakly finite and weakly infinite. As Dummett puts it,

> But to take vagueness seriously is to suppose that a vague expression may have a completely specific, albeit vague, sense; and therefore there will be a single specific totality which is the extension of a vague predicate . . . such totalities—those characterized as the extension

of vague predicates—can be both weakly finite and weakly infinite.[36]

For example, the totality of heartbeats of one's whole life is strongly finite since it has a last member that is immediately followed by death. The totality of natural numbers is strongly infinite since it is not finitely bounded. But the heartbeats of one's childhood can be shown to be both weakly infinite and weakly finite. This totality is weakly infinite; for every heartbeat in my childhood there is a successor (next heartbeat) in my childhood. Childhood and youth being continuous there is no last heartbeat of my childhood. This totality is at the same time weakly finite for there is a heartbeat, say, $(10^8 \times 25)$th one, which is distinctly recognized as not being a heartbeat of childhood. The tolerant nature of vague predicates makes the corresponding totalities weakly infinite. Still there is an upper bound beyond which the heartbeats cannot belong to the totality under discussion. So, though there is no last member, there exists an nth member which lies outside the given totality.

There are seeds of incoherence, it is obvious, inherent in the notion of a totality which is both weakly finite and weakly infinite. Dummett, therefore, is not very favourably disposed towards the philosophy of mathematics of strict finitism. Crispin Wright, on the other hand, maintains as against Dummett, that though the notion of a weakly finite and weakly infinite totality is incoherent yet such a totality is not unintelligible and therefore does not adversely affect the semantics, logic or mathematics.[37]

There is another consequence of the strict finitist notion of proof that continues to disturb us. We have already seen that no proof is accepted by a strict finitist unless it is actually surveyable. But isn't the predicate 'surveyable' itself a tolerant predicate? If tolerance lies at the root of the sorites paradox, then isn't there a chance of a paradox occurring at the meta-level too? Before we answer this question, we should explain how surveyability turns out to be tolerant.

In a sorites paradox from

Fa

by pairwise application of n pairwise steps of UI and MP we get

Fn

Here Fa is definitely true and Fn is palpably false.

It is, however, conceivable that the n step proof is not surveyable but there is a m<n and the proof up to the mth step is surveyable. We do not think that one pairwise application of MP and UI to the mth step can make the proof unsurveyable. But ultimately the proof becomes unsurveyable. This smooth passage from surveyability to unsurveyability is a mark of the predicate 'surveyable' being tolerant. Nevertheless Crispin Wright has shown that every surveyable proof does not necessarily lead to the sorites paradox.

So, despite Dummett's objections the strict finitist solution of solving the sorites paradox by shortening the chain of reasoning does not appear to be totally implausible. There is one important lacuna in the strict finitist position. It has failed to explain how in a long chain of reasoning the rules like MP, UI, etc., cease to be truth-preserving.

### 5.8 THE CONTEXT DEPENDENT SOLUTION

Wang's paradox has been given a totally different solution in terms of context dependence by Peter Bosch.[38] Vague expressions are context sensitive. These are usually defined and used in limited contexts. The sorites paradox can be avoided if we become aware of the fact that the same vague predicate stands for different concepts in different contexts. Bosch's solution depends on the Fregean thesis that no concept is vague. For each concept there is at least one context in which it is completely determined. The sorites paradox arises because we think that the vague predicate asserted in the first premiss can be used in the same sense all through the sorites chain independent of the context. When Bosch maintains that a vague predicate is context dependent he means two things:

(1) the predicate can be defined completely with respect to a context and (2) no predicate is applicable in the same sense in all contexts. Bosch formulates Wang's paradox as:

(i) 1 is a small number
(ii) If n is a small number, so is n+1
(iii) Any natural number $n \geq 1$ is small.

The root of the paradox lies in the assumption that 'is a small number' can be understood generally independent of the context. The second premiss gives rise to the paradox if it is applied recursively and recursion is warranted by the conceptual identity of small. This recursion can be stopped and the paradox can be bypassed if we construct specific context models for the application of 'small' in different premisses. Bosch, therefore, suggests that a predicate expression should be viewed as a function from context models to concepts and not as a constant. So, the context theoretic interpretation of the first premiss is: there is at least one context-model in respect of which the number 1 has a particular property which satisfies the predicate 'is a small number' for that context model.

Bosch has constructed a context model $CM_i$ that partially models the context that satisfies the premiss (1).

$$CM_i = \langle I, C, P \rangle$$
$$I = \{1\}$$
$$C = \{1^*\}$$
$$P = \{P_1\}$$
$$1^* = \langle \text{"1"}, \{P_1\} \rangle$$
$$P_1 = \langle \text{"is a small number"}, \{1\} \rangle$$

where I is a set of individuals, C is a set of characters and P is a set of properties. I contains the individual 1, C contains the character of 1, i.e. $1^*$ and P contains the property $P_1$. The character of an individual is represented by a pair of the name of the individual and the set of properties of the individual. The property $P_1$ is again a pair of the name of the property and the set of the extension of the property.

It has been assumed that in the second premiss too, the predicate 'is a small number' has been used in the same sense. So the antecedent of the second premiss which in this context is '1 is a small number' should be modelled by $CM_i$. But to accommodate the consequent, i.e. 1+1 or 2 is a small number we need to extend $CM_i$ to $CM_{i+1}$ which should include the individual 2 and its corresponding characters and properties. $CM_{i+1}$ would then take the following form and would be a partial model for the context covering both '1 is a small number' and '2 is a small number'.

$CM_{i+1} = \langle I, C, P \rangle$
$I = \{1, 2\}$
$C = \{1^*, 2^*\}$
$P = \{P_1\}$
$1^* = \langle \text{“1”}, \{P_1\} \rangle$
$2^* = \langle \text{“2”}, \{P_1\} \rangle$
$P_1 = \langle \text{“is a small number”}, \{1, 2\} \rangle$

$CM_{i+1}$ warrants the inference from '1 is a small number' to '2 is a small number'. Under similar reconstruction, any sentence of the form 'if n is a small number, then n+1 is a small number' will be true. Yet the sorites paradox will not be generated. For the second premiss cannot be applied recursively.

We have started with '1 is a small number' and have ended with '2 is a small number'. Now if we want to assert 'If 2 is a small number, so is 3', we shall have to construct another model for $CM_{i+1}$ will not be adequate for modelling this situation. Let us, therefore, construct a new model $CM_j$ to represent the context corresponding to '2 is a small number'.

$CM_j = \langle I, C, P \rangle$
$I = \{2\}$
$C = \{2^*\}$
$P = \{P_2\}$
$2^* = \langle \text{“2”}, \{P_2\} \rangle$
$P_2 = \langle \text{“is a small number”}, \{2\} \rangle$

This model like $CM_i$ can be extended to $CM_{j+1}$ to account for the consequent part of this particular instance of the second premiss.

$$
\begin{aligned}
CM_{j+1} = \ & \langle I, C, P\rangle \\
& I = \{2, 3\} \\
& C = \{2^*, 3^*\} \\
& P = \{P_2\} \\
& 2^* = \langle \text{“2”}, \{P_2\}\rangle \\
& 3^* = \langle \text{“3”}, \{P_2\}\rangle \\
& P_2 = \langle \text{“is a small number”}, \{2, 3\}\rangle
\end{aligned}
$$

It is obvious that we cannot simply move from $CM_{i+1}$ to $CM_j$. So we cannot insist that the property referred to by the predicate expression 'is a small number' remains the same in both contexts. By the models, it has been shown that the extension of 'is a small number' are different in two applications. In $CM_{i+1}$, the extension of the property is {1, 2} whereas in $CM_j$ it is {2}.

It may be objected that sometimes a predicate expression refers to the same property in different contexts. The above models will be inadequate in such a situation. Bosch does not find this objection formidable at all. He replies that when our knowledge of the context indicates a general context for several applications of the same predicate, we can, always construct a fuller context model by linking up models like $CM_i$, $CM_{i+1}$, $CM_j$, $CM_{j+1}$ and bringing all of them under the broader context. But as there is no such information contained in the premisses of the sorites paradox, it will not be legitimate to add this information generally in the context models of the premisses. And in absence of any such information, the second premiss will fail to apply recursively. In the language of Bosch,

> The crucial features of our reconstruction of the sorites-premisses then is, to sum up, that the two occurrences of the predicate 'is a small number' (or 'is a heap' or what not) in the second premiss must have the same property as their value (that is why the premiss is true); but on any new application of the second premiss to a particular number (or to any object that is a heap, for

> that matter) the property of being a small number (or a heap) that is at issue need not be identical to any other property of the same name that occurs in any other application of the premiss (that is why recursive application of the second premiss is excluded, and hence the paradox does not arise).[39]

Bosch's solution appears very effective on its own. But unfortunately Bosch's understanding of vagueness is not the same as ours. Bosch, like Frege, views vagueness as a result of incomplete definition and presumes that no concept is inherently incomplete. Incompletely defined concepts, only reflect our intellectual laziness. Bosch thinks that we usually try to cover up our epistemic inadequacy by using linguistic hedges like 'not really' 'hardly', etc., and 'hedges are appropriate when we cannot be bothered to get a full picture of the relevant context model.'[40] But, in our view, not all concepts can be completely defined. We are unable to specify contexts for essentially vague concepts however much we try to improve our knowledge. So Bosch's solution will be adequate and effective for those situations only where vagueness can be reduced to context dependence. The sorites paradox arising from the use of essentially vague predicates will remain unsolved.

The context dependent solution to the sorites paradox has been endorsed by Goldstein too.[41] While providing solution to the Mona Lisa version of the paradox, Goldstein draws a distinction between a logical proof and an informal piece of reasoning following Gilbert Harman.[42] A logical proof is a mathematical structure where interpretations of the terms are fixed but a piece of reasoning with vague predicates is context-sensitive. A logical proof is not affected by places, times, persons or neuronal discharges but a reasoning process is. Therefore with change in context we are justified in changing our beliefs concerning a particular state of affairs. Hence there is nothing to wonder if some one declares a particular reproduction of the Mona Lisa beautiful but finds another, almost indistinguishable, reproduction of the same ugly. This contingency cannot be taken care of by logic. A logical proof never tells us anything about the acceptability or unacceptability of a sentence involved in the proof, for acceptability varies depending on persons, time, speaker's frame of mind and many other contextual parameters. The sorites paradox arises because we confuse between a logical proof and a piece of reasoning. If we are concerned about the validity of an argument then we should see the relations between propositional forms. If on the other hand, we are concerned with a piece of reasoning expressed in imprecise natural language then the contexts of asserting premisses and the conclusion should be looked into. If due to change in context the reasoner changes his mind and asserts in the conclusion something not in consonance with what is involved in asserting the premisses, or holds a sentence false which he previously admitted to be true, 'this is not tantamount to his espousing a contradiction, in defiance of classical logic'.[43] So concludes Goldstein,

> These paradoxes are not paradoxical, for they do not lead to contradictions nor to the unacceptable conclusions that certain theorists have embraced. They serve only to illustrate a difference between natural languages and those artificial languages where the extensions of terms are not measured by the soft rubber rules of observation, but are fixed by *fiat.*[44]

Instead of providing a solution to the genuine paradox. Goldstein explains away the paradox itself. His outlook is, there is nothing unsatisfactory about this situation. Vague expressions are such that arguments involving vague expressions should not have any mechanical decision procedure. But in absence of any algorithm our natural language will not ever be machine-translatable. Not only that, there is every possibility of human communication going haywire. So it is always preferable to fall back on a logical solution—if such a solution is available.

## 5.9 FUZZY LOGIC AND APPROXIMATE REASONING

The fuzzy logicians, viz. Zadeh, Gaines[45] and Goguen[46] have provided logical solutions to the sorites paradox which have certain merits. I have shown in 4.6 how admission of degree of membership and continuous predication has enabled the fuzzy logicians to represent vagueness in terms of fuzzy set without harming its essence in any way. This gives us the confidence that a fuzzy logical solution to sorites paradox will not go against our intuitive understanding of vagueness. Secondly, the fuzzy logicians are very much aware of the context-sensitive nature of vague predicates. So, while assigning degree of membership to all objects falling under a particular vague concept, or specifying the truth-grade for a particular vague sentence, they always give proper attention to the contextual factors. Thirdly, it has been shown by Lakoff[47] and others that human beings really think through fuzzy concepts. Therefore, laying bare the rules of fuzzy reasoning amounts to laying bare the process of human thought. Those who are interested in mind simulation techniques find fuzzy logical tools and fuzzy logical ways of handling the paradoxical situations very effective. This type of solution to the sorites paradox can be fed to the computers with the expectation that the machine will yield correct results.

The fuzzy logicians have attempted to solve the sorites paradox by showing how M.P. fails to preserve truth in a long chain of reasoning and thus yields a false conclusion starting from a true premiss. Another variant of this solution is Zadeh's technique of approximate reasoning. Both these solutions possess the general feature of questioning the reasoning procedure underlying the sorites paradox so the fuzzy logical solutions belong to the second group of solutions mentioned earlier.

In section 4.6 we have discussed how M.P. can be taken to be truth-preserving even in a fuzzy situation. Modus poenens was generalized as

$$\vdash_{\alpha} p, \vdash p \rightarrow q / \therefore \vdash_{\alpha} q.$$

That is, if p is true at least to the degree $\alpha$ and $p \rightarrow q$ is true, q is true at least to the degree $\alpha$.

But in fuzzy situations it might be the case that $p \rightarrow q$ does not get the value 1. In order to explain these cases the fuzzy logicians have given alternative definitions of implication.

If $c = a \supset b$, then
(1) $c = \min(1, 1-a+b)$.
(2) $c = \min(1, b/a)$.

(1) is the accepted form of implication in many-valued logics as well as in probability logic and (2) is the definition of implication in conditional probability logic. Gaines has shown that both these forms of implication can explain the situation where $c \neq 1$, but $c = 1 - e$ with the help of the following derivations.

(1) $c = \min(1, 1-a+b)$
$= \max(a-b)$
or $c \geq (a-b)$
or $b \geq (a-c)$
or $b \geq (a-(1-e))$ .... (3)

Let us now consider (2)

$c = \min(1, b/a)$
$c \neq 1$ (hypothesis)
$\therefore c = \min b/a$
or $c \leq b/a$
or $b \geq a \times c$
or $b \geq (a \times (1-e)$, $\because c = 1 - e$ .... (4)

Gaines uses both (3) and (4) as the definitions of implication. His formulation of the sorites paradox is as follows:

Let *hair n* designate a person with n hairs on his head who has a degree of membership bald hair n to the fuzzy set of bald people.

The first premiss of the paradoxical argument says that there is at least one such bald man, i.e.

$B \neq \emptyset$ .... (5)

The second premiss states that a man with one more hair than a bald man is bald too. That is,

$\forall n$ (bald $hair_{n-1}$ is bald) $\supset$ (hair n is bald) .... (6)

Then by the classical rule of implication, we have

$\forall n$, bald hair $_n \geq$ bald $hair_{n-1}$ .... (7)

which yields by induction on n

$\forall n$, hair $_n \geq$ bald $hair_0$ .... (8)

That means a man with an arbitrary large number of hair is as bald as the man with no hair.

According to the fuzzy logicians derivation of (7) from (6) is not legitimate. This step would have been valid if (6) had the value 1. But in the context of a vague predicate, there is no guarantee that the conditional premiss will get the value 1, especially, when the vague sentence contains reference to the borderline cases of a particular vague expression. So, '$\supset$' in (6) should be taken in the sense of (3) or (4). By applying (3) or (4) to (6) then we shall get,

$\forall n$, bald $hair_n \geq$ bald $hair_{n-1}-e$ .... (9)

or,

$\forall n$, bald hair $_n \geq$ bald $hair_{n-1} \times (1-e)$ .... (10)

Then by induction we get either

$\forall n$, bald $hair_n \geq$ bald $hair_0-n \times e$ .... (11)

or,

$\forall n$, bad hair n $\geq$ bald $hair_0 \times (1-e)^n$ .... (12)

Thus in a long chain of reasoning, each step lowers our estimate of truth value of the result. That is why, starting from the true premiss by repeated application of logical rules we are arriving at a falsehood. This explains the sorites argument. According to Gaines the reasoning procedure underlying the argument comprising of steps 6, 9, . . ., 11 or 6, 10, . . . 12, is not invalid. Only the peculiar nature of the conditional premiss compels us to give up the truth-preserving character of M.P. In the above example the truth loss in each application of M.P. is to the tune of e, here e is an arbitrarily small quantity. Let us try to elucidate the process with a concrete example. Suppose we are dealing with the following conditional:

> If a man with 2000 hairs on his head is bald, then a man with (2000+1) hairs is bald.

Let us suppose further that the antecedent is nearly true, say, to the extent 0.96 and consequent is slightly less true, say, to the degree 0.95. The conditional, therefore, cannot be wholly true but very close to truth. So let the conditional have the value 0.99. Now if we apply modus ponens, then we get a conclusion having the value 0.95. In the next argument in the chain this sentence with the degree of truth 0.95 will be used as the antecedent of the premiss and the value of the conclusion will get slightly lower. The leakage of truth is very small for each application of M.P. but when the chain of argument is long enough, the truth value of the conclusion ultimately peters out to near zero.

Here, we have two important observations to make

(1) We have interpreted '$\wedge$' involved in the M.P. $(P \wedge (p \rightarrow q) \rightarrow q)$ as the product operation following Goguen but some fuzzy logicians want to interpret it as the 'Min.'

(2) The way we have defined implication, our chain of argument will never yield exact zero but the final conclusion will come very close to zero. That is, however, sufficient for resolving the paradox.

Gunter Todt[48] has revised the formulation of implication and modus ponens to show that the sorites chain yields a conclusion having the degree of truth 0 (not near 0) even when the chain is quite short. Todt has actually given two definitions of implication. The first definition is:

(i) $$[\alpha \rightarrow \beta] = \begin{cases} 1 & \text{if } |\alpha| \leq |\beta| \\ 1-(1-|\beta|)(|\alpha|-|\beta|) & \text{else.} \end{cases}$$

This subtraction-based implication, thinks Todt, is better suited for fuzzy logic than the versions of Gaines and Goguen. It follows from the definition that if $|\alpha| = 1$ or nearly 1, the value of the implication gets lowered the smaller $|\beta|$ is, and if $|\alpha| = 0$ or nearly 0, then the value of implication is 1 or nearly 1.

Todt's second definition of implication is:

$$\text{(ii)} \quad |\alpha - \beta| = \begin{cases} 1 & \text{if } |\alpha| \leq |\beta| \\ 1 - (|\alpha| - |\beta|) & \text{else.} \end{cases}$$

(i) has a further correction factor but (ii) will do in simple cases.

If $|(\alpha \to \beta)| < 1$, then

$|(\alpha \to \beta)| = (1 - |\alpha| + |\beta|)$

$\therefore |\beta| = |(\alpha \to \beta)| + |\alpha| - 1$

$\quad = |\alpha| + |(\alpha \to \beta)|$

But if $|(\alpha \to \beta)| = 1$, then

$\beta \geq \alpha$.

Next Todt offers his rule of modus ponens.

$$\begin{array}{ll} \alpha & i \\ \alpha \to \beta & j \\ \hline \beta & i + j - 1 \end{array}$$

If we apply this revised rule of M.P. in a chain, we can get a conclusion which is exactly equal to 0. The chain can be constructed as follows:

$$\begin{array}{ll} \alpha_1 & i \\ \alpha_1 \to \alpha_2 & j_1 \\ \hline \alpha_2 & i + j_1 - 1 \\ \alpha_2 \to \alpha_3 & j_2 \\ \hline \alpha_3 & i + j_1 + j_2 - 2 \\ \cdot & \cdot \\ \cdot & \cdot \\ \cdot & \cdot \\ \alpha_n \to \alpha_{n+1} & \cdot \\ \hline \alpha_{n+1} & i + \sum_{k=1}^{n} j_k^{\,-n} \end{array}$$

The value of $\alpha_{n+1}$ may be small though the values of $\alpha_1$ and $\alpha_k \rightarrow \alpha_{k+1}$ are close to zero. Take, for instance,

$$n = 99 \text{ and}$$

$$i = j_k = 0.99, \text{ then}$$

$$i + \sum_{k=1}^{n} j_k^{\ -n} = 0$$

Thus the chain of reasoning at the final step yields 0 and the chain need not always be too long. If '∧' in the M.P. rule is interpreted as the min value of the premisses, then depending on the difference between the values of α and β a pretty short chain will give 0.

The fuzzy logicians are not the only people who realize that in order to solve the sorites paradox, a revised rule of M.P. is required. Many other logicians of different persuasions also have offered quasi-transitive implications to solve the sorites paradox.[49] We have repeatedly pointed out that non-transitivity of non-discriminable differences are at the root of the sorites paradox. In the classical M.P. rule implication is always transitive. So if any implication can at all resolve the paradox then it has got to be quasi-transitive. One almost similar solution to that of the fuzzy logicians has been offered by Myers. We shall discuss Myers' solution right now.

Myers designates quasi-implication by 'Δ' and wants us to replace all occurrences of '⊃' or '→' in the sorites chain by 'Δ' to get rid of the paradox. He gives the following rules of value assignment for his logical system with the quasi-transitive implication.

(i) Each statement p, q, r, etc., is assigned both a verity value, e.g. V(p) and an error value like E(p).

(ii) Both the verity value and the error value lies between 0 and 1 such that $0 \leq V(p) \leq 1$ and $0 \leq E(p) \leq 1$.

(iii) $E(p) = 1 - V(p)$

(iv) If a sorites has n hypothetical premisses, then we can have a range of n+1 verity values and n+1 error values and each value is a multiple of 1/n.

(v) If $V(p) \geq V(q)$ then $V(p \Delta q) = 1 + V(q) - V(p)$

(vi) If $V(p) < V(q)$ then $V(p \Delta q) = 1 - V(q) + V(p)$

(vii) $V(\sim p) = E(p)$

(viii) $V(p \vee q) = \text{Max}\{V(p), V(q)\}$

(ix) $V(p \wedge q) = \text{Min}\{V(p), V(q)\}$

(x) $V(S_k) = (n - k+1)/n$, $S_k$ being the kth step in the argument chain consisting of n steps.

Given the above rules of valuation, the error value of quasi-implication linking the first step with the final step will be the following equation.

$$E(S_1 \Delta S_n) = \sum_{k-1}^{n-1} E(S_k \Delta S_{k+1})$$

That means the error value of the final step is the sum of error values of the mediating steps. It follows from the definition of relation between error value and verity value given in (*iii*) that the verity value decreases as the error value increases. So after a few successive applications of the revised rule of M.P., $V(S_k \Delta S_{k+1})$ will be less than 0.5. Myers stipulates that quasi-transitivity of implication fails where $V(S_k \Delta S_{k+1}) < 0.5$. Then $S_1$ would not entail $S_n$ and the paradox does not arise.

The solution of Myers and that of Gaines and Goguen do not differ in spirit. The only difference is that the fuzzy logicians do not always insist on the cut-off point of 0.5. They rather explain the complete story of falling down the sliding slope.

The most effective solution so far provided to the sorites paradox is by Zadeh.[51] It is his process of approximate reasoning that can neutralize the paradoxical effect of a sorites argument. By approximate or fuzzy reasoning is meant the process or processes by which a possibly imprecise conclusion is deduced from a collection of imprecise premisses. In order to perform approximate reasoning we need three different types of rules:

(1) Translation Rules
(2) Modifier Rules
(3) Rules of Inference.

*Translation Rules*
By translation rule is meant a set of rules that yield the translation of modified composite proposition from the translations of its constituents. There are four types of translation rules.

(i) *Modifier translation rules* for simple propositions: Given the proposition p = 'x is A' such that $\pi x = \mu_A$ find $\pi' x = \mu_A{}^*$ related to 'X is mA' where m is a modifier such as 'very', 'more or less', 'sort of', etc.

(ii) *Composition rules* pertain to the translation of a proposition p that is a composition of proposition q and r, such as conjunction, disjunction, implication, etc.

(a) The rule of implied conjunction or maximal restriction: Given x is P, y is Q we have x is P *and* y is Q ⇒ (x, y) is P × Q. If x = y, x is P *and* x is Q ⇒ x is P ∩ Q.

(b) The rule of disjunction: x is P *or* y is Q → (x, y) is $\overline{P} + \overline{Q}$ = (x, y) is ( P' × Q')', P' and Q' are the complements of P and Q and + denotes the union.

(c) *Maximin rule* of conditional propositions: If x is P then y is Q else y is S → (x, y) is P × Q + P' × S.
If x is P then y is Q → (x, y) is (P × Q) + P' × V where V is the interval in which the compatibility functions are mapped.

(d) *Arithmetic rule* of conditional propositions: If x is P then y is Q else y is S is defined as ( (P × V) ⊖ V × Q) + (P' × V ⊖ V × S) )'. Equivalently, (x, y) is $(\overline{P'} + \overline{Q}) \cap \overline{P} \oplus \overline{Q}$. And, If x is P then y is Q → (x, y ) is $\overline{P'} + \overline{Q}$). This is an adaptation to fuzzy sets of $L_{\Delta 1}$ material implication, viz. $V(r \rightarrow S) = \mathrm{Min}\,(1, 1 - V(r) + V(S))$

(e) *Quantification rules* work on propositions of the form p ≡ 'Fx are A' where F is a fuzzy quantifier (e.g. 'most', 'many', 'few', 'some' . . . ). F is a fuzzy set on [0. 1] usually.

(f) *Qualification rules:* One such rule is that of *truth qualification.* It may be stated as (x is Q) is $\tau \Rightarrow$ x is $\mu_Q^{-1}$ o $\tau$, where $\tau$ is a linguistic truth value (e.g. true, very true, false, more or less true, etc.); $\mu_Q^{-1}$ is a relation inverse to the compatibility function of A, a fuzzy set, and $\mu_Q^{-1}$ o $\tau$ is the composition of the non-fuzzy relation $\mu_Q^{-1}$ with the u-nary fuzzy relation $\tau$.

*Modifier Rules*

(i) *Semantic equivalence and entailment:* p and q are said to be semantically equivalent iff $\pi$ p = $\pi$ q and is denoted by p $\Leftrightarrow$ q; p semantically entails q is denoted by p $\Rightarrow$ q, p $\Rightarrow$ q iff $\pi$ p $\pi$ q

(ii) *Modifier rules for propositions:* If m is a modifier and p is a proposition, then mp is semantically equivalent to the proposition that results from applying m to the possibility distribution induced by p. For example, let m = very then very (x is A and y is B) $\Leftrightarrow$ 'x is very A and y is very B'. $\neg \forall x\, P(x) \Leftrightarrow \exists x \neg P(x)$

Not ('x is A is $\tau$') $\Leftrightarrow$ 'x is A is not true', etc.

*Rules of Inference*

(i) *Entailment principle* asserts that from any proposition p, we can infer a proposition q, if the possibility distribution induced by p is contained in the possibility distribution induced by q, e.g. from p = 'x is very large' we can infer q = 'x is large'.

(ii) *Generalized modus ponens or compositional M.P.*

x is P

If x is Q then y is S

---

y is P o $\overline{Q'}$+ $\overline{S}$

where '—' denotes cylindrical extension, '⊕' the bounded sum, ''' the operation of complementation and 'o' composition function. The definitions of all these operations are given below.

Alternatively,

x is P

If x is Q then y is S

---

y is P o $(Q \times S + \overline{Q}')$

Here $\overline{Q}'$, = def. $Q' \times V$.
It is to be noted that if P = Q and P and S are non-fuzzy, both formulations reduce to classical *modus ponens.*

In order to understand the process of approximate reasoning we have to learn a few other definitions:

(a) *Bounded sum:* This operator is defined as: $\forall x \in X$, $\mu_A \oplus \mu_B (x) = \min (1, \mu_A (x) + \mu_B (x))$

(b) *Bounded difference:* $A \ominus B$ is the fuzzy set of elements that belong to A more than to B. Bounded difference is defined as follows:

$\forall x \in X, \mu_{A \ominus B} = \max (0, \mu_A (x) - \mu_B (x))$.

The complement of any fuzzy set can be defined in terms of bounded difference,

$A' = X \ominus A$.

(c) *Extension principle*

*Definition*: Let X be a cartesian product of universes $X = X_1 \times X_2 \times \ldots\ldots \times X_n$ and $A_1, \ldots\ldots A_r$ be r fuzzy sets in $X_1, \ldots\ldots, X_r$ respectively. The cartesian product of $A_1, \ldots\ldots, A_r$ is defined as

$$A_1 \times \ldots \times A_r = \int_{x_1 \times \ldots \times x_r} \min\left(\mu_{A_1}(x_1), \ldots, \mu_{A_r}(x_r)\right) / (x_1, \ldots, x_r)$$

Let f be a mapping from $X_1 \times \ldots\ldots \times X_r$ to a universe y such that $y = f(X_1, \ldots\ldots\ldots, X_r)$.

$$\text{Then } \mu_B(y) = \sup_{\substack{x_1,\ldots,x_r \\ y = f(x_1,\ldots,x_r)}} \min\left(\mu_{A_1}(x_1),\ldots,\mu_{A_r}(x_r)\right)$$

$\mu_B(y) = 0$ if $f^{-1}(y) = \emptyset$ where $f^{-1}(y)$ is the inverse image of y.]

*Fuzzy Relations*

An n-ary fuzzy relation R in $U_1 \times \ldots \times U_n$ is a fuzzy subset of $U_1 \times \ldots \times U_n$. *The Projection of R* on $U_{i_1} \times \ldots \times U_{i_k}$ where $(i_1, \ldots, i_k)$ is a subsequence of $(1, \ldots, n)$, is a relation in $U_{i_1} \times \ldots \times U_{i_k}$ defined by Proj R on $U_{i_1} \times \ldots \times U_{i_k}$

$$\triangleq \int_{U_{i_1} \times \ldots \times U_{i_k}} V U_{j_1},\ldots,U_{j_l}\ \mu_R(U_1,\ldots,U_n)/(U_1,\ldots,U_n)$$

where $(j_1, \ldots, j_l)$ is the sequence complementary to $(i_1, \ldots, i_k)$ and $V\,U_j$ denotes the supremum over $U_{j_1} \times \ldots \times U_{j_l}$.

If R is a fuzzy subset of $U_{i_1}, \ldots U_{i_k}$, then its *cylindrical extension* in $U_1 \times \ldots \times U_n$ is a fuzzy subset of $U_1 \times \ldots \times U_n$ defined by

$$\overline{R} = \int_{U_1 \times \ldots \times U_k} \mu_R(U_{i_1},\ldots,U_{i_k})/(U_1,\ldots,U_n)$$

In terms of their cylindrical extensions, the *composition* of two binary relations R and S (in $U_1 \times U_2$ and $U_2 \times U_3$ respectively) is expressed by R o S = Proj ( $\overline{R} \cap \overline{S}$) on $U_1 \times U_3$, where $\overline{R}$ and $\overline{S}$ are the cylindrical extensions of R and S in $U_1 \times U_2 \times U_3$.

These complicated mathematical definitions can be clarified with the help of concrete examples.

Let U = 1+ 2+ 3+ 4.
P = Small $\triangleq$ 1/1 + 0.6/2 + 0.2/3
Large $\triangleq$ 0.2/2 + 0.6/3 + 1/4
Q = very large = .04/2 + .36/3 + 1/4

$$
\begin{aligned}
\text{Then}\quad P' &= 0/1 + 0.4/2 + 0.8/3 + 1/4\\
Q' &= 1/1 + .96/2 + .64/3 + 0/4.\\
(P' \times Q') &= 0/(1,1) + (1,2) + (1,3) + (1,4) + (2,4) +\\
&\quad (3,4) + (4,4) + 0.4/\ (2,1) + (2,2) + (2,3)\\
&\quad + 0.8/(3.1) + (3,\ 2) + .64/(3,3) + 1/(4,1)\\
&\quad + .96/(4,2) + .64/\ (4,3)\\
\therefore\ (P' \times Q')' &\quad 1/(1,1) + (1,\ 2) + (1,3) + (1,4) + (2,4) +\\
&\quad (3,\ 4) + (4,4) + 0.6/(2,1) + (2,2) + (2,3)\\
&\quad + 0.2/(3.1) + (3,\ 2) + .36/(3,\ 3) + (4,3) +\\
&\quad .04/(4,2) + 0/(4,1)
\end{aligned}
$$

$$
\begin{aligned}
\text{Let}\quad F &= .4a + .9b + d\\
G &= .6a + .5b
\end{aligned}
$$

Then

$$
\begin{aligned}
F \oplus G &= a + b + d\\
F \ominus G &= 0.4b + d\\
\text{Let}\quad P &= 0.6/2 + 1/3 + 0.5/4\\
Q &= 1/2 + 0.6/3 + .2/4\\
P' &= 1/1 + 0.4/2 + 0/3 + 0.5/4
\end{aligned}
$$

The next example is that of cylindrical extension. Given the universe U, we want to extend P' and Q to the domain U × U. Then,

| — = | | 1 | 2 | 3 | 4 |
|---|---|---|---|---|---|
| P' | 1 | 1 | 1 | 1 | 1 |
| | 2 | 0.4 | 0.4 | 0.4 | 0.4 |
| | 3 | 0 | 0 | 0 | 0 |
| | 4 | 0.5 | 0.5 | 0.5 | 0.5 |

| — = | | 1 | 2 | 3 | 4 |
|---|---|---|---|---|---|
| Q | 1 | 0 | 1 | 0.6 | 0.2 |
| | 2 | 0 | 1 | 0.6 | 0.2 |
| | 3 | 0 | 1 | 0.6 | 0.2 |
| | 4 | 0 | 1 | 0.6 | 0.2 |

Let us now consider the examples of approximate reasoning.

(1) Shefali is *tall.*
Shefali and Malini are *approximately equal in height.*
Malini is more or less *tall.*

(2) *Most* Swedes are *tall.*
Most tall Swedes are *blond.*
Karl is a Swede.

---

It is *very likely* that Karl is *tall* and it is more or less (very likely) that Karl is *blond.*

It is obvious that in both (1) and (2) truth values of the conclusions are lower than truth values of premisses. A few successive applications of *generalized M.P.*, mentioned above, in an argument chain will reach a conclusion having a truth value close to 0.

The general form of the first approximate reasoning is

(1) $x_1$ is tall.
(2) $x_1$ and $x_2$ are approximately equal in height.
∴ (3) $x_2$ is more or less tall.

In terms of fuzzy restriction (1) and (2) can be restated as

(1) R(u) = tall.
(2) R(u, v) = approximately equal in height.
∴ (3) R(v) = more or less tall.
Here R(v) = R(u) o R(u, v)

Now the compositional rule of inference is:

$$\mu_{AOB} = \bigvee_{U} (\mu_A(u) \wedge \mu_B(u, v)$$
$$= \max_{\mu \in U} [\min(\mu_A(u), \mu_B(u, v)]$$

This is actually a variation on generalized M.P.

Let $U$ = 1+ 2+ 3+ 4 as before
$\tilde{A}$ = tall: 1/1 + 0.6/2 + 0.2/3 + 0/4.
$\tilde{B}$ = approximately equal be represented in the form of a matrix.

$\tilde{B}$ = approximately equal:

| | 1 | 2 | 3 | 4 |
|---|---|---|---|---|
| 1 | 1 | 0.5 | 0 | 0 |
| 2 | 0.5 | 1 | 0.5 | 0 |
| 3 | 0 | 0.5 | 1 | 0.5 |
| 4 | 0 | 0 | 0.2 | 1 |

$\tilde{A} \circ \tilde{B}(1) = \max_U [\min \tilde{A}(u), \tilde{B}(u, 1)]$

(i.e. the extension will be first cordinatewise)

$= \max_U [(\tilde{A}(1) \wedge \tilde{B}(1, 1), \tilde{A}(2) \wedge \tilde{B}(2, 1)$

$\tilde{A}(3) \wedge \tilde{B}(3, 1), \tilde{A}(4) \wedge \tilde{B}(4, 1)]$

$= \max_U [1 \wedge 1, 0.6 \wedge 0.5, 0.2 \wedge 0, 0 \wedge 0]$

$= 1.$

$\tilde{A} \circ \tilde{B}(2) = \max_U [\min \tilde{A}(u), \tilde{B}(u, 2)]$

$= \max_U [\tilde{A}(1) \wedge \tilde{B}(2, 1), \tilde{A}(2) \wedge \tilde{B}(2, 2),$

$\tilde{A}(3) \wedge \tilde{B}(3.2), \tilde{A}(4) \wedge \tilde{B}(4. 2)]$

$= \max_U [1 \wedge 0.5, 0.6 \wedge 1, 0.2 \wedge 0.5, 0 \wedge 0]$

$= \max_U [0.5, 0.6, 0.2, 0]$

$= 0.6.$

$\tilde{A} \circ \tilde{B}(3) = \max_U [\min (\tilde{A}(u), \tilde{B}(u, 3)]$

$= \max_U [(\tilde{A}(1) \wedge \tilde{B}(3, 1), \tilde{A}(2) \wedge \tilde{B}(3, 2),$

$\tilde{A}(3) \wedge \tilde{B}(3, 3), \tilde{A}(4) \wedge \tilde{B}(3, 4)]$

$= \max_U [1 \wedge 0, 0.6 \wedge 0.5, 0.2 \wedge 1, 0 \wedge 0.5]$

$= \max_U [0, 0.5, 0.2, 0.5]$

$= 0.5.$

$$\tilde{A} \circ \tilde{B}\,(4) = \max_{U}\,[\min(\tilde{A}(u), \tilde{B}(U, 4))]$$
$$= \max_{U}\,[(\tilde{A}(1) \wedge \tilde{B}(4, 1), \tilde{A}(2) \wedge \tilde{B}(4, 2),$$
$$\tilde{A}(3) \wedge \tilde{B}(4, 3), \tilde{A}(4) \wedge \tilde{B}(4, 4)]$$
$$= \max_{U}\,[1 \wedge 0, 0.6 \wedge 0, 0.2 \wedge 0.2, 0 \wedge 1]$$
$$= \max_{U}\,[0, 0, 0.2, 0]$$
$$= 0.2.$$

$\therefore$ tall o approximately equal = [ 1, 0.6, 0.5, 0.2 ]

Hence the fuzzy restriction on $x_2$ is given by

$R(x_2) = 1/1 + 0.6/2 + 0.5/3 + 0.2/4$

tall = $1/1 + 0.6/2 + 0.2/3 + 0/4$.

Now using the definition of more or less tall = DIL (tall), we get

$1/1 + .77/2 + .45/3 + 0/4$

So by linguistic approximation comparing the value of R ($x_2$) and DIL (tall) we can derive the conclusion: $x_2$ is more or less tall. This shows that the difference in degree between the premiss (1) and the conclusion is not too much though the value of the conclusion is slightly lower than the premisses. By repeating this process of reasoning several times we shall reach a conclusion which will be nearly false, though the premisses with which we started were nearly true.

Such inferences are approximate in nature because (a) the matrix constructed for *approximately equal* is approximate since its formulation depends on a host of factors, (b) approximation has been resorted to in the computation of the projection relation and (c) linguistic approximation has been applied to the projection of the premisses by variables whose values are linguistic rather than numerical. A linguistic variable is a variable whose values are words or sentences in a natural or artificial language, e.g. age is a linguistic variable if its values are assumed to be young, not young, very young and more or less young, etc.

Zadeh's solution has a distinct advantage over the other solutions put forward from the fuzzy logical point of view. Other solutions have been devised with a view to solving the sorites paradox and appear to be somewhat *ad hoc*; but the procedure of approximate reasoning is far more general and is applicable to the wider fuzzy context.

## 5.10 APPROXIMATE IDENTITY

Towards the end of the second chapter we have discussed in detail how the tolerance of vague predicates leads to the notion of non-discriminable difference. Since non-discriminable difference among objects with respect to a particular property is non-transitive, it cannot be equated with identity among objects even to that respect since the latter is always transitive. To be able to say that A is the same shade of colour as B we must be able to assert 'For every x, if a matches x, then b matches x'. But if colour shades are arranged in a series, then we find that after some time this relation of matching or indistinguishability or non-discriminable difference becomes non-transitive. Thus in a chain the colour predicates always give rise to discrepancy between our logic and our observation. Indistinguishability cannot therefore be taken as the criterion of identity among two objects about which the same vague predicate can be asserted.

But if we relax our notion of *identity* and make the relation graded as has been done by fuzzy logicians, then in a non-crisp situation the gap between identity and indistinguishability will be bridged and the paradox can be avoided.

The fuzzy logicians working in this area have suggested different notions of graded identity and not all these identities are of equal strength. The notion of approximate identity that we have worked out in the last chapter can account for the notion of non-discriminable difference. But our notion is a much stronger notion, we can resolve the sorites paradox even with Menger's[52] probabilistic relation of approximate identity.[53]

Before we define Menger's notion of approximate identity ($E^M$) it is required that we define fuzzy identity in general. Let us first define $E_f$, the fuzzy equivalence on a fuzzy set $\tilde{A}$ such that elements of A are mapped into [0, 1]. Then $E_f : A \times A \rightarrow [0, 1]$ is a map such that

$E_f(x, x) = \tilde{A}(x)$ for all x in A.

$E_f(x, y) = E_f(y, x)$ and

$E_f(x, y) \wedge E_f(y, z) \leq E_f(x, z)$ for all x, y, z in A.

That means this fuzzy equivalence relation is reflexive, symmetric but weakly transitive $E_f$ coincides with $E_c$, the crisp equivalence relation on the set A when the characteristic function of A is defined on {0, 1} instead of [0, 1]. The fuzzy identity on $\tilde{A}$, $I_f$, is a special case of $E_f$ which may be defined as follows:

$I_F(x, x) = \tilde{A}(x)$, for all x in A and

$I_F(x, y) = 0$ where $y \in A$ is not x.

It is obvious that $I_F$ will be reduced to $I_c$ in the crisp situation.

Now $E^M$ can be defined as the fuzzy equivalence relation satisfying the following properties:

(i) $E^M(\langle x, x \rangle) = 1$ for all x in A

(ii) $E^M(\langle x, y \rangle) = E^M(\langle y, x \rangle)$

(iii) $E^M(\langle x, y \rangle) \cdot E^M(\langle y, z \rangle) \leq E^M(\langle x, z \rangle)$ for all x, y z in A

(Here '.' stands for the ordinary product of real numbers.)

We shall now apply $E^M$ to the bald man version of the sorites paradox. If we go on adding, say, 1 hair by successive hair-transplant method (though we must admit it will not be economically viable) to a bald head, at each stage, the head remains bald but in the long run it will turn into a shaggy head which is 'not bald'. Let $a_1, a_2, a_3 \ldots . a_n$ be bald persons at each successive stage. Then for each i, $a_{i+1}$

is bald because $a_i$ is bald. We can infer this since $a_i$ and $a_{i+1}$ are non-discriminable with respect to baldness. Then the rule of inference involved here is $a_i = a_{i+1}$ for each i. So the baldman paradox can be rewritten as:

(1) $Ba_1$ & $(a_1 = a_2)$ & $(a_2 = a_3)$ & ....... & $(a_{n-1} = a_n)$

where $Ba_1$ means '$a_1$ is bald'. If ' = ' in (1) is taken as crisp, then we reach a contradiction since, crisp identity being transitive and truth preserving, $Ba_1 = Ba_n$. So if $Ba_1$ is true so will be $Ba_n$. But $Ba_n$ in fact cannot be true if $a_n$ is a shaggy haired person. If, on the other hand, we take '=' in (1) to be *approximate* then $a_i = a_{i+1}$ should have a truth value $\alpha$ such that $0 < \alpha < 1$. If this approximate identity is of Menger's variety ($E^M$) then & in (1) should be interpreted as the ordinary predicate '.'. In that case the truth value of (1) will be $\alpha^{n-1}$. Now $\alpha^{n-1}$ is less than 1 and as n increases, the person becomes less bald. The value of $\alpha^{n-1}$ tends to zero as n tends to infinity. When the truth value of $Ba_n$ is very close to 0, $Ba_n$, no longer contradicts $Ba_1$; depending on the number n signifies, $a_n$ becomes less and less bald and the paradox is resolved.

## NOTES AND REFERENCES

1. W.E. Johnson (1964), p. 39.
2. W.V.O. Quine (1976a), p. 3.
3. R.M. Sainsbury (1988), p. 25.
4. Dummett (1970), p. 250.
5. Putnam (1986), p. 285.
6. Parikh (1983), p. 241.
7. L. Goldstein (1988), p. 441.
8. T.T. Ballmer and M. Pinkal (1983), p. 1.
9. An alternative analysis may be given by using M.P. and Mathematical Induction.
10. Dummett (1970), p. 250.
11. The distinction between a logical and a semantic paradox has been drawn by F.P. Ramsey (1931). He writes, the logical paradoxes 'involve no ideas but those of class, relation and number, could be stated in logical symbolism and can occur in the actual development of mathematics when it is pursued in the right direction .... On the other hand, the semantic paradoxes are none of them purely logical or mathematical but all involve

some psychological term, such as meaning, defining, naming, etc. . . . . .' p. 21.

12. Henceforth we shall not mention this 'with respect to' clause explicitly but it should be remembered that two things will be considered distinguishable or indistinguishable only with respect to some property or properties.
13. Vide Chapter 1.
14. For a detailed account of the principle of tolerance see Chapters 1 and 2.
15. In Chapter 2 we have discussed the problems related to observational predicates.
16. How much difference will be considered negligible depends on the purpose at hand, sometimes again on the capacity of human perception. When somebody weighs gold, a minute difference in the weight matters but when somebody weighs coal, a difference of the same quantity is neglected.
17. Dummett (1970), p. 258.
18. An ordered set is called well-ordered if every subset of it contains a first element. Any well-ordered set is totally ordered. Let A be a well-ordered set having two elements a and b. Then the subset {a, b} of A contains a first element which, therefore, must precede the other; hence any two elements of A are comparable.
19. More about this series will be discussed in connection with Wang's paradox.
20. The choice is arbitrary; any other version would have served the purpose.
21. For the details of Tye's logic see section 4.2.
22. S.C. Kleene (1952).
23. Pinkal (1983), p. 47.
24. Vide Section 4.3.
25. Fine (1975), pp. 285–86.
26. Though the sentence is neither true simpliciter nor false simpliciter.
27. Putnam (1986), p. 285.
28. Originally the intuitionists were concerned with mathematical propositions which they thought are assertible if and only if backed by some constructive proof. Later on attempts have been made to extend their logic to non-mathematical expressions too. So all their basic notions centre around 'construction' and 'proof'.
29. The famous Goldbach conjecture is an example of a weakly undecidable proposition. In 1742 Goldbach suggested that every even number greater than two equals the sum of two primes. Since then this assumption has been confirmed many times for all the even numbers for which it has been tested but it has not been possible to construct any proof of it.
30. Parikh (1983), p. 242.
31. Ibid., p. 258.

32. The original numbering of definitions, etc. have been retained.
33. Termini(1984), p. 222.
34. Dummett (1970), p. 256.
35. Ibid., p. 252.
36. Ibid., p. 258.
37. Wright (1987).
38. Peter Bosch (1983).
39. Ibid., pp. 205–6.
40. Ibid., p. 207.
41. L. Goldstein (1988).
42. Harman (1986).
43. Ibid., p. 450.
44. Ibid., p. 455.
45. B.R. Gaines (1978).
46. J.A. Goguen (1969).
47. Lakoff (1973).
48. Todt (1983).
49. C.M. Myers (1985).
50. T.K. Sarkar (1983).
51. Zadeh (1975a) and (1975b).
52. K. Menger (1951).
53. M.K. Chakraborti and M. Banerjee (1992).

CHAPTER 6

# Epistemic Vagueness

## 6.1 LOGIC FOR MODELLING EPISTEMIC VAGUENESS

The focus of our study throughout the book has been vagueness of essential variety—an ineliminable feature of any natural language. We have also mentioned *en passant* about non-essential vagueness which arises due to either some epistemic inadequacy or open texture of expressions, mainly observational words. These two types of non-essential vagueness are so divergent in nature that corresponding logics are bound to be different and deserve separate treatment.

Non-essential vagueness of the former type has held the attention of researchers in Artificial Intelligence and Knowledge Based Expert Systems. While developing logic and algorithm for computer applications in the fields where exact theories are missing, AI researchers find that human beings can derive conclusions from distorted and hazy information, from partially specified premisses. They, therefore, start enquiring into the nature of such reasoning processes with a view to discovering underlying rules of drawing reasonable conclusions from inexact premisses. The motivation is the same as Zadeh's. Only here the nature of inexactitude is different, which they call *ignorance* and according to them, vagueness and uncertainty are two most important forms of partial ignorance. No knowledge representation technique, therefore, can be deemed complete unless it can provide proper guidelines for modelling vagueness and uncertainty.

*Ignorance* results from a restricted reliability of technical devices (this type of ignorance has been exhaustively analyzed in connection with Parikh's theory), from partial knowledge, from inadequate observations, lack of propitious conditions, etc. Vagueness usually applies to observed facts or data and is generated from a host of causes like noise, resolution, lack of focus/contrast, imprecise definitions, masking. The conclusion of an argument may be imprecise if the information given in the premisses are imprecise or if the linkage between evidence and outcome is vague. Suppose, on a foggy day when a dark coloured car is visible only if the distance is thirty paces, a car is involved in a hit and run accident. According to the report of an eye-witness the colour of the car is blue. But the conclusion is imprecise due to restricted visibility condition, etc. The measured distance between an observer and the object observed has also been expressed in vague terms but that is quite in the fitness of things. On the other hand, when someone predicts rain from a sudden drop of atmospheric pressure there is some linkage vagueness. Our faith in weather reports based on expert knowledge of a meteorologist is, therefore, always shaky. This is an instance of uncertainty. Uncertainty is related to a valuation of some datum by a man reflecting his or her faith or doubt in its source. This sort of uncertainty in expert and user information can be represented by probabilities and can be handled very well by probabilistic logic. But modelling vagueness is a different proposition and requires different technique. In the AI parlance, however, any measure of tackling ignorance is known as artificial reasoning technique.

The AR techniques can be broadly classified under two heads (*a*) measure-theoretic and (*b*) linguistic. Measure-theoretic techniques are again mainly of two types—those based on probability, e.g. Bayesian technique and those based on fuzzy sets or on L-sets. Measurement of belief functions, e.g. by Demstar-shafer method also comes under this head. Under linguistic techniques can be listed a number of methods of which logic of likelihood, non-monotonic reasoning procedure, Folio, Endorsement, etc. have been widely used.

A number of studies in the AI field are in favour of using probabilistic technique not only for modelling uncertainty but also for vagueness. But several serious objections have been raised against the use of 'pure' probability theory in the context of vagueness on the grounds of efficiency as well as of sufficiency. It may appear that the fuzzy logical technique that we have described in detail in Chapter 4 is not sufficient to take care of this situation. Parikh, I would like to remind, has offered an intuitionistic supervaluational technique for handling vagueness that is improvable or refinable. Kreuse *et al.* are of opinion that a more appropriate representation may be given in terms of L-sets. They write,

> Vagueness, in our opinion, corresponds to the intuitive idea of 'gradednes', where different descriptions are obtained within different contexts. Thus we apply the calculus of L-sets, which are essentially layered sets. At the first approximation the reader may imagine each level as one shade of grey, for each of which a corresponding crisp picture of the entity in question is extracted from a hazy picture.[1]

The basic difference between the AR technique based on fuzzy set and one based on L-sets is that the former does not aim at precisification but with the help of the latter a crisp picture can be extracted from a hazy picture. The situation to be tackled with the second technique is different for here vagueness being a form of ignorance could have been made precise by addition to or alteration of the knowledge base but no question of improvement ever arises where vagueness is essential.

Parikh's technique differs from that of Kreuse *et al.* in being symbolic or logical whereas the latter is numerical. Let us now look at Kreuse's model.

Kreuse is interested in modelling epistemic vagueness so the reasoning process with which he is concerned is to determine the true but at the moment unknown state of the world. This situation can be best represented by layered sets signifying different degrees of acceptability.

While we try to determine the true state of the world we collect data through observation. These observations which may be precise usually restrict the set $\Omega$ of possible states of the world. But in general our observations have some inherent ambiguity. Only when we have accessible projections of the world, say, two dimensional pictures, the sets of possibilities are found to accord with observations. Otherwise we may only have several grey levels of hazy images which give rise to speculations. The vague datum that Kreuse and his associates are trying to represent actually mean vague projection of some precise observation resulting in such hazy images. They have illustrated this by the example concerning the location of ships with the help of a radar which provides vague outputs of three grey levels, viz. black, grey and white. In the example, the set of possible states of the world is denoted by

$$\Omega = \{ Z3, Z2, Z1, Ca, rd, ld\}.$$

It is assumed that Ca, rd and ld appear in black, Z1 in grey and Z2 and Z3 in white. On a radar screen white usually denotes that there might be some object at the concerned location. Now the information provided by the vague radar image may be given by the function

$$\mu : \Omega \rightarrow \{black, grey, white\}.$$

Here the different grey levels provide a scale of acceptability from which we may evaluate whether some region of the image covers the actual state of the world. Thus the basis of representation is a set L of different degrees of acceptability. We know by this time that 'white' contained in L gives us a possible location. But apart from 'white' L should contain at least one element corresponding to the lightest shade of grey actually appearing and denoting the basic level of absolute reliability, which is called the sure region, i.e. $\mu$-sure $\Omega$. However, it must be ascertained that $\mu$-sure covers the true value. That is, $\mu$-sure is the set of those elements of $\Omega$ that are possible in the light of the actual information. Inclusion of the lightest shade of grey in the sure region implies two things. First even what is absolutely sure has scope for improvement. Second, the sure region does not have a sharp cut-off point. Even in the epistemic context sure cases slowly merge with comparatively unsure ones.

If we now add a third 'grey' level, we obtain a second speculative description μ-spec. Even under the most conservative interpretation the region μ-sure corresponds to a reasonable degree of acceptability. But μ-spec can be considered reasonable only if we form an optimistic rather than a conservative evaluation of the available information. Thus μ-spec⊆μ-sure. But it is always possible to impose stricter restriction on Ω so that the final truth might be not among the elements of μ-spec. In general, a number of grey levels arranged in a natural order have to be considered where a higher level corresponds to a strong restriction thus leading to a high possibility of losing the truth. By restriction is meant the ability to separate things that are in accordance with some perception from those that are incompatible. Therefore, from our example we get,

μ-sure = { Z1, Z2, Z3}
μ-spec = {Z2, Z3}

A mathematical calculus of layered sets provides a suitable formal framework for dealing with cases like the abovementioned one in terms of a totally ordered finite set (L, ≤) of acceptability degrees. In the case of L= {white, black}, the layered set calculus coincides with the usual crisp set calculus.

Layered sets may be denoted by the function $\mu: \Omega \to L$ where $\mu(\omega)$, $\omega \in \Omega$, is the biggest value l of L such that $\omega \in \mu l$. In the above example,

black if $\omega \in$ {ca, rd, ld}
grey if $\omega \in Z_1$
white if $\omega \in \{Z_2, Z_3\}$

Since L in our example consists of three layers having an ordering relation, we are using L to depict the hierarchies of vagueness, viz. precision, imprecision and vagueness in general. The highest order of precision is considered totally free of vagueness. Precision, however, depends on the definition of frame of discernment used to represent the actual domain. In our radar example, the best possible situation would be to get an exact location of the ship, e.g. 'The ship is in Z2'. But rarely we have such exact knowledge. In most of the cases we receive information like 'The ship is either in $Z_1$ or in $Z_2$'. Formally the set of possible locations, if designated by $\Omega$, the last mentioned statement may be formalized as $\{Z1, Z2\} \subseteq \Omega$. So a vague image, according to this theory, can be represented by $\eta : \Omega \rightarrow L$ such that L is the set of physically existing grey levels, and degree of greyness is assigned to each point $\omega$.

The formal definition of an L-set is stated below following Kreuse.

*Definition 1*

Each function $\eta : \Omega \rightarrow L$ is called an L–Set of $\Omega$. Fl $(\Omega)$ denotes the set of all L-sets of $\Omega$.

It should be noted that we have defined L-sets with a view to discerning the actual location of the original entity $\omega_0 \in \Omega$

*Example:* Let $\Omega = \{Z3, Z2, Z1, Ca, ld, rd\}$
and let $\eta_1 : \Omega \rightarrow L_1 = \{\text{black, white}\}$
where

$$\eta_1(\omega) = \begin{cases} \text{white if } \omega \in \{Z3, Z2, Z1\} \\ \text{black otherwise} \end{cases}$$

be a radar image concerning some ship's location. Since the white region on the screen means 'there might be something', A= {Z3, Z2, Z1} constitutes a minimal set that necessarily covers $\omega_0$.

If we consider the possibility that the radar image contains three grey levels instead of two such that

$\eta_2 : \Omega \rightarrow L_2 = \{\text{black, white, grey}\}$

Where

$$\eta_2(\omega) = \begin{cases} \text{white if } \omega \in \{Z3, Z2\} \\ \text{grey if } \omega \in \{ld\} \\ \text{black, otherwise} \end{cases}$$

then we cannot be sure that the ship is necessarily at sea. For 'grey' signifies that the possibility of the ship being at the loading dock cannot be ruled out.

To handle vagueness by means of layered sets we presume a one-to-one correspondence between level $l \in L$ and the number of layers in an original space. Since we are interested in locating $\omega_0$ exactly within the range of possible locations, we have to introduce the layered sets for the images represent $\omega_0$ in different contexts each of which yields an imprecise description. So to each $l \in L$ a number $j(l)$ can be assigned that signifies the number of superposed layers such that $j : L \to \{0, \ldots, n\}$. Though the restrictions in various contexts may coincide yet let us assume for the moment that any vague datum $\eta : \Omega \to L$ corresponds to a mapping $\mu : \Omega \to \{0, \ldots, n\}$ and that there is an (unknown) subset A of $\Omega_n$ with the property $Vag_A^{6n} = \mu$.

This being the background framework now we need to find out whether $\omega_0$ can be located in A $\Omega$. That means we are to find out whether

(i) It is possible that $\omega_0$ is within a given set $A \subseteq \Omega$
(ii) It is necessary that $\omega_0$ is within a given set $A \subseteq \Omega$

We are also to formalize the idea that the dark areas of $\Omega$ are more likely to cover $\omega_0$ than light areas.

It is, therefore, imparative that we introduce the notions of graded possibility and necessity.

*Definition 2*
Let $\mu : \Omega \to \{0, \ldots, n\}$, $\omega \in \Omega$ is called j– possible with respect to $\mu$ if and only if $\mu(\omega) = j$. A subset $A \neq \theta$ of $\Omega$ is called j-possible if $A \cap \{\omega \in \Omega | \mu(\omega) \geq j\} \neq \theta$, but $A \cap \{\omega \in \Omega \geq j + 1\} = \theta$ where $\theta$ = 0-possible or impossible.

From this definition we get a set function

$$Poss\,\mu : 2^{\Omega} \to \{0, \ldots, n\}$$

that assigns to each subset $A \subseteq \Omega$ its degree of possibility. It is obvious that

$\text{Poss}\,\mu\,(A) = \max\,\{\mu\,(\omega) \mid \omega \in A\}$

Since Poss $\mu(A) = j$ signifies that given $\mu$, the degree of possibility for the unknown state $\omega_0$ to be within A is j. Now Poss $\mu$ possesses the following properties:

(i) $\text{Poss}\,\mu\,(\theta) = 0$
(ii) $\text{Poss}\,\mu\,(\Omega) \leq n$
(iii) $\text{Poss}\,\mu\,(A \cup B) = \max\,(\text{Poss}\,\mu\,(A), \text{Poss}\,\mu\,(B))$
(iv) $\text{Poss}\,\mu\,(A \cap B) \leq \min\,(\text{Poss}\,\mu\,(A), \text{Poss}\,\mu\,(B))$

Kreuse explains the definition by means of the following example:

Let the radar image be as follows:

$$\eta_2 : \Omega \rightarrow L_2;\ \eta_2\,(\omega) = \begin{cases} \text{white if } \omega \in \{Z3,\ Z2\} \\ \text{grey if } \omega \in \{ld\} \\ \text{black otherwise} \end{cases}$$

Let $\mu_2 : \Omega \rightarrow \{0, 1, 2\}$, then

$$\mu_2\,(\omega) = \begin{array}{l} 2 \text{ if } \omega \in \{Z3, Z2\} \\ 1 \text{ if } \omega \in \{ld\} \\ 0 \text{ otherwise} \end{array}$$

So, it can be said that $\begin{cases} j\,(\text{white}) = 2 \\ j\,(\text{grey}) = 1 \\ j\,(\text{black}) = 0. \end{cases}$

Thus we assume that there is a subset A of $\Omega_2$ which induces $\mu_2$. It is obvious that $Z2^1$, $Z3^1$ and also $Z2^2$, $Z3^2$ are contained in A but we do not know whether $ld^1 \in A$ or $ld^2 \in A$. So Z2 and Z3 are 2-possible, ld is 1-possible and the other elements of $\Omega$ are impossible with respect to $\mu_2$.

Next Kreuse defines the necessity measure.

*Definition 3*

Let $\mu : \Omega \rightarrow \{0, \ldots, n\}$. A subset $A \subseteq \Omega$ is called j-necessary, $j \neq 0$ with respect to $\mu$, if $\{\omega \in \Omega \mid \mu\,(\omega) \geq j\} \not\subseteq A$, but $\{\omega \in \Omega \mid \mu\,(\omega) \geq j - 1\} \not\subseteq$ A is defined to be 0-necessary (or not necessary) if there is no $j \neq 0$ such that A is j-necessary. The necessity measure said to possess the following properties:

(i) Nec μ (θ) = 0
(ii) Nec μ (Ω) ≤ n
(iii) Nec μ (A∩B) = min (Nec μ (A), Nec μ (B) )
(iv) Nec μ (A∪B) ≥ max (Nec μ (A), Nec μ (B) )

The definition of j-possibility and j-necessity with respect to a function $\mu : 2^{\Omega} \to \{0, \ldots, n\}$ depends on sets of the form $\mu j \overset{d}{=} \{\omega \in \Omega | \mu(\omega) \geq j\}$ known as *level sets.*

We know,

(i) $\mu_0 = \Omega$ and
(ii) $j < j' \Rightarrow \mu j \supseteq \mu j'$

The function μ is completely defined by the total number of level sets since

$\mu(\omega) = \max\{\min(j, \pi_{\mu j}, (\omega)) | j = 0, \ldots n\}$, where

$\pi_A(\omega) = n$ if $\omega \in A$ and $\pi_A(\omega) = 0$ otherwise. This is actually the representation theorem of Zadeh.[2]

The set μj is the minimal j-necessary set for j ≥ 1 and by using μj we can specify the given radar image the other way round.

There are other definitions and operations in Kreuse *et al.* which we are omitting for we are interested in presenting the bare outline of L-set technique of modelling vagueness.

Though L Sets are different from the fuzzy sets that we have employed yet we can bring L sets technique within the bounds of fuzzy logic for both the techniques deal with possibilistic measure and *not* with probabilistic measure. Besides both L sets and fuzzy sets are characterized by monotonicity and therefore share many basic principles. The monotonicity of L-sets can be grasped through the notion of specialization.

*Definition 4*

Let $\mu : \Omega \to \{0, \ldots, n\}$ and $\mu' : \Omega \to \{0, \ldots, n\}$. μ is called a specialization of μ' (written $\mu \subseteq \mu'$) iff $\mu(\omega) \leq \mu'(\omega)$ holds for all $\omega \in \Omega$. The intuitive rendering of $\mu \subseteq \mu'$ is the image represented by $\mu'$ is *at least as grey as* the one represented by $\mu$. The specialization relation enables us to compare the degrees of possibility derived for the elements of $\Omega$ with respect to $\mu$ and $\mu'$. Kreuse's theory of L-sets comes very close to Pultr's[3] theory of L-fuzzy sets and also can be linked with the notion of a flou set. Powlak's rough sets can also be used for modelling vagueness.

These observations lead us to conclude that representations of essential vagueness as well as of epistemic vagueness can be unified within the broad framework of fuzzy logic without any difficulty provided one can overcome ones reservations against the assignment of membership degrees to the elements of a fuzzy set and make measurements sufficiently objective.

## 6.2 OPEN-TEXTURED EXPRESSIONS AND NON-MONOTONIC REASONING

While we were describing different types of vagueness that may affect sentences of a natural language, we found that some expressions, though not actually vague, possessed the possibility of vagueness. Waismann calls such expressions open-textured. In his own words,

> A word which is actually used in a fluctuating way (such as 'heap' or 'pink') is said to be vague, a term like 'gold', though its actual use may not be vague, is non-exhaustive or of an open-texture in that we can never fill up all the possible gaps through which a doubt may seep in. Open-texture, then, is something like possibility of vagueness.[4]

Such expressions present a special difficulty because we can never be sure whether a particular predicate of this sort applies to a particular object or not. For such predicates have infinite possibilities. Suppose in our language we usually ascribe the predicate 'dog' to an animal that is a mammal, has four legs, one tail, a particular look, soft coat of hair all over its body and which barks. Now the question is, if a dog like animal is mute or roars like a lion, should we call it a dog? And when we take such cases into account can we ever validily argue that

All dogs bark
Chess is a dog
∴ Chess barks.

Or, suppose there is a crow in our garden which very often disturbs me by cawing while I write, sitting on a thin branch of a big tree. I call it Blackie the trouble-maker. I have watched it swinging but have never watched it flying. Am I justified in arguing that

All crows fly
Blackie is a crow
∴ Blackie flies.

Probably not. Because Blackie may be stiff winged or might have never learnt to fly. These examples may appear too unusual but I have used them only to highlight the fact that such instances often make deductive inferences involving open-textured expressions ineffective. The only effective way to handle such cases is by restricting the number of possibilities, by circumscribing the predicate having an open-texture. This technique has actually been tried by the AI researchers and is known as *circumscription*—a well-developed branch of non-monotonic reasoning.

Before we delineate the features of circumscription we need to analyze in detail the features of non-monotonic reasoning.

Deductive inferences of the traditional logic possess a property called monotonicity. According to Ginsberg[5] monotonicity means: as your set of belief grows, so does the set of conclusions that can be drawn from those beliefs. Let us consider the typical syllogism:

All men are mortal
Socrates is a man
∴ Socrates is mortal.

The conclusion of the syllogism remains valid even if we go on adding new premisses describing hitherto unknown facts about Socrates. Suppose, we come to know that Socrates could leap the Parthenon in a single bound, or he could single-handedly defeat the Spartan army, yet the conclusion remains true and the argument valid. The argument could be turned invalid only by removing one of the original premisses.

Now, contrast the Socrates-inference with the following one.

Birds fly.
Tweety is a bird.
∴ Tweety flies.

This argument remains valid until we add the premiss that Tweety is a penguin and then the conclusion is contradicted. But in absence of any information to the contrary we naturally assume that Tweety is a typical bird and as all typical birds fly Tweety also flies. The conclusion of this type of reasoning is defeasible unlike a valid deductive reasoning for this sort of argument lacks the property of monotonicity and hence gets the name non-monotonic reasoning.

Let us now present the characteristic feature of non-monotonic reasoning more formally. Let A be a set of formulae and let $\alpha$ be a single formula which can be derived form A. Then $A \vdash \alpha$ ( '$\vdash$' is the relation of consequence) can be looked upon as an operator, called a consequence operator, which maps the set of formulae to a single formula. Tarski has specified three properties of consequence relation.

(i) $A \subseteq Th(A)$ where $Th(A) = \{\alpha \mid A \vdash \alpha\}$. This condition is known as the overlap condition,
(ii) If $A \subseteq B$ then $Th(A) \subseteq Th(B)$. This is the monotonicity condition. In the literature this condition is also called the weakening principle or the dilution principle, and
(iii) $Th(TH(A)) = Th(A)$ or the closure condition..For any set A, Th (A) is the fixed point operator. Actually Th (A) is the smallest of all sets S such that $A \subseteq S$ and $Th(S) = S$.

Non-monotonic reasoning violates the condition (*ii*). Minsky[6] has pointed out that the property of monotonicity pertaining to the consequence relation follows from the permissive character of the classical rules of inference. A rule of inference is permissive, according to Minsky, if it is of the form: 'Q is a theorem, if $P_1, \ldots, P_n$ are theorems'. That means a classical rule of inference cannot invalidate previously established theorems.

But the non-monotonic rules of inference are generally of the form 'Q is a theorem, if $P_1, \ldots, P_n$ are *not* theorems'. This form makes the rules both permissive and restrictive.

Monotonicity condition imposes rigidity on the classical reasoning process. But the actual reasoning procedure of an ideally rational agent is characterized by flexibility. A rational agent can derive a conclusion depending on some premisses but can also retract the conclusion as and when necessary, particularly when some new evidence comes. Flexibility being the other name of non-monotonicity, computer programmes should also be developed in the line of non-monotonic reasoning.

Non-monotonic reasonings usually have two additional assumptions: (a) the *closed-world* assumption which states that there is no additional datum to contradict the conclusio; what sanctions an inference is failure to find a proof to the contrary, (b) the assumption of inheritance hierarchies states that 'absence of information to the contrary' can be extended to deal with hierarchies of defaults. For example, there may be no explicit information in our data base to assert that ostriches have feathers but if it has been explicitly mentioned that birds have feathers and ostriches are birds, then ostriches can inherit the property of having feathers by default.

There are three different approaches to tackle recalcitrant non-monotonic derivations: (i) Circumscription, (ii) Auto-epistemic logic and (iii) Default logic. Circumscriptive approach is model-theoretic or semantic whereas autoepistemic and default approaches are syntactic or proof theoretic. Moore[7] and Reiter[8] are the famous proponents of (ii) and (iii) respectively.

### 6.3 CIRCUMSCRIPTION

Circumscriptive reasoning was first propounded by McCarthy.[9] It is the most well known and well-developed semantic approach to non-monotonicity. Circumscriptive reasoning proceeds by minimizing the extension of any predicate to its known extensions. Let us assume that $\{\langle x_1, \ldots, x_n \rangle\}$ is known to satisfy a particular predicate P. Circumscriptive logic permits us to conclude that these are the only n-tuples that satisfy P.

Circumscription may be either (*i*) predicate circumscription which states that the entities satisfy a given predicate only if they have to, on the basis of a collection of facts or (*ii*) domain circumscription which takes for granted that the known entities are all that there are. Domain circumscription is a form of closed world assumption.

So in plain words the circumscriptive inference may be described as:

> If a sentence q can be obtained/inferred by deduction from the result of circumscribing P in A, we call it a circumscriptive inference of q from a and we write it as $A \mid \mid\!\!-_p q$

Let us now reformulate the Tweety example in terms of circumscription.

> It is known that Penguins and Ostriches are birds which do not fly.
> ∴ Penguins and Ostriches are the only birds which cannot fly.
> Tweety is neither a Penguin nor an Ostrich.
> ∴ Tweety can fly.

Now I would like to give a formal semantics of circumscription but there are some hurdles yet to be crossed. One such hurdle in the path of formalization of circumscriptive reasoning is the frame problem or the qualification problem. Ginsberg analyzes the root of frame problems in his book. He says,

> Whenever an action is performed, there are many 'hidden' preconditions that would prevent the action from succeeding. We know about these preconditions, since we understand that, if they were to happen, our intended action would be blocked. But we assume in a non-monotonic way, that they are not relevant to the particular situation in which we find ourselves.[10]

McCarthy's most startling example is that while starting a car in the morning we do not check whether there is a potato stuck in the tailpipe. We know, if there were a potato in the tail pipe, the car would not start. We do not have any proof to the effect that there is no potato, we simply overlook the possibility in a typically non-monotonic way. In circumscriptive reasoning we usually handle the frame problem in terms of minimization.

So the most important feature of circumscription is that it is a way of delimiting— a conjecture for jumping to the conclusion. In the words of McCarthy and Hays,[11]

> we know some objects in a given class and we have some ways of generating more; we jump to the conclusion that this gives all the objects.

It is evident from this feature of circumscription that mathematical induction is a type of circumscriptive reasoning.

To formally define circumscription we need to presuppose the usual first order language with identity.

Let A be a sentence (closed wff.) in which a predicate, say, P $(x_1, \ldots, x_n)$ or $(P(\bar{x}))$ occurs.

Let $\emptyset(\bar{x})$ be an n-place predicate expression (either a predicate symbol or a wff. in which there are free occurrences of $x_1, x_2, \ldots, x_n$).

$A\emptyset$ results from replacing all occurrences of P in A by $\emptyset$. Then the circumscription of P in A(P) is the following sentence schema:

$$A\emptyset \wedge \forall \bar{x}\,(\emptyset(\bar{x}) \supset P(\bar{x})) \supset \forall \bar{x}\,.\,(P(\bar{x}) \supset \emptyset(\bar{x}))$$

*Example :* Let A be: is block A $\wedge$ is bloc B $\wedge$ is block C.
Let P(x) be: is block x.

Then circumscription of P in A is the schema

(1) $\emptyset (A) \wedge \emptyset (B) \wedge \emptyset (C) \wedge \forall x. (\emptyset (x) \supset \text{is block } x) \supset \forall x. (\text{is block } x \supset \emptyset x)$

If we now substitute

$\emptyset (x) \equiv (x = A \vee x = B \vee x = C)$

into (1) and use the sentence A, i.e. is block A $\wedge$ is block B $\wedge$ is block C is taken to hold, then the left side of the implication is found to be true. So we get

$\forall x. (\text{is block } x \supset (x = A \vee x = B \vee x = C)$

Hence by circumscription, $\forall x. (\text{is block } x \supset \emptyset x)$.
Here one note of caution should be sounded; ø should be chosen properly.

This example is trivial for there is no provision in A for generating new blocks from old blocks. But the example is sufficient to show that circumscriptive reasoning is non-monotonic. For if we add is block D to A, then $\forall x.$ (is block $x \supset \emptyset x$) no longer follows.

We have already defined the notion of circumscription which can be written as $A \mid \vdash_p q$. Now we define a new notion called a Minimal Entailment.

*Definition*
A sentence q is minimally entailed by A iff q is true in all minimal models of A.

*Definition*
A model M of A is called minimal with respect to P iff $M' \leq_P M$ implies M' = M.

*Explanation*
Let M (A) and N(A) be models of the sentence A having the same domain. Let P be a predicate symbol in A such that all the predicate symbols in A besides P have the

same extensions in M and N. Let the extension of P be also in M and let it be included in the extension of P in N.

This is written as $M' \underset{P}{\leq} N$.

But the problem with circumscriptive inference is that minimal models do not always exist and when they exist they are nor always unique.

*Definition*

A minimally entails q with respect to P provided q is true in all models of A which are minimal relative to P.

There is an important theorem of circumscription. $A \Vdash_p q$ which states that any instance of the circumscription of P in A is true in all the models of A minimal relative to P. As a corollary of the above theorem it follows

If $A \Vdash\!\!-_p q$ then $\Vdash\!=_p q$.

This establishes the soundness of circumscriptive logic. Its completeness is yet to be proved.

We shall now define submodel.

Let M and N be two models of A. Let us assume that $M(P) \leq N(P)$. If P is a 3-place predicate then M(P) is a member of $D \times D \times D$ where D is the domain set. Then M is a submodel of N and is written as $M \underset{P}{\leq} N$.

We are now going to prove, if $A \Vdash\!\!-_p q$ then $A \Vdash\!=_p q$. This proof requires proving two lemmas which we shall just state.

(i) $A \Vdash_p q$ iff $B \vdash q$ where B is obtained by circumscribing A with respect to a certain predicate expression ø; and
(ii) any instance of circumscription of P in A is true in all models of A minimal in P.

*Proof*: If $A \Vdash\!\!-_p q$, then $A \Vdash\!=_p q$.

If $A \Vdash\!\!-_p q$, then $B \vdash q$ where B is an instance of circumscription of P in A. It follows from (ii) mentioned above that B is true in all minimal models of A and hence q is true whenever B is true. Therefore q is true in all the minimal models of A with respect to P. Hence A $\Vdash_p q$ (proved).

We have seen that in the Tweety inference 'Birds fly' needs to be symbolized properly. McCarthy suggests $B(x) \wedge \neg ab(x) \supset Fly\ x$ as the adequate symbolization. Here ab is a one-place predicate symbol. We have some axiomatized conditions of abnormality.

Let P be any predicate expression such that A(P) holds. Then circumscription allows us to conclude.

$$\forall x\ (P\ (x) \supset ab\ (x)\ ) \supset \forall x\ (ab\ (x) \supset P\ (x)\ ),$$

i.e. x's satisfying ab is exactly the same as x's satisfying P. Now, if the extensions of P are completely known by some means, the extension of ab is delimited with respect to that of P only. Thus ab is minimized so in the Tweety example, ab is minimized with respect to non-flying birds and it is assumed that Penguins and Ostriches are the only abnormal birds.

Non-monotonic reasoning has its own drawbacks. There are some general objections raised against non-monotonic reasoning as such and certain objections relate specially to circumscriptive procedure.

Kramosil[12] has raised two formal objections against non-monotonic reasoning in general. (a) No non-monotonic reasoning is even semi-decidable. The first order theory is semi-decidable for there is an algorithm to determine whether any wff. is a theorem of the first order system but if a wff. is not a theorem the programme will run forever. But non-semidecidability should not be taken as an unmixed curse for non-monotonic reasoning. For it enables us to explain the growth of knowledge. As Sarkar rightly points out,

> If all cases of new knowledge were analytical consequence of a basic set of tautologies (or indubitable truths) our knowledge might grow without giving us any new information in the process. We have to pay a price somewhere. It is better to trade off static cer-

tainty for dynamic growth so far as knowledge is concerned.[13]

(b) The second objection is that no non-monotonic reasoning is deductively closed. The multiple-extension problem[14] related to non-monotonic systems makes deductive closure impossible. Let us suppose that {p, q} is the original set of premisses and we can deduce certain conclusion from the premiss set. Now we come to know some new relevant data and another conclusion follows. The problem is what is to be counted as the theorem set? Some non-monotonic logicians have suggested that intersection of all extension sets should be taken as the theorem set. But the intersection set is not deductively closed in the usual sense of the term.

It has also been pointed out that the implementations of non-monotonic systems, especially of circumscription is excruciatingly slow. For here we proceed in the trial and error method. If the result is not arrived at we search for some hidden conditions rectify the premiss set and then make arrangements so that the result follows. This requires repeated consistency checking which is indeed very difficult and time-consuming. D.W. Etherington *et al.*[15] have proposed an extended use of circumscription with an automatic proof checker.

McCarthy[16] in one of his later papers has introduced a more powerful notion of *formula circumscription.* Formula circumscription is different from predicate circumscription. Predicate circumscription minimizes the extent of some particular predicate but formula circumscription allows the variation of the extents of other predicates. This modification is very useful. If only abnormal birds fail to fly then it is impossible to minimize the set of abnormal birds without varying the set of flying things. Lifschitz's prioritized circumscription[17] can be shown to be a special case of formula circumscription.

Formula circumscription can successfully rectify one of the defects of predicate circumscription as pointed out by Etherington that the predicate circumscription axiom can never introduce new positive instances of any predicate.

That means, it is not possible to employ predicate circumscription to conclude that a bird can fly. The problem arises because of the fact that predicate circumscription does not permit non-circumscribed predicates to vary when the circumscription is attempted. Just to rectify this weakness McCarthy introduces his notion of formula circumscription.

Lifschitz[18] and others have also shown that circumscriptive reasoning is also 'computationally tractable'. He has demonstrated that the general circumscription axiom can be replaced by a first order axiom in many cases. The most redeeming feature about the recent developments in circumscription is that Przymuzinski[19] has even successfully developed a resolution like algorithm to determine whether or not a particular formula follows from the circumscription axiom.

Another interesting point that is worth mentioning is that default reasoning process very closely resembles circumscriptive reasoning only the former is less general than the latter. So anybody attempting to argue with open-textured expressions can also proceed by applying default reasoning. We shall not, however, elaborate the default procedure. For circumscription is sufficient to prove arguments like:

> No normal cat ever grins, Tommy is a normal cat, Cheshire cat is known to be the only abnormal cat, (we can validly conclude) therefore, Tommy does not grin.

## 6.4 IGNORANCE AND SORITES PARADOX

The epistemic theory of vagueness or vagueness–rooted–in–ignorance view has been put forward by Cargile[20] and Sorensen[21] to devise an ingenious solution to the sorites paradox. According to them, vagueness is not a result of semantic indeterminacy; vagueness arises when we ignore the fact that some true sentences cannot be known to be true. Goldbach's conjecture may be taken as an example of such an unknowable vague sentence.

Timothy Williamson's example of such an unknowably true proposition is:

> Either 'The number of books in TW's room on 1 July 1989 is even and no one will ever know it' or 'The number of book in T.W.'s room on 1 July 1989 is odd and no one will ever know that it is'.[22]

But how does acceptance or denial of such unknowably true propositions account for or solve the sorites paradox? Let us consider the sorites series $a_1, \ldots, a_n$ for the predicate R such that R distinctly applies to $a_1$, does not apply to $a_n$ at all and there is no reason to maintain that there is an i such that $a_i$ is R but $a_{i+1}$ is not. Cargile and Sorensen think that there is such an i though we are never in a position to know which i that is. Consequently, they maintain that the sentence

'$a_i$ is R and $a_{i+1}$ is not R'

is true but not known to be true for we simply cannot determine which i it is that makes the above sentence true. So it appears that there is a very easy way out of the sorites paradox. Though $a_1$ is R and all contiguous samples in the series are indiscriminable yet $a_n$'s being not R can be explained by upholding $a_i$ is R and $a_{i+1}$ is not R true. Thus the paradox is resolved. But Cargile and others point out, it is our reluctance to admit any unknowably true proposition which makes us oblivious of such a simple solution.

Here, I feel, we need to probe deeper. It is not clear what stands in the way of our acquiring knowledge of such a true proposition. In Timothy Williamson's example, it is apparent, the structure of sentence hinders our knowledge. If we know or at least can reliably uphold that the number of books in T.W.'s room on July 1, 1989 is even then 'no one will ever know it' becomes false and hence the conjunction of the above propositions cannot be true. So we can know such a proposition to be true only on pain of contradiction. But the structure of the proposition underlying the sorites series is not exactly analogous. In some cases at least the sentence of the form

$a_i$ is R and $a_{i+1}$ is not R

can be known to be true. Only in some cases involving vague expressions we fail to know the sentences of the above form to be true because the cut-off point remains hidden from us. By improving our background knowledge we are supposed to lay bare the so-called 'hidden cut-off point'. But is it possible to lay bare the hidden divide in all cases? Can't vagueness be the result of necessary ignorance which can never be removed? And in such cases will not semantic indeterminacy be a necessary correlate? The solution to the paradox that Cargile and Sorensen have provided might have some appeal for an omniscient being. For by virtue of his omniscience he might be able to uncover several boundary lines in case of a sentence involving semantically indeterminate expression. But I doubt that where vagueness is essential, where no sharp line is to be drawn, even an omniscient being will be able to discover the cut-off point. Either he will have to overlook vague expressions or will have to opt for some logical solution. And it is the latter that we have been trying to achieve in the book. Hopefully, our effort to understand vagueness has not added to the general confusion prevailing in the scene, but has helped in a way to clear up the mystery around *vagueness.*

## NOTES AND REFERENCES

1. R. Kreuse, E. Sehwecke and J. Heinsohn (1991).
2. L. A. Zadeh (1971a).
3. A. Pultr (1983).
4. F. Waismann (1968), p. 38.
5. M.L. Ginsberg (1987).
6. M. Minsky (1975).
7. R.C. Moore (1984).
8. R. Reiter (1980).
9. J. McCarthy (1980).
10. M.L. Ginsberg (1987), p. 4.
11. J. McCarthy and P.J. Hayes (1969).
12. I. Kramosil (1975).
13. T.K. Sarkar (1992), p. 227.
14. For details see M.L. Ginsberg (1987), p. 11.
15. D.W. Etherington, R.E. Mercer and R. Reiter (1985).

16. J. McCarthy (1986).
17. V. Lifschitz (1985b).
18. V. Lifschitz (1987).
19. T.C. Przymuzinski (1986).
20. James Cargile (1969, 1979).
21. Roy Sorensen (1988).
22. T. Williamson (1990), p. 103.

# Bibliography


Adams, E.W. and H.P. Levine (1975), 'On the uncertainties transmitted from premisses to conclusions in deductive inference', *Synthese*, 30.

Alston, W.P. (1964), *Philosophy of Language*, Prentice-Hall, Englewood Cliffs, New Jersey.

Ballmer, T.T. and M. Pinkal (eds.) (1983), *Approaching Vagueness*, North-Holland, Amsterdam.

Ballmer, T.T. (1983), 'Fuzzy grammatical categories', *Approaching Vagueness*, edited by T.T. Ballmer and M. Pinkal, North-Holland, Amsterdam.

Ballweg, Joachim (1983), 'Vagueness or context dependence? Supervaluation revisited in a semantics based on scales', *Approaching Vagueness*, edited by T.T. Ballmer and M. Pinkal, North-Holland, Amsterdam.

Bencivenga, Ermano (1986), 'Free logics', *Handbook of Philosophical Logic*, III, edited by D. Gabbay and F. Guenthner, D. Reidel, Dordrecht, Holland.

Black, Max and Peter Geach (eds.) (1952), *Translations from the Philosophical Writings of Frege*, Oxford University Press, Oxford.

Black, Max (1954), 'Vagueness—an exercise in logical analysis' (1937), reprinted in *Language and Philosophy*, Cornell University Press, Ithaca, New York.

——— (1954), 'The identity of indiscernibles', *Problems of Analysis*, Routledge and Kegan Paul, London.

——— (1963), 'Reasoning with loose concepts', *Dialogue 2.*

Blau, Ulrich (1983), 'Three-valued analysis of precise, vague and presupposing quantifiers', *Approaching Vagueness*, edited by T.T. Ballmer and M. Pinkal, North-Holland, Amsterdam.

Bosch, Peter (1983), 'Vagueness is context-dependence; a solution to the Sorites paradox', *Approaching Vagueness*, edited by T.T. Ballmer and M. Pinkal, North-Holland, Amsterdam.

Braithwaite, R.B. (ed.) (1931), *The Foundations of Mathematics and Other Logical Essays,* Routledge and Kegan Paul, London.

Brennenstuhl, Waltraud (1983), 'A door's closing—a contribution to the vagueness semantics of tense and aspect', *Approaching Vagueness,* edited by T.T. Ballmer and M. Pinkal, North-Holland, Amsterdam.

Broome, John (1984), 'Indefiniteness in identity', *Analysis,* 44.

Burgess, J.A. (1989), 'Vague identity: Evans misrepresented', *Analysis,* 49.

Burns, Linda (1986), 'Vagueness and coherence', *Synthese,* 68.

Cargile, James (1969), 'The sorites paradox', *British Journal for the Philosophy of Science,* 20.

——— (1979), *Paradoxes: A Study in Form and Predication,* Cambridge University Press, Cambridge.

Carnap, Rudolf (1950), *Logical Foundations of Probability,* University of Chicago Press, Chicago.

——— (1956), 'The methodological character of theoretical concepts', *Minnesota Studies in the Philosophy of Science,* edited by H. Feigl, University of Minnesota Press, Minneapolis.

——— (1965), 'Testability and meaning', *Classics of Analytic Philosophy,* edited by R.R. Ammerman, Tata-McGraw-Hill, Bombay, New Delhi.

Chakraborti, M.K. (1988), 'Use of fuzzy set theory in introducing graded consequence in multiple-valued logic', *Fuzzy Logic in Knowledge Based Systems, Decision and Control,* edited by M.M. Gupta and T. Yamakawa, Elsevier Science Publishers B.V., North-Holland, Amsterdam.

Chakraborti, M.K. and A. Chatterjee, 'Approximate identity', (forthcoming).

Chakraborti, M.K. and M. Banerjee (1992), 'In search of a more appropriate identity: a categorical approach', *Fuzzy Sets and Systems.*

Chappell, V.C. (1964), *Ordinary Language: Essays in Philosophical Method,* Prentice-Hall, Englewood Cliffs, New Jersey.

Chihara, C. (1979), 'The semantic paradoxes: a diagnostic investigation', *The Philosophical Review,* 88.

Clark, Michael (1987), 'The truth about heaps', *Analysis,* 47.

Cohen, R.S. and M.W. Wartofsky (eds.) (1983), *Language, Logic and Method,* D. Reidel, Dordrecht, Holland.

Cook, Monte (1986), 'Indeterminacy of identity', *Analysis,* 46.

Copilowish, I.M. (1937), 'Borderline cases, vagueness and ambiguity', *Philosophy of Science,* 6.

Davidson, D. and G. Harman (eds.) (1972), *Semantics of Natural Language,* D. Reidel, Dordrecht, Holland.

Deas, Robert (1989), 'Sorensen's sorites', *Analysis,* 49.

Declaris, R.N. and R.E. Kalman (eds.) (1971), *Aspects of Networks and Systems Theory,* Holt, Rinehart and Winston, New York.

Dowlatshahi, F. and L.J. Kohout (1988), 'Intentional possibilistic approach to dealing with incompleteness, vagueness and uncertainty', *Fuzzy Sets and Systems,* 25.

Dubois, D. and H. Prade (1980), *Fuzzy Sets and Systems: Theory and Applications,* Academic Press.

Dummett, Michael (1970), 'Wang's Paradox', *Truth and Other Enigmas,* Duckworth, London, 1978.

——— (1973a), 'The philosophical basis of intuitionistic logic', *Truth and Other Enigmas,* Duckworth, London, 1978.

——— (1973b), *Frege: Philosophy of Language,* Duckworth, London, second edition, 1981.

Eikmeyer, H.J. and H. Reiser (1983), 'A formal theory of context dependence and context change', *Approaching Vagueness,* edited by T.T. Ballmer and M. Pinkal, North-Holland, Amsterdam.

Eikmeyer, H.J. and H. Reiser (1983), 'A nominalistic approach to ambiguity and vagueness, considered from a mildly Platonistic point of view', *Approaching Vagueness,* edited by T.T. Ballmer and M. Pinkal, North-Holland, Amsterdam.

Engel, R.E. (1989), 'On degrees', *The Journal of Philosophy,* 86.

Etherington, D.W., R.E. Mercer, and R. Reiter (1985), 'On the adequacy of predicate circumscription for closed-world reasoning', *Readings in Non-monotonio Reasoning,* edited by N.L. Ginsberg and M. Kaufmann, Stanford University Publishing Inc., Los Altos, California.

Evans, Gareth (1978), 'Can there be vague objects?,' *Analysis,* 38

——— (1976), 'Semantic structure and logical form', *Truth and Meaning,* edited by G. Evans and J. McDowell, Oxford University Press, Oxford.

Evans, Gareth and J. McDowell (1976), *Truth and Meaning,* Oxford University Press, Oxford.

Feigl, H. (ed.) (1956), *The Philosophy of Science,* University of Minnesota Press, Minneapolis.

Fine, Kit (1975), 'Vagueness, truth and logic', *Synthese,* 30.

Fitch, F.B. (1976), 'The relation between natural languages and formalized languages', *Philosophy of Logic,* edited by S. Körner, Blackwell, Oxford.

Flew, A. (ed.) (1968), *Logic and Language,* Blackwell, Oxford.

For, J. (ed.) (1965), *System Theory,* Microwave Research Institute Symposia Series XV, Polytechnic Press, Brooklyn, New York.

Forbes, G. (1983), 'Thisness and vagueness', *Synthese,* 54.

Frege, Gottlob (1952), *Translations from the Philosophical Writings of Frege,* edited by Peter Geach and Max Black, Oxford.

——— (1979), *Posthumous Writings,* edited by H. Hermes, F. Kambartel, F. Kaurbach, translated by P. Long and R. White, Basil Blackwell, Oxford.

French, S. and M. Redhead (1988), 'Quantum physics and the identity of indiscernibles', *The British Journal of Philosophy of Science,* 39.

Gabby, D. and F. Guenthner (eds.) (1986), *Handbook of Philosophical Logic,* D. Reidel, Dordrecht, Holland.

Gaines, B.R. (1978), 'Fuzzy and probability uncertainty logics', *Information and Control,* 88.

Garrett, B.J. (1988), 'Vagueness and identity', *Analysis,* 48.

Garrett, B.J. (1991), 'Vague identity and vague objects,' *Nous*, 25.

Giles, Robin (1979), 'A formal system for fuzzy reasoning', *Fuzzy Sets and Systems*, 2.

Ginsberg, M.L. and M. Kaufmann (eds.) (1987), *Readings in Non-monotonic Reasoning*, Stanford University Publishing Inc., Los Altos, California.

Goguen, J.A. (1969), 'The logic of inexact concepts', *Synthese*, 19.

Goldstein, Laurence (1988), 'The Sorites as a lesson in semantics', *Mind*, XCVII.

Goodman, Nelson (1977), *The Structure of Appearance*, third edition with an introduction by G. Hellman, D. Reidel, Dordrecht, Holland.

Gupta, M.M. and T. Yamakawa (eds.) (1988), *Fuzzy Logic in Knowledge-Based Systems, Decision and Control*, Elsevier Science Publishers B.V., North-Holland, Amsterdam.

Hardin, C.L. (1988), 'Phenomenal colours and sorites', *Nous*, 22.

Harman, G. (1986), *Change in View*, MIT Press, Cambridge, Massachusetts.

Hempel, Carl (1939), 'Vagueness and logic', *Philosophy of Science*, 6.

Hospers, John (1977), *An Introduction to Philosophical Analysis*, Allied Publishers Private Limited, New Delhi, Calcutta.

Jackendoff, R. (1983), *Semantics and Cognition*, MIT Press, Cambridge, Massachusetts.

Johnsen, Bruce (1989), 'Is vague identity incoherent?', *Analysis*, 49.

Johnson, W.E. (1964), *Logic*, Part I, Dover Publications, New York.

Kamp, Hans (1981), 'The paradox of the heap', *Aspects of Philosophical Logic*, edited by U. Monnich, D. Reidel, Dordrecht, Holland.

Kenny, Anthony (1973), *Wittgenstein*, Penguin Books, Harmondsworth, Middlesex, England.

Khatchadourian, H. (1962), 'Vagueness', *Philosophical Quarterly*, 12.

Kindt, Walther (1983), 'Two approaches to vagueness: theory of interaction and topology', *Approaching Vagueness,* edited by T.T. Ballmer and M. Pinkal, North-Holland, Amsterdam.

Kleene, S.C. (1952), *Introduction to Mathematics,* North-Holland, Amsterdam and Princeton.

Körner, S. (ed.) (1976), *Philosophy of Logic,* Blackwell, Oxford.

Kramosil, I. (1975), 'A note on deduction rules with negative premises', *Proceedings of the Fourth International Joint Conference on Artificial Intelligence,* Cambridge, Massachusetts.

Kripke, Saul (1972), 'Naming and necessity', *Semantics of Natural Language,* edited by D. Davidson and G. Harman, D. Reidel, Dordrecht, Holland.

Kreuse, R., E. Schwecke, and J. Heinsohn (1991), *Uncertainty and Vagueness in Knowledge based Systems in Numerical Methods,* Springer-Verlag, New York.

Lakoff, George (1973), 'Hedges: a study in meaning criteria and the logic of fuzzy concepts', *Journal of Philosophical Logic,* 2.

Lewis, David (1988), 'Vague identity: Evans misunderstood', in *Analysis,* 48.

Lifschitz, V. (1985a), 'Closed world databases and circumscription', *Artificial Intelligence,* 27.

——— (1985b), 'Computing circumscription', *Proceedings of the Ninth International Joint Conference on Artificial Intelligence,* Cambridge, Massachusetts.

——— (1987), *Pointwise Circumscription, Technical Report,* Stanford University, Stanford, California.

Linsky, B. (1984), 'Phenomenal quantities and the identity of indistinguishables', *Synthese,* 59.

Lowe, E.J. (1989), 'What is a criterion of identity?', *The Philosophical Quarterly,* 39.

Machina, K.F. (1976), 'Truth, belief and vagueness', *Journal of Philosophical Logic,* 5.

McCarthy, J. and P.J. Hayes (1969), 'Some Philosophical problems from the standpoint of artificial intelligence', *Readings in Non-monotonic Reasoning,* edited by M.L.

Ginsberg and M. Kaufmann, Stanford University Publishing Inc., Los Altos, California, 1987.

McCarthy, J. (1977), 'Epistemological problems of artificial intelligence', *Proceedings of the Fifth International Joint Conference on Artificial Intelligence,* Cambridge, Massachusetts, reprinted in *Readings in Non-monotonic Reasoning,* edited by M.L. Ginsberg and M. Kaufmann, 1987.

McCarthy, J. (1980), 'Circumscription—a form of non-monotonic reasoning', *Artificial Intelligence* 13, pp. 27–39, reprinted in *Readings in Non-monotonic Reasoning,* edited by M.L. Ginsberg and M. Kaufmann, 1987.

McDermott, D. and J. Doyle (1987), 'Non-monotonic logic-I', *Readings in Non-monotonic Reasoning,* edited by M.L. Ginsberg and M. Kaufmann.

McDowell, John (1984), 'Wittgenstein on following a rule', *Synthese,* 58.

Menger, K. (1951), 'Probabilistic theory of relations', *Proceedings of Natural Academy of Science,* 37, USA.

Minker, J. and H. Gallaire (eds.) (1978), *Logic and Databases,* Plenum, New York.

Minsky, M. (1975), 'A framework for representing knowledge', *The Psychology of Computer Vision,* edited by P. Winston, McGraw-Hill, New York.

Moore, R.C. (1984), 'Possible world semantics for auto-epistemic logic', *Proceedings of Non-monotonic Reasoning Workshop,* American Association for Artificial Intelligence, New Paltz, New York.

——— (1985), 'Semantic considerations on non-monotonic logic', *Artificial Intelligence,* 25.

Monnich, U. (ed.) (1981), *Aspects of Philosophical Logic,* D. Reidel, Dordrecht, Holland.

Myers, C.M. (1985), 'Vagueness, arbitrariness and matching', *International Logic Review,* 31.

Noonan, H.W. (1982), 'Vague objects', *Analysis,* 42.

——— (1984), 'Indefinite, identity: a reply to Broome', *Analysis,* 44

——— (1986), 'Relative identity: a reconsideration', *Analysis,* 46.

Noonan, H.W. (1988), 'Substance, identity and time', *Aristotelian Society,* supplementary volume 62.

Over, D.E. (1989), 'Vague objects and identity', *Analysis,* 49.

Parikh, Rohit (1983), 'The problem of vague predicates' in *Language, Logic and Method,* edited by R.S. Cohen and M.W. Wartofsky, D. Reidel, Dordrecht, Holland.

Peacocke, Christopher (1981), 'Are vague predicates incoherent?', *Synthese,* 46.

Peirce, C.S. (1902), 'Vague', *Dictionary of Philosophy and Psychology,* edited by J.M. Baldwin, London.

Pelletier, F.J. (1989), 'Another argument against vague objects', *The Journal of Philosophy,* 86.

Pena, Lorenzo (1984), 'Identity, fuzziness and non-contradiction', *Nous,* 18.

Pettit, P. and J. McDowell, (eds.), (1980), *Subject, Thought and Context,* Oxford University Press, Oxford.

Pinkal, Manfred (1983), 'Towards a semantics of precization in *Approaching Vagueness,* edited by T.T. Ballmer and M. Pinkal, North-Holland, Amsterdam.

Popper, Karl (1974), 'Autobiography', *The Philosophy of Karl Popper,* edited by P.A. Schilpp, The Library of Living Philosophers, Open Court, La Salle, Illinois.

Prior, A.N. (1961), 'On a family of paradoxes', *Notre Dame Journal of Formal Logic,* 2.

Przymusinski, T.C. (1986), 'Query-answering in circumscriptive and closed-world theories', *Proceedings of the Fifth National Conference on Artificial Intelligence,* USA.

Pultr, A. (1983), 'Fuzziness and fuzzy equality', *Aspects of Vagueness,* edited by H.J. Skala, S. Termini, E.O. Trilas, D. Reidel, Dordrecht, Holland.

Putnam, Hilary (1979), 'What theories are not', *Mathematics, Matter and Method,* Philosophical Papers 1, second edition, Cambridge University Press, Cambridge, reprinted in 1987.

——— (1986), 'Vagueness and alternative logic', *Realism and Reason,* Philosophical Papers 3, Cambridge University Press, Cambridge, first published in 1983, reprinted in 1986.

Quine, W.V.O. (1960), *Word and Object,* MIT Press, Cambridge, Massachusetts.

Quine, W.V.O. (1969), *Ontological Relativity and Other Essays*, Columbia University Press, New York.

——— (1976a), *Ways of Paradox and Other Essays*, Harvard University Press, Cambridge, Massachusetts.

——— (1976b), 'Grades of discriminability', *Journal of Philosophy*, 73.

Quine, W.V.O. (1981), 'Things and their place in nature', *Theories and Things*, Harvard.

Ramsay, F.P. (1931), *The Foundations of Mathematics and Other Logical Essays*, edited by R.B. Braithwaite, Routledge and Kegan Paul, London.

Rea, George (1989), 'Degrees of truth versus intuitionism', *Analysis*, 49.

Reiter, R. (1978), 'On closed world databases', *Logic and Data Bases*, edited by H. Gallaire and J. Minker, Plenum, New York.

——— (1980), 'A logic for default reasoning', *Artificial Intelligence*, 13, reprinted in *Readings in Non-monotonic Reasoning*, edited by M.L. Ginsberg and M. Kaufmann, Stanford University Publishing Inc., Los Altos, California, 1987.

——— (1987), 'Non-monotonic reasoning' in *Annual Reviews of Computer Science*, 2.

Richards, I.A. (1936), *The Philosophy of Rhetoric*, Oxford, London.

Rolf, Bertil (1980), 'A theory of vagueness', *Journal of Philosophical Logic*, 9.

——— (1981), *Topics on Vagueness*, Lunds Universitel Filosofiska Institutionen Kungshuset, Lund, Sweden.

Russell, Bertrand (1923), 'Vagueness', *Australian Journal of Philosophy*, 1.

Russell, B. and A.N. Whitehead (1927), *Principia Mathematica*, second edition, Cambridge University Press, Cambridge.

Sainsbury, R.M. (1988), *Paradoxes*, Cambridge University Press, Cambridge.

——— (1988/89), 'Tolerating vagueness', *Proceedings of the Aristotelian Society*, 89.

——— (1989), 'What is a vague object?' *Analysis*, 49.

Salmon, N.U. (1982), *Reference and Essence,* Blackwell, Oxford.

Sarkar, T.K. (1983), 'Language, thought and reality modelling–I', *Journal of Indian Council of Philosophical Research,* I, New Delhi.

——— (1990), 'Some systems of deviant logic: a unifying approach', *Foundations of Logic and Language: Studies in Philosophical and Non-standard Logic,* edited by P.K. Sen, Allied Publishers in collaboration with Jadavpur University, Calcutta.

Sarkar, T.K. (1992), *Knowledge, Truth and Justification,* Allied Publishers in collaboration with Jadavpur University, Calcutta.

Savage, C.W. (1967), 'The paradox of the stone', *Philosophical Review,* 76.

Scheffler, Israel (1979), *Beyond the Letter, a Philosophical Inquiry into Ambiquity, Vagueness and Metaphor in Language,* Routledge and Kegan Paul, London.

Schrader, D.E. (1979), 'A solution to the stone paradox', *Synthese,* 42.

Sen, P.K. (ed.) (1990), *Foundations of Logic and Language: Studies in Philosophical and Non-Standard Logic,* Allied Publishers in collaboration with Jadavpur University, Calcutta.

Skala, H.J. (1978), 'On many-valued logics, fuzzy sets, fuzzy logics and their applications', *Fuzzy Sets and Systems* 1.

Skala, H.J., S. Termini and E. Trillas (1984), *Aspects of Vagueness,* D. Reidel, Dordrecht, Holland.

Slaney, John (1988), 'A note on "Most" ', *Analysis,* 48.

Sorensen, Roy (1985), 'Vagueness and sorites', *Analysis,* 45

——— (1988), *Blindspots,* Oxford University Press, Oxford.

Stalnker, R. (1988), 'Vague identity', *Philosophical Analysis: A Defense by Example,* edited by D.F. Austin, Kluwer, Holland.

Tarski, Alfred (1956), 'Methodology of deductive sciences', *Logic, Semantics, Metamathematics,* Oxford.

Termini, S. (1984), 'Aspects of vagueness epistemological problems related to their formalization', *Aspects of*

*Vagueness,* edited by H.J. Skala, S. Termini and E. Trillas, D. Reidel, Dordrecht, Holland.

Thomason, R. (1982), 'Identity and vagueness', *Philosophical Studies,* 42.

Thorpe, D. (1984), 'The sorites paradox', *Synthese,* 49.

Todt, Gunter (1983), 'Fuzzy logic and modal logic', *Approaching Vagueness,* edited by T.T. Ballmer and M. Pinkal, North-Holland, Amsterdam.

Travis, Charles (1985), 'Vagueness, observation and sorites', in *Mind,* 94.

Trillas, E. and A. Valverde (1984), 'An inquiry into indistinguishability operators', *Aspects of Vagueness,* edited by H.J. Skala, S. Termini and E. Trillas, D. Reidel, Dordrecht, Holland.

Tye, Michael (1989), 'Supervaluation and the law of excluded middle', *Analysis,* 49.

——— (1990), 'Vague objects', *Mind,* 99.

Unger, Peter (1979), 'I do not exist', *Perception and Identity: Essays presented to A.J. Ayer,* Macmillan, London.

——— (1984), *Philosophical Relativity,* Basil Blackwell, Oxford.

van Frassen, B. (1966), 'Singular terms, truth value gaps and free logic', *The Journal of Philosophy,* 67.

——— (1968), 'Presupposition, implication and self-reference', *The Journal of Philosophy,* 69.

Waismann, F. (1953), 'Verifiability', *Logic and Language,* edited by A. Flew, Basil Blackwell, Oxford.

Wiggins, David (1979), *Sameness and Substance,* Basil Blackwell, Oxford.

——— (1980), 'On singling out an object determinately', *Subject, Thought and Context,* edited by P. Pettit and J. McDowell, Oxford University Press, Oxford.

Wildgen, Wolfgang (1983), 'Modelling vagueness in catastrophetheoretic semantics', *Approaching Vagueness,* edited by T.T. Ballmer and M. Pinkal, North-Holland, Amsterdam.

Williamson, Timothy (1990), *Identity and Indiscrimination,* Basil Blackwell, Oxford.

Winston, P. (ed.) (1975), *The Psychology of Computer Vision,* McGraw-Hill, New York.

Wittgenstein, Ludwig (1953), *Philosophical Investigations,* translated by G.E.M. Anscombe, Basil Blackwell, Oxford.

——— (1958), *The Blue and Brown Books,* Basil Blackwell, Oxford.

Wittgenstein, Ludwig (1961), *Tractatus Logico Philosophicus,* translated by D.F. Pears and B.F. Mcguiness, introduction by B. Russell, Routledge and Kegan Paul, London.

Wreen, M. (1985), 'Vagueness, values and the world/word wedge', *Australasian Journal of Philosophy,* 63.

Wright, C.C.J. (1975), 'On the coherence of vague predicates', *Synthese,* 30.

——— (1976), 'Language mastery and the sorites paradox', *Truth and Meaning,* edited by G. Evans and J. McDowell, Oxford University Press, Oxford.

——— (1987), *Realism, Meaning and Truth,* Basil Blackwell, Oxford.

——— (1987), 'Further reflections on the sorites paradox', *Philosophical Topics,* 15.

——— and S.L. Read (1985), 'Hairier than Putnam thought', *Analysis,* 45.

Zadeh, L.A. (1965a), 'Fuzzy sets', *Information and Control,* 8.

——— (1965b), 'Fuzzy sets and systems', *System Theory,* edited by J. For, *Microwave Research Institute Symposia, Series XV,* Polytechnic Press, Brooklyn, New York.

——— (1971a), 'Towards a theory of fuzzy systems', *Aspects of Networks and Systems Theory,* edited by R.E. Kalman and R.N. Declaris, Holt, Rinehart and Winston, New York.

——— (1971b), 'On fuzzy algorithms', *REL—M 325,* University of California, Berkeley, California.

——— (1971c), 'Quantitative fuzzy semantics', *Information Sciences,* 3.

——— (1972), 'A fuzzy set theoretic interpretation of linguistic hedges', *Journal of Cybernetics,* 2.

——— (1975a), 'Calculus of fuzzy restrictions', *Fuzzy Sets and Their Applications to Cognitive and Decision Process,* edited by L.A. Zadeh, K.S. Fu, K. Tanaka and M. Shimura, Academic Press, New York.

——— (1975b), 'Fuzzy logic and approximate reasoning', *Synthese,* 30.

——— (1975c), 'A relational model for approximate reasoning', *IEEE International Conference on Cybernetics and Society,* San Francisco.

Zadeh L.A., K.S. Fu, K. Tanaka and M. Shimura (eds.) (1975), *Fuzzy Sets and Their Applications to Cognitive and Decision Process,* Academic Press, New York.

Zadeh, L.A. (1976), 'A fuzzy–algorithmic approach to the definition of complex or imprecise concepts', *Man Machine Studies,* 8.

——— (1981), 'Test score semantics for natural languages and meaning representation via PRUF', *Quantitative Linguistics 12: Empirical Semantics* I, edited by B.B. Rieger.

——— (1983), 'A computational approach to fuzzy quantifiers in natural languages', *Computer and Mathematics with Applications,* 9.

——— (1984), 'Syllogistic reasoning in fuzzy logic and its application to reasoning with dispositions', Electronics Research Lab, University of California, Berkeley, to appear in *Proceedings of the International Symposium on Multiple-valued Logic,* Winnipeg, Canada.

# Index